If you had told me six or seven years ago I'd be designing and manufacturing a nationally sold line of shapewear, I would have laughed you out of your chair. It was a divine accident!

Carol Columbus-Green/Laracris Corporation

We've been in business five years. Five and a half years ago, if you had asked me if I ever thought I would be running a flight school, I'd be like, "No way!" Even a month before I started, I would have told you, "No way!"

Robin Petgrave/Bravo Helicopters

When I look back, I can't believe this all happened. (Laughs.) I'm just totally flabbergasted by it! I never really planned on all this—never! I just thought I'd work for the state the rest of my life.

Mary Ellen Sheets/Two Men And A Truck

This was never something I sat down and said, "Oh, I'm going to build a business." It was done for love. It certainly wasn't done to make a lot of money or develop a company. It evolved, but it wasn't what I started out to do.

Judi Sheppard Missett/Jazzercise

I really can't believe it happened! A lot of people have asked, "Is this something you envisioned?" The fact is, this is a glorious accident!

Hyrum Smith/FranklinCovey

GLORIOUS ACCIDENTS

HOW EVERYDAY AMERICANS CREATE THRIVING COMPANIES

MICHAEL J. GLAUSER

SHADOW MOUNTAIN

Library of Congress Cataloging-in-Publication Data

Glauser, Michael J.
    Glorious accidents : how everyday Americans create thriving companies / Michael J. Glauser.
        p.   cm.
    Includes bibliographical references and index.
    ISBN 1-57345-391-9 (hc.)
        1. New business enterprises—United States. 2. Entrepreneurship—United States. 3. Success in business—United States. 4. Businessmen—United States—Interviews. I. Title.
    HD62.5.G59   1998
    658.1'1—dc21   98-26636
                                                                                        CIP

Printed in the United States of America   72082-6373

10   9   8   7   6   5   4   3   2   1

*To all who create and
maintain free enterprise*

CONTENTS

PROLOGUE

Sean Nguyen fled from Vietnam when he was seventeen years old. He sailed to Indonesia in a homemade boat with his father, brother, and thirty-six other castaways. During the voyage, the tattered band was attacked by pirates, who stole their meager possessions and raped the women. After finally arriving in America, Sean was offered a job at an electronics manufacturing company, even though he couldn't speak English. With the company's blessing, he began taking work home to his father and brother, who were unable to find jobs. A few years later, President Clinton honored Sean as the Young Entrepreneur of the Year for his thriving new venture, Nguyen Electronics.

Sally Gutierrez was forced to accept welfare when her husband left her with their two small children. She worked at a Hallmark card shop even though it reduced her monthly welfare benefits. Before long, she was cleaning the owner's home for extra income. Within a few years, she owned one of the largest cleaning services in Spokane. When she sold her business, she had seventy-five residential and commercial accounts.

Jon Huntsman grew up in a dust bowl in Idaho. During high school he had only one shirt, which his mother washed on weekends. The first company Jon started, Huntsman Container, pioneered the polystyrene clamshell for the McDonald's Big Mac. Today, Huntsman Chemical is the largest privately held petrochemical company in the world with more than eighty plants in more than twenty countries.

Robin Petgrave came to America from Jamaica. As a helicopter flight instructor, he refused to fly one day because his helicopter had not been properly maintained—so his boss grounded him for four days. With three hundred dollars and a handful of students, he rented a helicopter and started his own company. Today, with fifteen helicopters, fourteen airplanes, and nearly sixty employees, Bravo Helicopters is one of the largest flight-instruction and charter-tour companies in America.

How do these and other American entrepreneurs conceive their business ideas? How do they create their initial products and services? How do they make the leap from their former jobs to their new ventures? Where do they find their first customers? How do they survive the ups and downs of the start-up phase? How do they grow and develop their companies over time? Why do they later describe their business successes as unplanned accidents?

This book helps answer these questions by portraying the human drama of entrepreneuring in America: the summons and uncertainty, the passion and fear, the surge and reprieve, the laughter and tears, the freedom and restraint, and the ultimate triumph. The actors are business founders from New York to California who, in their own words, describe the exhilarating and exhausting process of conceiving an idea, implementing a concept, and building a successful enterprise. The cast of characters represents all of America: male and female, Caucasian, African-American, Hispanic, Asian, and Native American. These uncelebrated heroes own and operate companies, large and small, that make products, transport goods, sell merchandise, feed communities, serve customers, and entertain audiences. And in the process, they meet their own needs for autonomy, achievement, self-reliance, and financial stability.

My purpose in gleaning the intricate details from nearly a hundred business success stories was twofold: First, to shed light on what

American entrepreneurs *actually do* to get new ventures off the ground—as opposed to what they *should* do. Second, to identify the common trends that run through a diverse group of successful start-ups. And there are definite trends! A careful analysis of the interview transcripts reveals ten keys that appear over and over in the stories. While these findings are not earth-shattering, this book highlights how important they are in practice. This is by far the most important contribution of my three years of shoe-leather research. Clearly, the more these ten keys are present in a business startup, the greater the chance of success; if several or most of them are missing, the probability of failure goes up dramatically. In essence, the book is an operating manual for getting new ventures off the ground, complete with highly credible role models who demonstrate each principle. In our current era of turbulent change, these ten keys to entrepreneurial success will benefit organizations of all types. While the book has obvious relevance for anyone interested in starting and growing a business, it also has value for company executives, middle managers, educators, students, and politicians—anyone with a burning desire to create excellence in organizations.

THE SURGE OF ENTREPRENEURSHIP

This process of creating new ventures—entrepreneurship—is one of the more significant dramas played out in America today. Not since the birth of our nation has the need for entrepreneuring been greater or the opportunities more abundant. Just a few decades ago, economists and business gurus heralded the warning, "Small business is soon to become obsolete as mammoth corporations take over America!" Surprise! No one really expected the significant upheaval of entrepreneurial activity currently shaping our new economy. In each of the past three years, more than 800,000 new businesses were incorporated in America, and the number continues to grow. When you throw in sole proprietorships and partnerships, the annual total exceeds 1.3 million. In addition, only 3 percent of our corporations now employ more than one hundred people. By contrast, 80 percent of the businesses in this country employ fewer than twenty people. These smaller companies are outsmarting the teetering giants and introducing many of our new products and services; they also happen to create two out of every three new jobs in America. Many of these jobs surface as imaginative and resourceful entrepreneurs conceive a business script, give birth to an enterprise, and enlist a handful of people to share in their dream.

This recent flurry of entrepreneurial activity has many explanations. One obvious factor is technology. Today's computers, unlike past innovations which generally affected only specific jobs or industries, have affected nearly every household, occupation, business, and industry in America. As communication and computer technologies continue to become more compact, more powerful, and more affordable, more of us computer-ize, cable-ize, cellular-ize, satellite-ize, and Internet-ize our lives. Not only has technology created whole new industries and markets, but it has also changed the way we work. Companies of any size now have access to the same powerful systems once available only to large corporations. In addition, we can now do business anywhere we want: at home, from a car, on an airplane, or in a hotel room. This phenomenon has aided the explosion of home-based businesses; since 1991, approximately 4 million have been formed. Amazingly, 44 percent of the new enterprises launched in 1996 were started in the owner's home.

A second force driving the bustle of business startups is the globalization of our economy. Stiffer competition throughout the world has forced giant corporations that once dominated industries to scale back growth, sell off extraneous operations, cut costs, and reduce their work forces. In 1996, the *New York Times,* sensing an economic cataclysm, ran a weeklong series on the history, frequency, and impact of mass layoffs in American corporations. During my years as a business consultant, I have helped a dozen such companies restructure in an attempt to become more competitive. When downsizing or, the more politically correct term, "rightsizing" occurs, a considerable number of seasoned executives and managers find themselves out of work. Feeling little loyalty to their former employers, many of these individuals seek to establish their independence by starting a business, acquiring a franchise, or launching a consulting practice. At the same time, the struggling organization begins using outside help for a variety of services once performed inside the company—outsourcing. Ironically, many uprooted executives end up providing services to the very companies that lay them off: market research, personnel services, product development, or consulting of one kind or another. In 1996, outsourcing became a $100-billion industry, and some experts predict it will triple in the next five years.

So corporate downsizing initiates a startup frenzy. And once the entrepreneurial wheel starts to spin, it sets off a chain reaction of additional business activity, often with other small independents. For example, new ventures need computers, telephones, office space, furniture, supplies, and a variety of other resources—including a few helpers.

The changing American family is a third catalyst that has transformed American business in diverse ways. The number of women in the work force has grown steadily in recent decades. The traditional family—working dad and stay-at-home-mom—is no longer the common arrangement. This has created opportunities for a wide variety of home-support businesses: child care, maid services, catalog shopping, take-out food, and anything else that makes managing a household easier. It has also exposed women to a host of unmet needs in the world of work. Women have a much keener sense for what women want than do men. I thoroughly enjoyed my interviews with Gail Frankel, who designed the Stroll'r Hold'r because she couldn't find one anywhere; Zia Wesley-Hosford, who created a line of natural cosmetic products; and Carol Columbus-Green, who launched an attractive line of shapewear lingerie for women who bulge a bit after having babies.

Women also create businesses because they want more flexibility in juggling career, marriage, and children. Diane Dimeo started Pony Haven so she could stay at home with her daughter; Frieda Caplin entered the produce business to obtain the flexible hours she needed to breast-feed her children. An interesting aspect of this new dual-career household is that it allows one spouse to work for the bread and butter while the other can explore, dabble, and play at creating something that brings in the gravy. In recent years, the number of businesses started by women has grown twice as fast as those started by men. In 1970, women owned just 5 percent of the businesses in America; today, they own nearly 40 percent. In 1996, 32 percent of the new ventures formed were launched by women. While the female forte of the past decade has been the retail and service trades, today's women are writing business scripts and playing entrepreneurial roles in all industries: manufacturing, transportation, construction, and wholesale trade. Companies owned by women now provide as many jobs as the Fortune 500.

No doubt other factors help explain the changing American economy, but the fact is that more and more people are choosing or being forced to look at jobs and careers differently. Seeing more opportunities, feeling a lack of loyalty from big corporations, and wanting more flexible and fulfilling lifestyles, we are looking for ways to take care of ourselves, become independent, and do what excites us. As this trend continues, many more of us will play out the passionate drama of striking out on our own. A recent study by Paul Reynolds, a sociologist at Marquette University, reveals that roughly 4 percent of American adults—that's one in twenty-five—say they are in the process of starting a new business. In addition, surveys show that around 50 percent of the students in our business schools say they want to start their own companies rather than work for an existing corporation. Even more astonishing is a study cited by Elizabeth Myers, deputy assistant to President Clinton, which suggests that "over 64 percent of women aged 18 to 34 want to become business owners." Finally, a recent nationwide survey by the Entrepreneurial Research Consortium reveals that 35 million U.S. households—about one in three—have had some experience with starting a business, trying to start a business, or helping to fund a small business. Inarguably, we

Americans are keenly interested in starting and running our own companies.

But despite this growing gusto to strike out on our own, the business failure rate in America continues at a healthy cadence. According to the U.S. Bureau of the Census, one business fails in the United States each year for every ten new businesses created. Government statistics also show that nearly half of our new ventures fail within the first five years. However, a recent study by Donald Hicks at the University of Texas suggests that startups today may fail in half the time they did in previous decades. In other words, 50 percent of the new ventures launched in today's rapidly changing world may fail in two years rather than five years. So how do we find sound business opportunities? Where do we go to gain the required skills? How do we take astute first steps? Most important, how do we keep from becoming a failure statistic in the government annals?

Unfortunately, little is known about the complex and elusive process of creating new ventures. For decades, the entrepreneur was omitted almost completely from economic theory and organization design. The focus was on capital formation and equilibrium between supplies and demands—not the process of creating new products or services and influencing markets. When I started my career as a university professor, it was not even fashionable to teach, let alone do research on, the topic of entrepreneuring. The emphasis was managing, marketing, and expanding existing corporations. Those who taught the business start-up classes were usually part-time faculty members with outside interests in the real world of work. As a result, academic studies on entrepreneurship are relatively new. What research there is has generally focused on the traits of entrepreneurs or a single aspect of the more elaborate and ongoing process. While the "how-to" books are plentiful, they mostly espouse principles derived from traditional corporate practices: how to write a business plan, how to incorporate, how to find capital, how to buy a franchise, how to hire employees, how to increase sales, how to budget, and so on.

Clearly, it's time to start at the beginning with a more detailed description of the entrepreneurial drama over time. Throughout history, social anthropologists have spent years living in the field, walking the streets, peeking around corners, conducting in-depth interviews, taking exhaustive notes, and providing rich description of human cultures and processes. Only when we observe what's happening from the inside can we adequately theorize or hypothesize about new and intriguing social phenomena. This book takes a step in this direction by portraying the enigmatic process of creating new enterprise in America. In the tradition of oral history, it takes the three-dimensional world in which we live and casts it across the fourth dimension of time, enabling us to see real people in real-life situations stumbling onto opportunities, drafting plans, mitigating risks, concocting dreams, tasting success, falling short, revising plans, starting again, and enjoying the outcomes of their actions. The stories are thus slices of reality with the intensity of theater. Throughout the production, we realize that the dramatis personae—these seemingly distant and somewhat heroic characters—are actually very much like you and me, our friends and family, our neighbors and co-workers: they start each day uncertain of its outcome; they experience the same euphoria, ire, failure, and fortune; they possess similar peculiarities, strengths, foibles, and ambitions. No previous book documents so completely the character of the entrepreneur or the process of creating new ventures from the perspective of those who actually do it. And during the episodes, the seed of identification is planted: *"If she can do it, it just might be possible for me."*

EXPERIENCE AS MASTER TUTOR

My own interest in using personal and vicarious experiences to learn about organizations germinated during my college days. While I was a young graduate student, my professors extolled the virtues of the scientific method for unclasping the shackles of human mysticism. I can still picture one red-faced pedagogue pounding exuberantly on his podium, telling us to discount human experience, question all our assumptions, believe nothing we see or hear unless it can be supported with empirical data. Then one day, a fellow student brought a study to class revealing that practicing managers can predict with a high degree of certainty the outcomes of scientific research in management. In other words, from experience, they know the answers to many questions before scientists conduct the research. The reaction of my fellow student was, "Why are we quantifying common sense?" The reaction of the professor was, "Empirical data is far superior to experience because managers get some things wrong!" My reaction was that real-world experience, coupled with objective, scientific data, may provide the best understanding. I filed this conclusion away—fairly deep at test time—but added "experience" to my arsenal of tools for comprehending organizations.

After finally securing my highly coveted degree, I walked in to teach my first MBA class as "Dr. Glauser," wrote my name on the board, and turned around to greet students who were unquestionably older than I was—some nearly twice my age. My fascination with the study of organizations had propelled me through three degrees at the ripened age of twenty-seven; these guys (I don't recall any women in the class) were full-time managers and executives in a part-time MBA program. While I was clearly on top of the intellectual heap having just completed my exams, I was noticeably "out-experienced" by almost every student in the class. I knew a lot about the organizational literature; they knew a lot about organizations. Though I impressed them with my intellectual bravado, I knew I was masquerading as a business authority.

Fortunately, the schools at which I taught during those years not only allowed but also encouraged outside consulting work. The thinking was logical enough: when you consult with companies, you further the reputation of the university; you are able to place students in internships and jobs more easily; and you expand your own expertise as an organizational scholar—everybody wins! So for me, the imminent passage from full-time professor to full-time business consultant was smooth, orderly, and fairly predictable. And it was during those consulting years that my corporate education intensified tenfold. I had numerous clients, large and small, national and international—everything from startups to colossal corporations. I consulted on a variety of topics—management development, strategic planning, market research, corporate restructuring, acquisition planning—anything my partners and I could sell. I trained computer sales forces, helped displaced executives find new jobs, assisted geologists in looking for an ore body, promoted teambuilding in an underground mine, taught Catholic nuns how to administer schools, and helped morticians provide better service to grieving families.

On one occasion, a client called to say his company needed help announcing a layoff to the press. My partner—who was much more proficient at selling my services than I was—responded enthusiastically, "Hey, Glauser's a communication expert. I'll have him bring a program to your next executive meeting." It turned out they were ready to proceed *now*—their next meeting was that afternoon. Since we didn't have a "program," I had two hours to cook something up. I asked my assistant to round up all the newspaper and magazine articles she could find that announced layoffs during the past year. As I studied them, a clear pattern emerged: first, they announced the specific action to be taken (twenty employees laid off); second, they explained the cause of the action (increasing costs of production); third, they explained the effects on the company (50-percent drop in net income); and finally, they outlined a strategy for improvement (modernizing the plant). En route to the client's office, I ruminated on the pattern . . . action, causes, effects, strategy . . . action, causes, effects, strategy . . . As I rode the elevator to the top floor, I wrote the four words on a yellow pad . . . *Action, Causes, Effects, Strategy* . . . I had it just as the elevator door opened! I walked into the board room and said, "Ladies and gentlemen, I'm here to introduce our *ACES* program for communicating layoffs to the press." The client called a week later and raved about our exceptional *ACES* program—it had thwarted a company disaster. We now had a new program to sell!

And so my consulting experience was a master tutor, coaching me on the stage of professional life. It continuously stretched my wit and adeptness in innovative and peculiar ways. Largely, it consisted of drawing on experience, my own and that of others, to help companies more competently achieve their ambitions and, hopefully in the process, become more gratifying places for people to work. It was heady, cerebral stuff: racking my brain, getting creative, exuding confidence, doing my darnedest, braying boldly, swaggering with a big-city gait, and occasionally skating fast over thin ice.

Somewhere along the way, I started feeling antsy to launch a venture of my own. The summons started small, then grew to the gnawing crescendo of a pile driver. At this point in my career, I had studied organizations, taught about organizations, and consulted with organizations; now I wanted to start, own, and operate one. After a year of looking around, my wife Mary and I had the concept. We linked my interest in management with her training in nutrition and fitness and opened a couple of retail outlets that offered healthy, frozen desserts. The next thing we knew, we had seven, then thirteen, then twenty-five, then forty-two, then sixty; and it continued to grow from there. Along the way, we also launched a wholesale division called Northern Lights and started selling our products to the food-service industry. It seemed as if overnight we had stores scattered all over the place, a team of seasoned and talented executives, our own proprietary recipes, a wholesale food-service company, and more than 500 employees. By employee head counts, we were suddenly and surprisingly in the top 1 percent of the companies in America.

Then in the spring of 1997, I received a call from Michael Serruya, chairman of Yogen Fruz World-Wide Inc., a giant in the frozen dessert industry based in Toronto. Michael said, "I want to talk to you about buying your company." "It's not for sale!" I said. And he replied, "I really think you're going to like what we're doing in the industry!" Yogen Fruz had recently raised $30 million on the Toronto Stock Exchange and was trying to consolidate the frozen dessert/specialty foods industry. They had purchased Bresler's Ice Cream, I Can't Believe It's Yogurt, and Java Coast Fine Coffees. The company had more than 3,000 retail locations in eighty countries but few sites in the western United States. They really liked the tandem relationship between our sixty Golden Swirl retail stores and our Northern Lights wholesale division. They wanted to franchise the retail concept throughout the west and turn Northern Lights into their premium national brand. So after two months of productive and spirited talks, our executive group decided to sell the business. We signed the documents on June 6, 1997. A few days later, as Mary and I headed for the mountains to catch our breath, we marveled at what had happened in a relatively short period of time.

Anyway, along the way people have asked, "Did you plan all this?" The truthful answer is, "Not exactly!" Next they ask, "Then how did it happen?" The honest answer is, "By accident!" This doesn't mean we didn't formulate annual plans; it doesn't mean we didn't aggressively develop products; it doesn't mean we didn't seriously court customers; it doesn't mean we didn't work with undaunting tenacity. What it means is this: where we ended up wasn't exactly what we envisioned for ourselves in the beginning—we didn't plan on growing as big as we did as fast as we did—nor did we anticipate the zigs and zags that took us to our destination. As I've told this story—and continued consulting, lecturing, and reading the business literature—I've found more and more entrepreneurs who echo my sentiments: "I never planned on this!" "It was a divine accident!" "It sort of just evolved!" "I never dreamed we would be this big!" "If you would have suggested a few years ago I'd be doing this, I would have thought you were crazy!" And on and on.

So how does someone create a $300-million business by accident? For that matter, how does anyone create a $30-million, $3-million, or even a $300,000 business by accident! The fact is, entrepreneurship is a complex, messy business. It involves scrambling, falling down, shifting directions, trying again . . . and again . . . and again. And for some reason, inherent in the process is a reaction of surprise toward the final achievement. While contemplating this phenomenon, I was re-reading *Working*, by Studs Terkel, a fascinating book full of real people describing their real-life jobs and how they feel about them. The thought occurred to me: What could we learn if we heard the stories of the entrepreneurs who created the companies that created the jobs for the people in Studs's book? Would it cast new light on the mystery of entrepreneuring? Would it expose common patterns thriving entrepreneurs enact over time that people who fail don't? Would it help explain the riddle of the glorious accident?

And so began the three-year endeavor of tracking down entrepreneurs across America, hearing their dramatic presentations, transcribing hours of tape, and portraying the real-life saga of creating a new enterprise. The final product reveals that common Americans do create glorious accidents all the time by following similar paths:

- They know the terrain.
- They seize the opportunity.
- They find a mentor.
- They radiate zeal.
- They work with tenacity.
- They give mind-boggling service.
- They build a powerful team.
- They get more from less.
- They notch it upward and onward.
- They passionately give back to their community.

While these ten keys may not guarantee triumph, they dramatically up the odds that a new enterprise with "take," stabilize, expand, and prosper. And because nothing stays the same very long anymore, these entrepreneurial skills are critical to leadership of the future. To survive long term, all organizations need to constantly update, innovate, and redefine their very nature. So the ten keys presented here can help any leader find new opportunities, move an organization off dead center, and make dazzling things happen.

THE APPROACH

As you read the chapters that follow, keep in mind that I was not looking for high-profile companies—the ones written about all the time. I was looking for a wide variety of people in a wide variety of places in a wide variety of businesses in a wide variety of industries. I wanted the book to "look like America" as much as possible—the full gamut of types. In a sense, I was looking for a scientific sample—a smattering of businesses that might represent the larger population of companies. I called attorneys, consultants, professors—anyone who could help locate these entrepreneurs. I also scoured numerous publications to hunt them down: *Inc., Entrepreneur, Independent Business, Small Business Opportunities, Black Enterprise, Hispanic Business, The Franchise Handbook,* and others. The final sample included male and female entrepreneurs from various ethnic backgrounds who own small, medium, and large companies in the full spectrum of American industries: manufacturing, high tech, petrochemical, transportation, wholesale, retail, service, health care, real estate, entertainment, restaurant, food service, and the arts.

The process was fairly simple: I sent each business founder a letter explaining the project, then followed up with a phone call. Next I conducted and recorded a detailed interview, either in person or on the phone, depending on my travel schedule. The interview format was completely open-ended and unstructured. I simply asked, "Tell me the story of your business from its early beginning up to today." Most got right after it, as they had told their stories many times before. A few needed prodding, so I typically inquired, "What were you doing before you started your company?" "How did the idea come to you?" "How did you take the first step?" "How did you find your customers?" "How have you grown your business?" In the end, I asked them to give any advice they might have for aspiring entrepreneurs. In most cases, I followed up with a second interview to clarify facts, figures, dates, names, and other relevant information.

Uncovering these stories was the most remarkable experience any student of entrepreneuring could imagine. I sailed on Marti McMahon's yacht, *The San Francisco Spirit;* toured Pam Walsh's candle factory; dined at Babe Humphry's Bar-J Ranch; and attended two of Annie Meadows's concerts. I flew over L.A. in one of Robin

Petgrave's helicopters, visited Alvina Quam's home (which doubles as her jewelry shop), toured the morgue and crematorium at Palm Mortuaries, and rafted the Snake River with Jackson Hole Whitewater. Perhaps my most surprising experience was interviewing Jon Huntsman, founder and chairman of Huntsman Chemical Corporation. I had hoped to include a few billion-dollar companies in the book but figured these entrepreneurs would be the hardest to track down. On my first visit to Jon's office, he asked a number of questions, then asked me to call his assistant, Ronnie, to squeeze in the interview. Each time I called during the next few months, Jon was traveling, closing a deal, or visiting plants—but Ronnie assured me he wanted to participate. One day she called and said, "Jon is taking a day off Thursday and would love to meet with you at his summer home in Deer Valley." Of course, that Thursday I found a way to be in Deer Valley, a resort town in the mountains of Utah, and spent three hours with the founder of a $5-billion corporation—the largest privately held petrochemical company in the world.

After collecting the stories, I transcribed the tapes, then performed a detailed content analysis to identify common patterns, trends, and themes. This process led to the ten keys to entrepreneurial success featured in this book. Keep in mind, these principles emerged from the interview transcripts rather than being squeezed, bent, and twisted into some preconceived theory of success. In other words, the actions portrayed here represent the *actual* practices of these successful entrepreneurs. Each chapter that follows features one of these important business concepts.

While many of the stories I collected are mentioned throughout the book, I highlight three at the end of each chapter that are particularly strong examples of the principle being portrayed. For the most part, these stories contain the actual words the entrepreneurs delivered to me. I edited the manuscripts only to clarify chronology, eliminate redundancy, and improve overall readability. I wanted you, as vicarious participant, to savor the extraordinary experience of sitting down with each actor, hearing the dialogue, feeling the energy, sensing the drama, and following the saga of ensuing success as I did. Though these stories have been shortened to highlight the principle discussed in each chapter, you will notice many of the other keys throughout each transcript.

One important note about the approach. While my goal was to write inspiring and informative literature, not conduct sophisticated science, I was still concerned about self-selection bias. That's when a hundred or so people are asked to participate and only a few respond. When this occurs, you have to ask, "What is different about the few who responded?" Most likely they don't represent the whole group, so you can't draw accurate conclusions about common trends. To my amazement, during the entire period of story collection, only seven of the entrepreneurs on my original list failed to participate. Two of the seven told me no; the others simply failed to respond to my letters and phone calls or couldn't fit me into their schedules in my time frame. In other words, over 90 percent of the people I contacted agreed to participate. This means entrepreneurs either like to talk about themselves or really want to help others—perhaps both. It also means the keys to success threaded throughout these stories are highly representative of the larger population of thriving entrepreneurs. Following them can help you discover your own path to successful entrepreneuring.

THE TEN KEYS TO SUCCESS

Key 1: Knowing the Terrain

Nearly all the entrepreneurs I interviewed were already heavily involved in the industry or marketplace in which they started their business. Most worked for another company in the same industry; some were serious and frequent consumers of the products or services. Being in the industry not only hones future entrepreneurs' skills and abilities, but it also exposes them to the products, services, mentors, customers, networks, opportunities, sources of distribution, major players, strengths and weaknesses of competitors, and so forth. The fact is, you can't create a successful new enterprise in a vacuum. I didn't interview a single entrepreneur who quit a job, refused to work for someone else, and sat around trying to think up something to do. While it may happen, it doesn't happen very often. To the contrary, many of these entrepreneurs were extremely successful in their jobs, well-liked by their companies, and highly regarded in their industry. Being in the thick of the action gave them ideas to contemplate and test while still drawing a paycheck. In nearly every case, this higher level of *knowing* revealed the missing piece that led to the idea that led to the new enterprise.

Key 2: Seizing the Opportunity

Successful entrepreneurs lock onto a *true* business opportunity, then take action. A legitimate opportunity includes these components:

1. An idea for meeting or better meeting a need.
2. A uniquely credible position in the industry.
3. Access to the resources required to implement the concept.
4. A handful of customers who are ready to buy the product *right now!*

Naively, many wanna-be entrepreneurs believe that the idea—component 1—is everything, and that once you have it, anyone can do the rest. While this may have been the case in past decades, today's swirling economy requires superb *execution*—components 2 through 4. Being intimately involved in the industry dramatically enhances the odds that all four components will align themselves at some point in time. And when they do, the entrepreneur-to-be must have the courage to take the risk and face the challenge—as the actors in our stories did. Actually, stepping up to the challenge is much less risky when these four components are present in sufficient strength. When many of our entrepreneurs launched their ventures, they were amply equipped with knowledge, skills, experience, resources, contacts, and built-in customers—the key elements of a true business opportunity!

Key 3: Finding a Mentor

During the process of formulating an opportunity, the hopeful entrepreneur needs support from a significant character—a parent, spouse, sibling, customer, friend, professor or boss. It must be someone with the credibility to endorse the notion and champion the plunge. Nearly all the entrepreneurs in our stories received some type of support at launch time: serious encouragement, seed money, a first contract, free consulting, feedback on ideas, introductions to vital contacts, ongoing financial support, and so on. In some cases, the encouraging mentor was a luminous ray in a murky tunnel of snarl-faced naysayers. Many of our entrepreneurs warn against listening to people who discourage the new venture. Apparently, opposing comments heard by aspiring entrepreneurs can be offset by a credible and assuring voice—a voice that seems to be necessary for launching the startup. Without support from a mentor, many of our business founders confessed they would not have started the heartrending journey.

Key 4: Radiating Zeal

The dictionary defines zeal as "eager and ardent interest in the pursuit of something." Its synonyms are *fervor, enthusiasm,* and *passion.* I witnessed this attribute in every entrepreneur I interviewed, and it's absolutely critical to successful new venturing! Like a series of concentric circles from a rock thrown into a pond, zeal washes forward, lapping at everything it touches. It draws people to the idea; it attracts members to the team; it entices customers to buy; it enables an average bunch of folks to beat the more talented teams. Zeal is captivating! Zeal is infectious! Zeal is power! I don't think it's possible to get a new venture off the ground without a hearty dose of zeal.

Of course, this finding is not surprising. One of the more common beliefs about starting a business—taught by educators, consultants, and authors of "how-to" books—is that you must love what you are selling to be successful. A love for the product is definitely the source of zeal for many of our entrepreneurs: Judi Sheppard Missett loves to dance, Robin Petgrave is enamored with helicopters, and Becky Brevitz adores animals. In an equal number of stories, however, the zeal is for independence, excellence, accomplishment, and success—not the products or services involved. In my case, I never experienced a pounding pulse to open a chain of frozen-dessert stores, but I did have a longing to create an excellent company—one that would be an envy in the industry. In a like manner, Dave Burbidge wasn't all that fond of garbage, Mary Ellen Sheets had no special affinity for moving vans, and Beth Stewart never bonded with billboards on buses. Rather, they had a zealous urge to build a successful business and thus become independent—the product simply facilitated the opportunity. So zeal definitely needs to be there; when it's not, fledgling entrepreneurs won't have the energy to make it up the steep hills. People who are naturally pessimistic, overly cautious, excessively critical, or unduly obsessed with *the numbers* can never generate the power necessary to make new enterprise happen.

Key 5: Working with Tenacity

Arduous effort, teeth-gritting tenacity, galvanized resistance—all recurrent themes in these stories. I always say, the real advantage of running your own business is getting to choose when to work your eighty hours each week. As these stories clearly show, our entrepreneurs work exhausting hours, do the work themselves to keep costs down, and hang in there long enough to realize good fortune. Rather than bailing out when times get tough, these folks do whatever it takes to make their business work! They find ways to go over mountains, under hurdles, and around roadblocks—they simply don't take no for an answer! Part of it is a love for the business—the zeal! Another part is a strong belief about personal control. The message came through loud and clear in my interviews: these entrepreneurs take full responsibility for their lives, their businesses, and the outcomes of their actions. They simply don't play the blame game! This hearty yet sometimes stressful attitude of personal control empowers them to act courageously, change courses, try again, whittle away, start something new, and relentlessly persist. Apparently, this posture is essential to conquering the rocky road of entrepreneuring. The fashionable trend in America to blame others for things that don't go right wasn't found in these stories. Neither was the all-too-frequent and halfhearted American hope of getting something going, letting others do the work, then making money while lying on a beach. So if your objective in life is to pile up lots of money without doing much, you probably need to inherit it, marry it, or try your luck in Las Vegas.

Key 6: Giving Mind-Boggling Service

An elated customer is really the only requirement for initiating a new business. Realizing this, and wanting desperately to stabilize their fragile new ventures, the actors in this drama go *way* beyond industry standards in serving customers. You'll see them offer stupendous support, astounding speed of delivery, unheard of prices, money-back guarantees, lots of face-to-face interaction, and real insights into people's needs. In sum, they seriously overshoot their customers' expectations, which boggles people's minds. This "customer is everything" attitude is absolutely critical to the early survival of a new venture; it wins the accounts, produces important long-term relationships, and renders a splendid competitive advantage. When people receive service beyond their loftiest expectations, they bond with the company, tell all their friends about it, go back again and again, and even stop going to competitors' businesses. And because a handful of loyal customers ends up being the lifeblood of the new startup, successful entrepreneurs establish systems to maintain this brilliant customer focus as the business grows. In doing so, they have little trouble competing with their bigger, bureaucratic rivals—often stodgy companies in their second or third generation of ownership—where customer service has become a routine function.

Key 7: Building the Team

Entrepreneurs are often portrayed as "Lone Rangers" who have trouble working with other people. While this may be the case with some new venturists, the entrepreneurs I interviewed thrive on the experience of others. Most realize they lack some of the deftness required to maneuver their expanding enterprise, so they enlist cohorts to fill in the voids—and in some cases, straddle the chasm. Indeed, they seem to have a knack for finding players with compensating talents, enthusiasm for teamwork, and a fervor for the start-up environment. In other words, these entrepreneurs are super team builders who quickly put the puzzle pieces in place. Throughout the stories, you'll hear them praise their mentors, partners, managers, and board members. Not only do they share the credit for their success, but many also share ownership. You'll love the example of Hyrum Smith (chapter 7), cofounder of FranklinCovey, who brought in partners to provide administrative, marketing, and financial leadership to a growing business. The company made more than thirty people millionaires when it went public in 1994, including Karma, the company's first order-entry clerk. Apparently, bringing in strong team members early, then sharing the credit and rewards, are critical to getting new ventures over the inevitable humps of entrepreneuring. Would-be entrepreneurs who hold onto everything and try to do it all themselves usually sputter, then tumble.

Key 8: Getting More from Less

Effectiveness is achieving your goals; efficiency is doing it with as few resources as possible. The characters in this book are masters of efficiency. They've been able to create something from practically nothing, get more out of less along the way, and keep costs beneath industry levels. Contrary to popular belief, many of these entrepreneurs are not lavish risk-takers—very few of them bet the farm in the beginning. Instead, they use an abundance of assets other than money to get started: they fiddle with ideas while they're still getting paid, enlist others who are also willing to fiddle, work on old desks in basements, partner up with their first customers and use someone else's plant rather than build one. Consequently, the capital meter doesn't tick very long before revenue is generated, which greatly increases the chance of financial success.

Not only do these entrepreneurs keep start-up costs down, but they also orchestrate remarkable efficiencies during the stages of business growth—the lessons learned in early bootstrapping apparently carry over. Throughout the stories, these folks defer salary, work extra hours, hire one person when two are needed, stretch cash flow, lease rather than buy, incur new costs only after increasing revenues, and build with cash flow. This keen eye for getting more from less has enormous competitive advantages with the big boys, often fat with corporate and industry tradition. It yields lower costs, better prices, superior products, and finer services than many better-established companies can provide. While we must give our entrepreneurs some credit for this genius, not having any money goes a long way toward sharpening this skill. Those who have cash spend it; those who don't learn to finagle without it. It's difficult to fully comprehend this mindset of *getting more from less* without wearing the entrepreneurial moccasins. Those steeped in traditional corporate life may never fathom the multitude of ways to solve problems and generate "big-time" results with small means.

Key 9: Notching It Upward and Onward

Today's bumpy environment can wreak havoc on new businesses, particularly if they are not able to adjust and move forward. The entrepreneurs I interviewed are masters of transformation, which helps explains the "unplanned" nature of the glorious accident. Here's what happens over and over again in the stories: First, our entrepreneurs set a rather small, attainable goal. Second, they devise a simple plan for accomplishing that goal. Third, they jump in with zeal and tenacity. And fourth, they achieve their objective and enjoy the thrill of success. This process provides experience, new contacts, increased confidence, and energy to tackle something a little more challenging. Now the cycle begins again as the same sound principles are applied at a higher level: objective, plan, work, success. In other words, successful entrepreneurs cycle through an upward spiral of incremental steps, each building upon the last. I call these cycles *propelling events* because they thrust the entrepreneur forward following each success and as new opportunities arise.

Two types of forward movement are observed throughout these stories. First, our entrepreneurs continue to *expand* what they are already doing—*notching it upward*. And second, they *extend* into new products and services outside the initial business—*notching it onward*. Our role models offer superb examples of this process. June Morris is a master! (See chapter 9.) Amazingly, she transformed her company from a travel agency to a leisure travel business to a charter airline service to a full-fledged airline in a relatively short period of time. This ability to alter the very nature of a business is critical for long-term survival in today's economy. It's really the practice of quickly shifting resources to new and more fruitful opportunities over time. Is it all that surprising that aggressive entrepreneurs who constantly monitor their customers' changing needs are surprised by the course of their journey? I find it more surprising that some corporations still cling to their prized ten-year business plan.

Key 10: Giving Something Back

This final pattern intrigued me the most. I guess I wasn't prepared for the enthusiasm many of these entrepreneurs would show for charitable giving and participation in community affairs. But the more I reflected on it, the more it made sense. Here's how it happens: By offering mind-boggling service, the entrepreneur attracts a handful of willing customers who help get the new venture off the ground. During the initial growth phase, incredible service is perpetuated with all customers as a survival strategy. Over time, the process endears both business founder and loyal customer to one another. From there, the story goes like this: "I wasn't sure this new venture was going to work. I can't believe we've been so successful. It's really our customers who got us where we are today. I would really like to do something to show our appreciation to this community." The result? These entrepreneurs get involved in cancer research, feeding the poor, aiding the homeless, supporting schools, lowering grocery costs, rebuilding cathedrals, disseminating health information, helping families of the chronically ill, and so forth. Community members soon begin to reason, "This business supports us, so let's support this business." And so the outcome of this generosity is often very positive for the business, even though this was not the objective sought in the beginning. But the fact is, the business gets an extra boost from people expressing gratitude and hoping to continue receiving resources from the company. Apparently, this key is important to getting fragile new ventures up and running.

RECAP

In sum, these ten keys illuminate the puzzling process of hammering out new ventures. The first three explain how entrepreneurs get into business; the last seven shed light on how they grow their companies over time. What we have here is a recurrent method for success used by everyday Americans: While knocking around in some real-world business situation, future entrepreneurs discover some unmet need, and after receiving hoorays from a major player, they step up to the opportunity with a zealous response. They work exceptionally hard, give mind-boggling service, build a strong team, orchestrate amazing efficiencies, constantly transform their organizations, and enthusiastically give back to their communities. After zigzagging around over time, they end up in a place that was not completely planned or expected—a place beyond anything they envisioned for themselves initially. Hence, the glorious accident!

So can entrepreneurship be taught, or is it an art form? Are we born with the talent, or can we develop the skills? The debate has gone on for years and will probably continue for some time. But my findings suggest that, for the most part, entrepreneurship is something you do; it's a set of actions that can be observed, learned, and enacted in the real world. The chapters that follow elaborate on these important keys and provide tips for mastering them. And in my opinion, there is real value in the clever, inspiring, and hilarious stories from a marvelous cast of American role models. Each story is packed with gems of business wisdom. Collectively, the tales display rich description of an important and dramatic human process—a process that constitutes the leadership model of the future. I think you'll adore the actors, enjoy their grit and quirks, and love their narratives.

Finally, in the epilogue, you'll have an opportunity to assess your readiness to launch a new venture. The tools provided will help you determine if you have adequate knowledge of the terrain, a sound business opportunity, a strong dose of zeal, and just the right mentor for you. You'll also have a chance to evaluate your service plan, the gaps to be filled by team members, and your ability to finagle with limited resources. The results of this self-assessment will tell you whether to jump in with both feet or keep your day job and continue your preparation. My hope is that all the factors will eventually come together to put you on the path to entrepreneurial success.

Happy entrepreneuring!

Chapter · 1

KNOWING
THE TERRAIN

Alvina Quam comes from a family of jewelry makers. At a very young age, she was exposed to every stage of the business. She used to sit on her great-grandfather's lap while he used the tools of the trade. She also helped her grandparents grind and set stones. While going to college, she made jewelry on the side to earn extra income. "I was working with my family," she says, "getting experience and establishing contacts with all the different traders and jobbers." After completing her master's degree, she applied for various jobs in education. Following a handful of rejections, she said, "Forget it, I'll just do my jewelry!" Since she already had her tools, she converted her garage into a shop and went to work. Over the past decade she has produced some of the finest Southwestern jewelry in the industry. A manager at Palms Trading Company in Albuquerque, says, "Alvina's work is very creative, very unique; she is clearly one of the top Indian artists in the area."

Knowing the terrain is the first key to success in any new venture. Industry knowledge can be obtained in a variety of ways, but without it, the odds of survival are not good. It's really more than a keen intellect for some field. Rather, it's an understanding of the lay of the land, the major players, and the ability to navigate through the territory.

Generally, this degree of *knowing* is obtained only through direct experience with the products, services, suppliers, and customers.

LEARNING FROM THE INSIDE

Most of the entrepreneurs I interviewed worked in the industry in which they started their business. Terry Neese, for example, held several jobs in personnel offices before creating Terry Neese Personnel Services in Oklahoma City. Babe Humphry managed a chuck-wagon ranch before debuting his Bar-J Ranch in Jackson Hole. June Morris was a travel agent with American Express before launching Morris Travel, and later Morris Air. And Rob Olson worked in an auction gallery before becoming a full-time auctioneer. The list goes on and on.

These entrepreneurs not only held jobs in the industry, but many were also star performers, thus acquiring solid expertise and hardy reputations; some rose to the highest levels within their organizations. Debrah Charatan, for instance, was the vice president of a real estate company before launching her own real-estate business in New York City. Wiley Mullins was the brand manager for the Mott's line at Cadbury/Schweppes before creating Uncle Wiley's, a company that produces healthy Southern food with an African-American bent. And "Ad Guy A" (his pseudonym) was an executive in the advertising industry before debuting his wacky marketing company "The Unknown Ad Guys." He and "Ad Guy B" wear paper bags over their heads so no one in their current organization will recognize them moonlighting in their new venture.

Working in the industry gives the future entrepreneur many distinct advantages. First, you learn all about the products, services, systems, processes, channels of distribution, and strengths and weaknesses of the competition. Second, you develop this industry savvy on someone else's nickel—it's like being paid to go to school. Third, you develop relationships with mentors and key contacts who can help down the road. But most important, you get to know the customers and where the *holes* are in the topography. If you pay attention, you gain answers to critical questions: How can products or services be modified to better meet needs? What do people want that they aren't getting? What would thrill customers more than the status quo? What systems or processes can help people become more effective? Indeed, the pieces required to make a strong run at new venturing are revealed in the flow of industry participation.

While businesses fail for many reasons, not knowing the terrain tops the list for an early demise. A small investment company I started years ago blew up for this very reason. I found a partner, raised some funds, and relied on others to give me critical industry information. Over the next few years, I watched our investments fall apart. One of the entrepreneurs I interviewed describes a similar experience:

> *I bought a chemical company that I thought would be a great deal. Maybe having succeeded in business made me think I was indestructible, that it didn't matter what type of business I ran. I worked hard at it, but I didn't know what I was doing. What it took was a chemist to get all the mixes right, and I hated chemistry in school! I lost money and ended up selling the company to a guy in the field who does that sort of thing all day long. Now it's doing phenomenal! He's branched out into hand cleaners, floor strippers, and other products. I mean, he's really done a number on that company.*

The advantages of on-the-job preparation are so great that I always advise young "wanna-be" entrepreneurs to first take a job in their chosen industry. I encourage them to give their very best effort, go beyond the job description, solve problems for the company, volunteer for challenging assignments, make as many friends as they can, save some money along the way, and keep their eyes and ears open. Opportunities usually come to those who are good at what they do. In the stories at the end of this chapter, notice how Frieda Caplan developed a real expertise in a niche no one else in her company wanted—mushrooms! Her reputation and contacts led to a unique business opportunity on the L.A. Produce Market. This pattern is seen over and over in the stories.

LEARNING FROM
USING THE PRODUCTS

Some of our entrepreneurs, while not employed in the industry, learned the terrain as serious and frequent consumers of the products. It's not quite as good as learning from the inside, but it's the next best thing. Gail Frankel, for example, purchased juvenile products during the years she was raising her children. Most of her inventions are items she and other mothers needed but couldn't find anywhere in the marketplace. Kevin Olson loved sports paraphernalia but could find items from specific teams only in their stadium or arena. He started The Pro Image to bring together a wide variety of team paraphernalia under one roof. Rafael Rubio ate fish tacos on his business trips to Mexico but couldn't find them anywhere in the states. The recipe that launched Rubio's Fish Tacos came from a street vendor in the Baja town of San Felipe. John Kittelsen, a hockey player in high school, couldn't find a mouth guard that would stay in when he took a good hit. He started EZ-Gard Industries to put a safer and more functional product on the market. In the stories that follow, notice how Joe Montgomery of Cannondale Bicycles keeps his finger on the pulse of the industry by hiring only avid bike riders. He argues that you don't need market research if all your team members are serious product consumers and thus know as much as anyone in the industry.

But far too often, hopeful entrepreneurs get excited about a product or service and move down the road of development only to find they are playing in the minor leagues—their product awareness and industry knowledge are too incomplete for the fragile venture to survive. That said, occasionally things do work out. Several entrepreneurs I interviewed had little knowledge of their industry yet became wildly successful. Tony Conza admits to knowing very little about the fast-food business when he started Blimpie Sandwiches. Fortunately, his youthful tenacity and a great-tasting sandwich pulled him through the operational disasters. Likewise, Lan England knew very little about the publishing business when he created *The Great American Bathroom*

Book. He spent a great deal of time and money in trial-and-error marketing before he got his bestseller on the shelves.

Unfortunately, few businesses are able to survive the short-term stumbling, the missed delivery dates, the products or services that don't quite work yet, the disappointed customers, and the burning of capital that occurs while the founders muddle along the learning curve. Thus, when I counsel aspiring entrepreneurs, I ask a number of questions to determine their readiness to launch the venture: What is your previous business experience? Who are the major competitors? What products currently exist on the market? Who has the best products? How is your product different from what's out there? What is your unique competitive advantage? What potential customers do you know that will buy the product right now? If they can't respond favorably to these inquiries, I suggest they keep their day job. Although I do think we learn from our failures, I never intentionally send anyone into an entrepreneurial abyss.

KEEPING UP TO DATE

Once new ventures are up and running, entrepreneurs often get the "big head," particularly if they are gaining customers, making money, and taking on bigger companies and winning. At this point, they often neglect the industry information that helped them succeed in the first place. "We're the best!" "Nobody will ever catch us!" How important it is to stay humble and constantly scan the environment for changes in trends, technology, preferences, products, and services. Successful entrepreneurs realize that large companies can quickly revamp and change direction. And as Joe Montgomery articulates later in this chapter, there is always the "guy in the garage" creating products to compete with yours, and you don't even know his name.

Many of the entrepreneurs I interviewed have established ongoing systems for acquiring up-to-date market knowledge. These are usually simple rather than sophisticated systems. For example, many of them attend trade shows, join industry associations, and participate in information-sharing groups (the Executive Committee, the Young Presidents' Organization, and so on). Some buy, analyze, and take apart their competitors' products. Others regularly visit their competitors' businesses looking for fresh ideas. One company has a program called "One Good Idea." They pile team members into a van and drive around looking for things their competitors do well. And of course, Sam Walton, the founder of Wal-Mart, was known as the master of shopping the competition. He believed that much of Wal-Mart's success was a function of his regular trips to K-Mart, Sears, and other discount retailers.

At Golden Swirl, we established a consumer feedback program to give us up-to-date market information. Using double-blind testing procedures, we had frequent yogurt consumers compare our products to other brands in the industry. This data formed the basis for our research and development program. When 70 percent of those sampled selected our product, we proceeded to scale up production; if less than 70 percent chose our brand, we went back to the lab. Some flavors took two months to get right, and some took two years. While this standard was strict, it guaranteed that our products were the finest in the market—and we had objective data to support our claims. Ultimately, this strategy enabled us to introduce a full line of nonfat products that tasted better than most low-fat brands. Our product line was a real key to our success.

In the stories featured in this chapter, notice how our three role models have created policies, strategies, and systems to keep them well informed. Frieda Caplan, for instance, has a policy of listening to everyone about everything, whether it's an oxygen-retardation system, some exotic new fruit, or a better way to ship produce. Sean Nguyen works closely with his customers and produces whatever products they want. And Joe Montgomery hires passionate consumers to bring the latest industry trends into his company.

BUYING INDUSTRY KNOWLEDGE

Although a growing number of men and women want to start their own businesses, many will never realize this dream: some will struggle with the idea, others will lack the knowledge, and many will fall short on experience. Here's where the format of franchising might help. Essentially, buying a franchise is paying someone else to get you up to speed, keep you current, and worry about the *industry knowledge* part of the equation. And the opportunities are endless! The *Franchise Handbook* runs numerous ads and articles every quarter. Each year *Entrepreneur Magazine* lists the top 500 franchises in America. *Black Enterprise* publishes a top-50 list for black entrepreneurs. And every good bookstore will have several current books on franchise opportunities.

Here's how franchising works. A company with a proven track record sells you the rights to duplicate their concept in a specific territory. For an up-front fee and an ongoing royalty, you get access to their products, trademarks, training, marketing strategies, advertising materials, and ongoing product research and development. It sounds great in theory; too bad it doesn't always work in reality. Buying a franchise definitely has its pros and cons. The obvious advantages are that you don't have to reinvent the wheel, you get training and help where you might be weak, and you have a much bigger partner keeping your products, systems, and services state-of-the-art. These factors make buying a franchise a lower risk than starting something new. Statistics from the U.S. Department of Commerce show that only 5 percent of franchised units fail each year. Those are pretty good odds.

The down side of franchising includes the high fees, the strict conformity to someone else's system, and the inherent conflict between franchiser and franchisee. These problems are magnified tenfold when the franchiser is a relative newcomer to the industry and knows the terrain no better than you do. While this may sound far-fetched, I could tell horror stories about companies that open one unit, enjoy brief success, then sell franchises all over the country. When the franchiser lacks industry knowledge, you end up in the worst of all worlds:

you have to worry about keeping the concept alive yourself, and you have to pay fees while doing it! Because more and more companies are expanding through franchising, we may see more of this in the future. If this trend continues, the failure rate from franchising may be the same as starting your own company. So you need to be careful if you decide to buy ongoing industry knowledge from someone else. Things will probably work out fine if the franchiser has (1) a long-term track record in the industry, (2) aggressive research and development that keeps the business state-of-the-art, (3) patents, technology, or trade secrets that are difficult to duplicate, and (4) reasonable fees that allow the business to work for *you!* In other words, a Wendy's franchise may be a better bet than Billy's Barbecued Burgers.

Six of the entrepreneurs I interviewed have successfully expanded their businesses through franchising. In each case, the entrepreneur has strong systems in place to support franchisees. Judi Sheppard Missett, founder of Jazzercise, is a particularly impressive role model. (See chapter 4.) Briefly, her franchisees pay $650 up front for an intensive three-day workshop that includes materials, testing, training, and basic business education. For an ongoing royalty, they get newsletters, video tapes, and updated materials, including thirty new choreographed routines every ten weeks. Her franchisees love the relationship! So under the right conditions, buying a franchise is a good way to acquire up-to-date industry knowledge.

In summary, knowledge of the terrain—derived from passionate involvement in the industry, serious use of the products, ongoing knowledge systems, and in some cases, buying a franchise—seems to up the odds that a new venture will succeed long-term. Knowing the terrain, however, does not guarantee success—obviously, other factors are involved. But it *is* a matter of probabilities: the more you know, the greater your chance of survival; the less you know, the more likely you will muddle, stumble, and fall.

OUR ROLE MODELS

Frieda Caplan

Frieda Caplan is the first woman in America to successfully develop, own, and operate a major produce business. She is the founder of Frieda's, Inc., a California company specializing in exotic fruits and vegetables. In 1986, she received the first Harriet Alger Award from Working Woman *magazine for being an exceptional entrepreneurial role model for women. In 1990, the* Los Angeles Times *listed Frieda as one of a dozen individuals from southern California who shaped the course of American business during the previous decade. Again, it was Frieda's excellent performance and industry contacts in her prior job that facilitated her entry into the produce business. Here's her story:*

I got into the produce business by accident. When I had my first child, Karen, I wanted a job where I could breast-feed. At the time, I was a production manager at a nylon factory. They actually paid me full salary for three months while I was off having the baby. Wanting to breast-feed and needing flexible hours, I looked for something else that would satisfy those needs.

I called my husband's aunt and uncle who were managing a major company on the L.A. Produce Market. It was just a regular produce house; they sold to anybody that came onto the market, primarily supermarkets and restaurants. I knew they had unusual hours in that business, so I called to see if they knew anybody that was looking for office help. They said, "My goodness, you called the right day! Come on down. We're desperate!" So I started working in their accounting department upstairs.

About a year and a half later, they went on a vacation and asked me if I'd come downstairs to cashier. While I was down there, I noticed they had small quantities of mushrooms—a specialty item at that time—that the salesmen were not selling. So while I was cashiering, I started offering the mushrooms to various customers. When my aunt and uncle came back a couple of weeks later, I said, "Gee, this was a lot of fun! Can I continue working downstairs?" They said, "Yes, if you'll work upstairs also." Eventually, I built the mushroom business up to the point that I stopped working upstairs altogether.

As my mushroom sales increased, I started becoming a factor in the mushroom industry. After a while, a business next door that I had sent customers to offered me a job as an independent contractor. I went to my aunt and uncle and said, "What do you think?" And they said, "Hey, go for it!" So with their blessing, I went to work for the people next door selling mushrooms. This was a citrus house, but they felt I would be very advantageous to their business. It was also an opportunity for me to build up a larger clientele of my own.

A few years later, they decided to go out of business. At that time, Southern Pacific Railway—the company that owned the produce market and leased the space—came to me and said, "Frieda, we want you to go into business for yourself." And I said, "You're crazy! I have no business experience. I'm just a salesperson for the mushroom growers." But they were very, very pushy and said, "We've been watching you for years; we feel you'll be very, very successful; we'll make it easy for you." They had the right to lease those doors to anybody in the market, and they offered them to me. This was on the Seventh Street produce market in L.A.

So I talked to my mushroom growers because I had no money, and they said, "Go for it! We'll continue to consign our mushrooms to you, you can sell them, then pay us after you collect the money." That was basically the financing. So I had ten days to get the licenses, organize a lot of things, and go into business for myself. Fortunately, the state and federal licensing people rushed everything through. Meanwhile, I linked up with other salespeople on the market who handled unusual items: pineapples, avocados, papayas. So in almost no time, I was in business, really pushed by the Southern Pacific Railway. I never had any desire or plans to go into business for myself. (Laughs.)

What happened next was rather interesting. The Taiwanese mushroom growers invaded the U.S. market with cheap canning mushrooms, which suddenly ruined the canning market for the U.S. mushroom growers. So right at that very time, southern California mushroom growers were forced to go onto the fresh market. I became their answer because I had been selling mushrooms fresh all along. That's why they were so supportive, not because I was a nice kid. It was one of those things where the timing was just right. I must say, however, that my father was extremely helpful too. I had asked him if this was the right thing to do, and to show his support, he took me to his bank and got me a $10,000 loan. As we left the bank, he said, "Pay it back as fast as you can so you'll have good credit." I paid it back in four months.

I guess a number of things really put me in good stead. For one, the media adopted us very quickly. What probably triggered things was a major story in the L.A. Times. They featured me as the only woman on the produce market and played up the fact that I had two small children. The lead to the story was "A sturdy mother of two . . ." They didn't want to say I was on the heavy side, so they called me "sturdy!" But the oddity of a woman in a man's world had some appeal. In addition, being the first woman in the United States to actually start, rather than inherit, a produce business attracted a lot of articles and stories. Of course, back then it was very unique, which certainly helped.

I think there was another factor in our success: the market itself became a source of products. During our first year, we stumbled onto a new product that eventually set us up internationally. Safeway came to us looking for something called a Chinese gooseberry; one of their customers had eaten them as a missionary in New Zealand. I told them I had never heard of it. A couple months later, a new broker on the market started offering Chinese gooseberries. No one was interested, but they all told him to go see Frieda. So he came to us, and the minute I heard Chinese gooseberries I said, "I've got a customer!" He had 2,400 pounds, which was a lot at the time. I said, "We'll take 'em!" We eventually named and marketed that product as the kiwi fruit. We brought it over here, developed a tasting program, and even asked the growers in New Zealand to change the name, which they did. So we have been given credit both nationally and internationally for introducing the kiwi fruit. Of course, it took eighteen years for it to be accepted the way it is today, so we call it our eighteen-year "overnight" success story. (Laughs.)

Anyway, that really propelled us forward. From then on, chambers of commerce, merchant associations, trade commissions, the National

Academy of Science, the USDA, the California Department of Agriculture, and the media all started funneling questions to us about anything odd or unusual. So I suppose the single thing that really helped us grow our business was our open-door policy of listening to anybody on anything. The other wholesalers on the market were only interested in high-volume items: apples, pears, bananas, tomatoes, strawberries. So when farmers came onto the market with small, low-volume items like limes or horseradish or ginger, everybody said, "Go see Frieda." Not only did we have an open-door policy on new items, we were the first in the industry to put recipes and explanations for consumers on our packages. We were also the first to do air freight with TWA, and we've been on the forefront of experimenting with oxygen retarding systems to extend shelf life. But we've listened to everybody on everything, whether it's been produce, packaging, transportation, or new products.

> The single thing that really helped us grow our business was our open-door policy of listening to anybody on anything.

I'm also very optimistic—the kind of person that thinks everything comes out for the best. And a lot of our successes in selling have come from turning negatives into positives. Even when we have a disaster—which we had a few years ago when our ammonia system broke down and we lost everything in the place—we try to turn it into a positive experience. An example is a customer in Boston who ordered some English peas. He wanted fresh English peas, and we sent him dried ones 'cause we had a program on rehydrated beans and peas at the time. So we messed up the order but convinced him to put them out in his store anyway, and they became a success for us. So those are the kinds of things we try to turn around. We were shifting our paradigm long before it was the thing to do. We are just very proactive; we refuse to accept negatives.

We now handle between 400 and 500 items at any one time. If you pick up a current edition of Food and Wine Magazine, we list our top sellers. Our top-selling items last year were shallots, jicama, dried red tomatoes, pearl onions, and fresh chilies. We were credited with the explosion of hot chilies when we introduced the habanero in 1990. We're also the ones that introduced the sugar-snap pea, tofu, wonton, the spaghetti squash, elephant garlic, black-eyed peas, ginger, and cherimoyas. Probably the oddest thing we've ever introduced is the kiwanos horned melon out of Africa. So exotic specialty items is the nature of our business. Supermarkets in the United States and Canada are our major customers. If you go into Von's or Ralph's you'll see some of our items on ad every week.

Anyway, we stayed on the L.A. Produce Market until 1983; our space was about 5,400 square feet. We moved to a facility that had about 44,000 square feet about a mile off the market. In July of 1994, we moved here to Los Alamedos with about 82,000 square feet—a very sophisticated, modern facility. We now have over a hundred employees and are around $25 million in sales.

One of the things that really helped our growth was turning the leadership of the company over to my oldest daughter, Karen. I never encouraged either child to come into the business, but they both did. It was totally a surprise, but I consider myself very lucky. When Karen took over the presidency, we were doing something like $10 or $11 million, and in five years she doubled that. She has a lot of training in management and put it to great use; she brought the structure we needed to go from the entrepreneurial into the corporate world. When you hit beyond $15 or $16 million you really have to change your thinking 'cause you're no longer a small business.

Another exciting thing is that Karen and Jackie are very complementary to each other. Karen definitely loves to be in charge, and Jackie is a super salesperson. They really support each other, so it's a great team! I think a lot of women will have this kind of joy in business because they're more nurturing than men. So I have something few people have—I'm working with my daughters every day! They both have two children each, and I've had the joy of seeing them breast-feed their babies. They used to bring them down to work, so I would have my daughters and my granddaughters here. Now that's what I call a different kind of dream!

So anyway, this industry's been very exciting! And with the direction things are going in our country, the fresh-produce industry has no place to go but up. Many organizations, including schools, the government, and cancer societies, are encouraging people to eat five servings of fruits and vegetables every day. So it's not just a fad. In fact, it's the best medicine in the world! The way to fight heart disease, cancer, and a lot of other debilitating illnesses is with a broad diet of fruits and vegetables, including the unusual fruits and vegetables because they are high in trace minerals. You now find food retailers expanding produce departments all over the country.

I guess the thing I would recommend to budding entrepreneurs is to really learn the industry—join associations, network, take leadership, and become part of things. I have also found that having an open door and an open mind makes a big difference. Never reject out of hand anybody's ideas—explore them, then go with your gut feeling. I always tell my daughters, "I feel it in my elbows, good or bad." But after you've been in an industry for a while you just develop a base of resources and thought, and you can tell when something is right. And I depend on that a great deal!

> After you've been in an industry for a while you just develop a base of resources and thought, and you can tell when something is right.

Sean Nguyen

Sean Nguyen is the founder and former president of Nguyen Electronics Incorporated (NEI), a Minnesota-based company that manufactures electronic components for the computer, medical, communication, and automobile industries. Sean founded the company in 1986 when he was twenty-three years old. In 1993, the Small Business Administration named Sean the National Young Entrepreneur of the Year—he received the award from President Bill Clinton at the White House. Notice how the industry experience Sean gained with his first employer led to his *business opportunity. In 1997, having achieved $10 million in sales with 200 employees, Sean sold the company to Plexus, a large contract manufacturer in Wisconsin. Here is his story:*

In 1980 I escaped from Vietnam in a homemade boat built by my family. I came with my father and my brother and another thirty-six people. We left my mom and two sisters in Vietnam. We lived on a farm there, but the communist government took it over in 1975. They took everything we had, so that's why we escaped. When we left Vietnam, we had a 50 percent chance of making it—if you got caught you would be in jail for a long time. But we passed through that section and sailed for four days and four nights to Thailand. During the trip we had a big storm, and everybody got sick because the boat was so small. Then pirates stopped us and took everything we had and raped all the women.

When we got to Thailand, we stayed in a refugee camp for Vietnamese for three months. Then we went to another refugee camp in Indonesia and stayed there for six months. Finally, we got a sponsor in the United States, a cousin who lived in Minnesota, and came here in September of 1981. First we landed in San Francisco, and then we went to Minnesota. I was seventeen, almost eighteen years old. I was very cold because the weather was very different. We didn't have a penny when we got here, but we were allowed to stay because we were refugees and we had a sponsor. You have to be here five years to become a citizen, so we became citizens in 1988.

My cousin had a big family of nine members in a two-bedroom apartment. His family just barely came to United States, too; they came over three or four months before we did. They lived in that apartment, and only my cousin worked. We couldn't afford to rent an apartment, so we lived with them. My cousin and his wife stayed in one bedroom, and the girls all stayed in the other bedroom. All the boys and my father slept in the living room for almost a year.

We wanted to go to work, but my father was almost sixty years old, so it was very difficult for him to find a job. I was lucky. A friend of my cousin knew a company called MultiTech Systems, a company that was manufacturing computer modems. I went to work for $4.00 an hour to do final assembly—I put the modems in the box. I worked there for six months and couldn't speak English at all. It was very difficult, but I learned very quick and I worked very hard. They liked the work I did, so they decided to let me work long hours—I worked about fourteen hours a day. The company was really growing, so they had no problem paying overtime. So that's how I started at MultiTech.

When I first started working, I used most of the money to send clothes and stuff to my mother and sisters in Vietnam. You couldn't send the money, so we just sent them materials. After a year I got promoted to group leader and supervised a few employees. I moved from final assembly to computer-board assembly, which meant I put all the components on the circuit board—I did the soldering and inspecting, so I was doing very well. My English was still not very good, but I tried to learn, and people liked me a lot. Then some engineers and technicians wanted me to work for them, so I got promoted from supervisor of assembly to technician. Since I didn't have any schooling, they sent me to night school for a year. I went to work all day, then went to school at night.

My father and brother were still without employment. It was very difficult for them to find a job. I tried to get them on at MultiTech, but they wouldn't hire them because we are family. So one day I said to my boss, "Is it possible that I can bring home work for my father and my brother to do?" I was a technician testing modems, so you don't need a lot of equipment; you just need the terminals and the telephones. So we put some telephones in the basement and were doing the functional tests. At the end of the day, I would bring home 1,000 modems, then bring them back the next day. We worked very hard, so MultiTech loved the service. I was still going to school two nights a week, but I helped them whenever I didn't have school. Sometimes I would go to work, then go to school, then come home and help them, too.

During that first year, MultiTech's business really picked up. Because the technology was moving very fast, they wanted a very quick turnaround. They didn't want to start a second shift, so one day I told them, "You can't find anywhere better than us." So they decided to send all the work home with me. We were doing modems all the time, then got into assembly, too. I hired more people, mostly Asians because they like to work long hours. Because we work for $4.00 or $5.00 an hour, we have to work more than eight hours to have a good living . . . you understand that. Anyway, while we were doing this service, I said, "We're good at this; why can't we just open a business?" So that's how it started. Interesting, right?

I worked for MultiTech from 1982 until 1986. Even after I opened my business, I worked there part time, so I still had some salary. We were saving the money we were making, and we still lived together—my father and brother and me. During that time I bought a home, so I hired more people to work in my basement. I kept asking MultiTech for more and more work. First we were doing the labor only, then we started buying all the materials and manufacturing products for them. After some time, we got work from other companies, too. The first year, which was 1986, we did $50,000. The next year we did about $150,000. Then we moved out of the basement and leased a space, about 2,500 square feet, and did $450,000 in sales. So that's how it started, and we have grown very nicely. We grew from $450,000 to $750,000, then $1.2 million, $2.4 million, $4 million, $4.7 million. Now we are in two locations and have about 50,000 square feet. We were able to lease our new buildings and buy all the parts we need with the earnings from our business. We are in the process of getting a line of credit from a lender, but mostly we have built our company with our own cash flow. We do around $10 million in sales.

We now provide a variety of electronic contract manufacturing services . . . any electronic device, we can manufacture. Let's say a customer wants to design a computer. We go out and buy the parts and manufacture the computer. If they want to do medical products, we can do medical products. We do about 20 percent of the medical products for Medtronics, a big medical company in Minnesota. We also manufacture computers for Unisys and Xerox. Most of our people are Asians, so they are very flexible. We have one division that does very high-tech products and one that does low-tech, labor-intensive products. In the high-tech division, we do the boards for laptop communication modems, the high-tech medical products, and the industrial controls. We also do some high-tech consumer products. We do sensors for Honeywell that go into the Cadillac. We also do a very high-tech dog collar, which is interesting; it controls the dog; it shocks him in the neck if he goes too fast. So we are very well diversified in the industry.

Since technology is getting smaller and smaller, you need more high-tech equipment to produce these products. During our growth, we invested $3 million in electronic-manufacturing equipment. This has made us very competitive in getting contracts. We get most of our work from our reputation. You service one company well, then you get work from other companies. We've been working for MultiTech for many years and service them well, so they are a very good reference. It's just word of mouth in the community. People say, "NEI is great! They service us well, with on-time delivery, at very competitive prices." That's how we grow the business.

> Our success has come from hard work, using common sense to run the business, and treating people well.

I think our success has come from hard work, using common sense to run the business, and treating people well. I have always tried to treat our employees just like our customers—to me they are the same. You can't just make your customers your priority and forget about your employees. Customer service has been very important to us, but let me tell you, how can you service the customer well if you don't take care of the employees? Right? They are the same—they are both important. If I commit to deliver a product to my customer, and my employees can't commit to meet the delivery, then we have a problem. So it is important to have teamwork. I learned this from MultiTech—they take care of their employees—it's very nice. I was lucky to work with them for my first company. When I opened my business, I used a lot of things I learned from them.

Another thing that is very important is to run your business with honesty—honesty will take care of everything. I'm honest with my employees, and I work well with them. I think this has helped a lot. You also need to work, not just harder but smarter. It's hard because bigger companies have more advantages, so you have to work harder and smarter to compete with them. I think this is why we're successful: we're a team that works hard and smart so nobody can beat us. Teamwork makes a difference!

Actually, I never, ever thought I would be doing something like this. (Laughs.) It's a big surprise! My goal when I was making $4.00 an hour was to make $8.00 an hour. But I'm looking back and I say, I treat my employees equal to how I treat my customers, I create teamwork, I'm honest with people, and we work harder and smarter. So it makes sense, right? There really isn't anything unique about our company. America is such a wonderful land of opportunity; there is no way I could have done this in Vietnam. I certainly am living the American dream. (Laughs.)

Joe Montgomery

Joe Montgomery is the founder of Cannondale Bicycles. He started out selling a wide variety of bike accessories. When he introduced his first aluminum-frame bicycle in 1983, he was deeply entrenched in the industry. Cannondale went on to "write the book" on how to make aluminum bikes. Today, with sales approaching $200 million, the company has the reputation of producing the finest bicycle frames in the world!

I was born and raised on a fruit farm in central Ohio. My mother and I ran the farm from as far back as I can remember because my father was doing another business. So I was hiring and managing people when I was twelve years old. Somewhere in there I decided I wanted to go into business for myself. My grandfathers had their own businesses, my father had his, and we had the farm. So I just kind of assumed that's what you did when you grew up. At one point I was pretty hot on some kind of agriculture endeavor because I loved the outdoors. As a farm boy you're up before it's light, you go outside, and you come in sometime after dark. So I loved anything outdoors: hiking, fishing, cycling, whatever.

My father used to get after me because I was always taking apart everything he bought me. I think you become mechanically oriented when you work on a farm because you're fixing stuff all the time. I don't think you can work on a farm and not be messing around with something, whether it's an apple grader or a tractor or a plow or a sprayer or something. It's never a problem when it rains because you have plenty to do in the barn on those days. So I think that was a lot of it, but my father told me at one point, "I'm not going to buy you anything anymore because you just tear it apart." And I said, "Well dad, the guys that make these things obviously don't use them or they wouldn't make them the way they do." Whether it was a fishing vest, a hunting jacket, a tent, a bicycle, or whatever, it just didn't work the way it ought to.

After high school I went to a couple of colleges but ultimately dropped out. I ended up in the Caribbean working on charter boats. I spent a lot of nights on sailboats listening to the lines bang on the aluminum mast. In those days, the newest and most modern ocean-racing boats had oversized aluminum masts because they were stronger and much lighter. I actually got the idea for fat-tubed aluminum bikes while I was on those boats. I was interested in how you could make a bicycle frame lighter because our farm was on top of two large hills and I rode my thirty-five pound Schwinn up them all the time. I would pump real hard to get a run from the bottom, judge the stoplight just right, and still end up walking—there was just no way to pump a bike to the top! So when I was on those sailboats I'd think about this. Aluminum was obviously a better medium than steel, if it was engineered properly. So that was the beginning of the idea.

After I'd been in the Caribbean for a while, I took a job in New York as a research analyst on Wall Street. I knew I wanted to go into business for myself, but I wanted to get a bird's eye view of the possibilities. I had three ideas every two days, most of which were no good. I finally narrowed my interests to two industries: one was the camping-equipment industry, like Coleman or L. L. Bean; the other was the cycling industry. Within the bicycle industry, I saw three opportunities. The first was innovation. I thought the technology was way behind where it could have been. And of course, Cannondale has been on the innovative side of the bicycle industry right from our first product, which was the bicycle trailer. The second opportunity was in distribution. At the time, everybody used distributors, which meant they were selling the product twice. I mean, you would sell it to the distributor, then take his sales guy with you to the dealer and sell it again. I thought we could go direct and put a little money in our pocket, a little money in the dealer's pocket, and give the consumer a better cut too. The third thing was above-average growth, which usually comes out of the first two: innovation and changes in distribution.

Anyway, I got fired from my job in New York and eventually took a job with another brokerage company. But in the meantime I borrowed $7,000 from the Bank of New York and opened up a restaurant and bar on the upper west side of New York with a couple of friends. In fact, it's still there—it's called "Under the Stairs." It's on Columbus Avenue between 94th and 95th on the west side of the street. Anyway, that turned out to be a very fortuitous investment because I sold the business and used the money to start Cannondale.

I started working with an industrial designer in Wilton, Connecticut, on various ideas I had. One day I was going to his house in my car, and there's a long hill with a pretty steep grade that runs a couple miles. At the top of the hill there was this cyclist, a young guy with a big ladder pack—he had pumped all the way up the hill. I mean, it was hot, and this kid was not enjoying life. (Laughs.) As I turned the corner, I thought if I had to carry that thing, I would put it on a couple of wheels and lower the center of gravity—it would be an easier way to do the same job. By the time I got to John's house, I actually had a picture of this thing in my head. He was a very clever guy, and within a couple of days we were pulling prototypes around.

Once we had the trailer where we wanted it, we started showing it around the country. It was a frame with two wheels and a fabric pack; it hooked onto the bike right underneath the seat. We were buying all the parts and putting these things together in an old building down in Stamford. One of the guys that worked with me had an aunt in New Jersey who ran a stitching operation. She and her husband put some old machines in their basement, and that's where the cloth part was assembled. Well, we thought we were going to make zillions of dollars. As it turned out, we way overestimated the number we could sell and were going broke. Actually, we already were broke! We just weren't able to generate enough cash flow. But one day I was standing in a store down in Baltimore with one of our dealers, and I said to him, "What else can we make out of this fabric?" And he said, "Well, you see these little bright-colored bags hanging on the wall? We can't keep those in stock." So I bought one of 'em, and it was the same fabric we were using on the trailers. It wasn't long before we were making panniers, handlebar bags, and all kinds of stuff. That was at the time when cycle touring was really growing very quickly, and we rode that whole thing.

In 1977 we opened our first stitching facility because we had grown way beyond the basement volumes we had subcontracted out. It was 4,500 square feet at one end of a trucking terminal. After a few years, we moved into an old IGA store in downtown Bedford which was about 14,000 square feet. Then in 1980 we found this old shoe factory in Bedford. It was 70,000 square feet or something like that. Two or three shoe companies in a row had gone broke there, and this building was a political hot potato because they had invested a lot of money into it, but nothing was coming out of it—no jobs or anything. I made a bid for $300,000, which was what I thought it was worth, but they had to sell it for $500,000 or it would have been a big black eye for them. So we bought it for $500,000. They financed it at 100% and loaned us one million dollars to fix it up. The interest rate was 2% and the term was thirty years. So it was an offer we just couldn't pass up.

We were making so many things at the time, all the different bicycle bags and, of course, the trailer. We wanted to make aluminum bikes right from day one but didn't have the kind of capital we needed. But when we hit $5 or $6 million in sales, our balance sheet was at the point we could really get serious about bikes. We bought every aluminum bike we could find, rode them, tested them, and did all kinds of things. We were very encouraged because we knew aluminum was the right way to go; we also knew that nobody was utilizing the material in the right way. Then in the fall of 1981, I got this letter from a young engineer who wanted to make aluminum bikes. He had designed several but didn't have the wherewithal to make them. To make a long story short, he came down and talked to me and ended up working here. His name was David Graham. We went very quickly from the design to the first product. Because we knew the aluminum bike was coming, we'd reserved about half the shoe factory for bicycles and started making them in that space.

Our first bike hit the market in 1983. We went to the trade show that year geared up to make 6,000 units, and we sold them all out at the show. We promised delivery in May but delivered in August. (Laughs.) Oh man, what a time! We really had to come back and figure out how to mass-produce them. See, making steel bikes is relatively easy. You can literally go out and buy a book on how to do it, and all the parts and equipment are readily available. Of course, they aren't going to be any different than the next guy's bikes, so you're going to end up with a low-margin product. But aluminum was something totally different. The real competitive advantage is the weight of the bike plus the stiffness. As you increase the diameter of the tubes, the stiffness goes up by the cube. And of course, that's what you want in a bicycle. When you step on the pedal you want to go forward—you don't want the frame to bend or twist and absorb that energy. You want the energy from your foot and leg to go right into the wheel to propel you forward.

We also chose to weld the tubes rather than hard-tool them like most bikes. You see, most bikes are made with straight tubes that you forge and then glue together. You can make a bike that way, but it's not going to be the ultimate bike. By welding, you eliminate all the overlap on the tubes and end up with a lighter, stiffer, stronger unit. Additionally, you are able to change the design and improve it all the time because you don't have any investment in expensive forging or casting tools. So we are cutting, bending, and welding aluminum tubing, and we can do a lot of new and different things quickly. It's really an important part of our culture to make everything better tomorrow than it is today. It's the way we've built the company from day one, and we're all very passionate about it. We've got a lot of people around here saying, "Gee whiz, I know this bike weighs twenty-two pounds, but we can make one that weighs twenty-one pounds, and this one has too much of this and too little of that." Sometimes I think we've done too good a job in that regard—it's almost a disease here. (Laughs.) I have to remind people every now and again, "Hey guys, I know we can make the one we just made better, but we also have to meet payroll, so let's sell some of these things."

The quest for the best not only pervades the product end of the business but also the systems. We now have a very sophisticated system in place that we have innovated. We ride each bike on a given terrain with certain weight riders at certain speeds and collect data on the strains and stresses being radiated in that frame. We then take the information, put it into our CAD system, and multiply it by a safety factor to make sure we produce the strongest bicycle possible. That information then becomes the benchmark for design activities in our CAD system. We have guys that are very good at using CAD, and they sit down with the benchmark data and say, "Well, I want a frame that's going to do this or that," and they design it the way they want. Then I say, "Yea, I think we ought to ride that frame." So they push a button that sends the data over the telephone to our production facilities. We then use lasers and other sophisticated equipment to cut and bend the frame.

Next, we have a patented method of putting frames together so we don't need any fixtures. We cut little tabs and slots in each one of the tubes so they fit together accurately. And because the tolerances are so tight, it won't go together in the wrong way. Then it's tacked, welded, sanded, painted—components are put on, and it becomes a bike. The system is very customer responsive; we can make changes to designs in no time. An example: Shaq O'Neal wanted a bike, but it had to be so big. We designed it on the computer and cut the frame. It was the biggest thing I've ever seen in my life. It didn't look like a real bike, I mean, the top tube was up around my Adam's apple! It was just unbelievable . . a huge bicycle!

Anyway, all along we funded our growth with debt. I mean, we were 50/50 partners with the banks for a long time, boy oh boy! We did asset-based borrowing—they'd lend against our inventories and receivables. This was good for us because it kept us in line. If the inventories got too big relative to sales, they wouldn't lend against them. Or if the receivable got too big or too old, they wouldn't lend on them. So there were strong incentives when we made something to ship it and get paid. But we were always into the banks. It was sad in some ways, but it was the only way we could do it. So the pucker factor was pretty high at different times of the year. (Laughs.)

Once we grew the company into a sizable business we were able to tap the public markets, which we did in the fall of 1994. It's done a tremendous amount for our profitability because we don't pay much interest anymore. All the money that used to go to the banks now falls through to the bottom line. On top of that, we never negotiated discounts for our bills. Our first question was never "What's the price?" It was always "How soon do we have to pay for it?" So when we got the capital from the public offering we went back to these vendors and said, "Now we're going to play by a different set of rules because there's less risk. The price needs to be better and the terms need to be just as good, unless you're willing to give us an attractive discount on the bill." Our margins have gone from the high 20s to the mid 30s.

But I'll tell you, I don't think we'd be as strong as we are if we hadn't done it the way we did. We've learned how to manage with very limited resources, and it's helped us become very competitive in the market. I mean, the best news in the world for us is that we've got a big competitor. Oh boy, not a problem, not a problem . . . And conversely it

> I'm not worried about this big competitor or that big competitor. I'm worried about some guy in a barn someplace whose name I don't even know right now.

also scares me because we're getting big! We now have plants in Bedford, Pennsylvania, Holland, and Japan. I'm not worried about this big competitor or that big competitor. I'm worried about some guy in a barn someplace whose name I don't even know right now—that's the guy I'm worried about.

Anyway, we now produce most categories of bikes: tandems, road bikes, mountain bikes, hybrid bikes, touring bikes, track bikes. We have reps all over the world who sell in over sixty countries. Thousands of retailers sell our products worldwide—between here and Europe alone we have well over 2,000 retailers. There are certainly other companies in the United States that do what we do, but they're relatively insignificant in the overall scheme of things. But there's going to be more competition all the time because the consumer has clearly stated that all things being equal, "Give me aluminum!" We are just about to announce a new frame technology that's going to set them all back on their ears again because it is very unique—it is considerably lighter and considerably stronger. It's going to do again what we did in 1983. So I feel very confident we can continue to kick everybody's hind end, which is a lot a fun to do!

My advice to people who want to start a business is to hurry up! Don't do any market research. If you're not a user of the product, if you're not involved with it all the time, if you don't know enough about it to know it's a good idea, if you don't know that it's truly unique, then don't waste the money you have on market research, because you're going to fail. What we've always done is hire our customers: people who are passionate about cycling, people who know the sport and want to make it more fun, people who have the tools with which to work, people who want to get greater performance out of every product, whether it's a trailer, a bag, or a bicycle. You know, we're just always trying to make the product better.

TIPS FOR KNOWING THE TERRAIN

1. **TAKE A JOB IN THE INDUSTRY.**

   Give your very best effort, take on special or unusual projects, meet as many people as you can, rise to the highest level possible, keep your eyes open for better ways to meet needs.

2. **JOIN INDUSTRY ASSOCIATIONS.**

   Get involved in trade shows, take leadership positions in associations, join information sharing groups, subscribe to and read the trade journals and magazines.

3. **CREATE ONGOING KNOWLEDGE SYSTEMS.**

   Get customers involved in your research and development, hire customers who are passionate about your products, constantly follow competitors' products, visit their places of business, listen to everyone about everything.

4. **LEARN FROM OTHER INDUSTRIES.**

   Watch for products, services, systems, and technologies that might transfer and provide a competitive advantage for your company.

5. **DON'T GET THE "BIG HEAD."**

   Stay humble, watch how large companies react, and realize there are always people in garages tinkering away.

Chapter • 2

SEIZING THE
OPPORTUNITY

---

*J*anet Yorgason received her cosmetology license and started working in
hair-care salons. She noticed that parents with larger families had a
terrible time getting their children in for haircuts. The "wait—take your
turn—wait some more" cycle was more than some children and their
parents could handle. During this time, Janet also had several standing
appointments in her own home and her customers' homes. The idea came
to her: why not start an in-home, hair-care service for families? She
already had her license, her experience, her equipment, and a beginning
clientele. She created a business card, circulated a flyer, and bought a
"Mary Poppins" bag to carry her gear. Within a short time her new business, "At-Your-Door Hair Care," was serving forty to fifty families in the
convenience of their own homes.

This pattern repeats itself over and over in the stories: the entrepreneur works in an industry, develops some expertise, sees a way to do
something better, has the experience to meet the need, has the
resources, has a handful of potential customers, musters the courage,
and takes action. Frieda Caplan did it. Sean Nguyen did it, Joe
Montgomery did it. You'll see this pattern again in the stories that
follow.

OPPORTUNITY OR PIPEDREAM?

One of the favorite pastimes in our home is to think up new products or services for business ventures; over the years we've schemed up dozens of them. Here is one of the latest: a homing device that can be planted in the soles of children's shoes so when you push a button, a tone will help you locate these all-too-frequently missing items. This ingenious gadget could save parents hours of time and countless bouts of depression during their child-rearing years. I know many parents who would pay handsomely for this product right now!

Unfortunately, Mary and I know very little about the electronics industry—we have no training, we have no experience, we have no contacts. Nor do we have any knowledge of the shoe-manufacturing, marketing, and distribution business. We could probably raise some money, launch the venture, and stumble along the industry learning curve, but we'd most likely run out of enthusiasm, interest, and money long before we enjoyed success. So it's a great idea but not a realistic business opportunity for us.

Naively, many aspiring entrepreneurs believe the idea is every-thing—once you dream it up, you're home free—anyone can do the rest. While this may have been true in past, it certainly isn't the case today. An interesting study conducted in 1982 revealed that 80 percent of the *Inc.* 500 CEOs credited their companies' success to "novel, unique or proprietary ideas." The same study repeated in 1992 showed that 80 percent of the *Inc.* 500 CEOs said their companies' ideas were rather "ordinary or mundane." The key to their success, they said, was "superb execution!"

Obviously, there are a lot of good ideas in our rapidly changing world, but there are not a lot of good ideas coupled with people who can and will make things happen. From my interviews with the entre-preneurs, sensational execution is much more likely when a legitimate business opportunity presents itself. Here are the critical components: (1) an idea for meeting or better meeting a need, (2) a credible posi-tion in the industry, (3) the resources required to meet the need, and (4) customers who are ready to buy the product or service *right now!*

When these four ingredients are present, the new venture has a good chance of taking off; when several are missing, the idea is nothing but a pipe dream.

To elaborate, most of the entrepreneurs I interviewed first observed a need that was *not* being met in the marketplace or a better way to meet a need that *was* being addressed (better quality, better price, more features, better service). After mulling the observation over, they realized they were uniquely positioned to meet the need; they had the education, experience, skills, training, credibility, certification, and so on. Next, they realized they had the resources required to make things happen: equipment, tools, partners, contacts, access to money, offices, a studio, and so forth. Finally, and most important, they had customers who were ready and waiting for the products or services at the time the business was launched—and in some cases, beforehand! Recall from our previous stories that Frieda Caplan already had customers buying mushrooms; Sean Nguyen's first customer was the company he was working for, MultiTech Systems; and Joe Montgomery was already selling bike accessories to dealers who were willing to buy his bicycles.

The story of Teresa McBride, founder of McBride and Associates, is a great example of a legitimate business opportunity waiting to be pursued. While managing her parents' restaurant in Grants, New Mexico, Teresa wanted more time to spend with her son. She was doing all the bookkeeping on the weekends, so she decided to buy a computer to speed up the process. She researched various systems, bought a computer, got some training, and successfully completed the conversion. When customers at the restaurant learned what she had done, they started asking her to do the same thing for their businesses. According to Teresa, "Having been through it, I knew the ropes . . . so I just took the experience I had and used it to help other people get started." It wasn't long before she had real expertise in a variety of information systems.

When her family decided to sell the restaurant, Teresa thought she might go back to school. But a friend encouraged her to bid on a large government computer contract. To her amazement, she won the bid! With a handful of customers and a government contract, she now had a real opportunity. She quickly set up shop in her home, hired a few helpers, and started bidding on other projects. The typical contract would involve identifying an organization's information needs, researching available hardware and software, installing the system, and training people to use it. During the past ten years, Teresa has developed a national reputation for designing "turnkey" information solutions. She has received the "Businesswoman of the Year" award from the National Hispanic Chamber of Commerce and the "Small Business Person of the Year" honor from the U.S. Small Business Administration. McBride and Associates now employs several hundred people in a dozen offices, doing $100 million plus in annual sales. Now that's a legitimate business opportunity!

Jayne Tsuchiyama, founder of the New York design firm Cross Check, is another notable role model. In 1990 she joined Lifetime Television as the director of creative services. Her major responsibility was to promote the network through advertising, print campaigns, merchandising, and special events. After winning a dozen industry awards, she was promoted to vice president. About this time, the president of Lifetime left the company and set up his own business. He called Jayne and asked her to come to work for him. She didn't want to work for his company full time but agreed to a consulting arrangement. With the blessing of Lifetime, she also turned her current job into a consulting contract. With two initial contracts, she now had a sound business opportunity. As Jayne recalls, "Because I was able to negotiate projects in advance with both accounts, I felt comfortable enough setting up shop." So Cross Check was launched to help companies create identities, design promotions, and carry out special events. Since its inception in 1993, the firm has done creative work for Comedy Central, Court T.V., The Ms. Foundation, Vanity Fair Magazine, and others.

THE COURAGE TO SEIZE

Of course, it takes courage to seize an opportunity once it presents itself. The aspiring entrepreneur must be enthusiastic about the challenge and willing to accept some degree of risk. It also helps when a strong mentor provides a gentle nudge—the topic of our next chapter. The risks of launching a new venture, however, are reduced dramatically when you have a great idea, credibility in an industry, adequate resources, and a handful of customers. These components produce immediate sales and enhance the probability of early profit—the lifeblood of any startup. Businesses that fail are generally missing one or more of these important ingredients. Sometimes it's the idea, but more often it's one of the other components: inadequate experience, insufficient resources, or a lack of access to customers. When "wanna-be" entrepreneurs chase a pipe dream, it almost always vanishes into thin air. The message? Be patient and wait for all four ingredients to come together. When they do, it's an easy transition from employment to your own business. So be brave and step up to the challenge! All you have to lose is your job, and you can always find a new one of those. The three stories that follow are noble examples of viable business opportunities that were seized with courage.

OUR ROLE MODELS

Diane Dimeo

Diane Dimeo is the owner of Pony Haven, a business that provides ponies for birthday parties, barbecues, carnivals, reunions, and neighborhood get-togethers. She owns twenty-two ponies and averages twenty-five parties a week. Her flyer reads, "Give Your Youngster a Birthday Party to Remember, Make Your Church Picnic the Best Ever, Be the Center of Attention at the Family Barbecue . . . Call Pony Haven." When Diane started her business she had the previous experience, the ponies, and access to customers. She explains:

It really started as a children's business. My parents moved from the city into the country. My brothers wanted a job to make extra money, so they started working in the onion fields. After a couple of days, they came home sunburned and said, "There's got to be an easier way to make a living." My dad said, "You got a pony out there, why don't you rent him out to the neighbor kids?" We had one pony at the time and a couple of horses. So they started going out to bigger and better neighborhoods and renting the pony. They would take it to people's homes, let the kids ride it, and take their pictures on it. With that money, they bought another pony. Then one of the horses had a colt. From there, it just skyrocketed. This was back in the '50s when we were all kids.

We had a step-grandfather who liked to build things. He came out here and started building a frontier town for the kids. Instead of taking the ponies to the people's homes, kids would come here to play in the frontier town and ride the ponies. We had everything in the town: a saloon that sold soda pop, a sheriff's office with a jail, a gallows behind the jail, a hotel. We had dummies in all the buildings and a dummy hanging from the gallows. We had boot hill with the boots sticking out of the graves with little sayings on 'em. It was really just a play place where kids could spend the day. We had lots of birthday parties in the saloon. Church groups would come out for hayrides and bobsled rides in the winter. We'd set up a bonfire and cook hotdogs. We didn't have enough room to separate the horses from the frontier town, so after we'd turn the horses out, people would be walking back and forth and the horses would walk up to 'em. We'd be roasting hotdogs over the fire and the donkeys would come over and eat the hotdogs.

We advertised the frontier town through word of mouth. We had a certain clientele, like we had a group from the air base that came out all the time to go riding. It was just a weekly thing—every Saturday and Sunday they'd spend their days out here. We also had a lot of neighbor kids whose parents would drive 'em here and leave 'em all day long. They would drop 'em off at eight in the morning and pick 'em up at nine o'clock at night. We were a good daycare. (Laughs.) We always had extra boys just staying around and helping us if they could come. Girls, too! They were always horse crazy, so they'd just come and hang out. Our swimming pool is an interesting story. The kids that worked here dug it in between taking horse rides. They wanted something they could cool off in, so they hand dug the hole. Also, once a year we had the mentally retarded come out. Their school would come, and we'd give 'em a day of hayrides, pony rides, pop, and hotdogs.

One year we had an article about us kids in Life Magazine. It was three pages long with pictures of the frontier town. I don't know how they heard about us, but they were interested because it was an all kids' business, run by kids. My parents were here to support and help, but they always said, "It's yours." Anyway, E. K. Edwards at Walt Disney saw the article and came out. He thought our business would make a great feature film. It was about the same time the series Spin and Marty was on— I don't know if you remember that or not. He wanted to do something like that and shoot it in our frontier town. He stayed with us for a few days each time he came. They got the summer shots done, the spring shots done, but waited a long time to finish the winter shots because we didn't get a lot of snow that year—that held 'em up for a while. Eventually, it was shown on their weekly show—the Mickey Mouse Club. It was before they had the Disney Channel.

We had to rebuild our frontier town three times 'cause we have a lot of wind out here. We sometimes get winds of 100 or 120 miles an hour. When this happened, there'd be nothing left of the town. We'd have to start all over and build it up again. We had antiques in the buildings, so we'd have to go get more of them. We kept the frontier town going long enough to put us all through college; we just tore it down about four years ago. We were still using it for hayrides up until then.

During those years, we also had a riding academy with the horses. We basically took kids on horseback rides—sometimes night rides, sometimes midnight rides. Then we extended it and started building wagons. We started taking those around to parades and renting them to people for store openings. We'd also do 'em out here; we'd hook 'em up and give people rides. We eventually stopped the academy because homes started going up and there was no place to ride. No one wants to go riding through a subdivision.

All along, I was working with my brothers. I was the only girl in the family of three boys. I took over the business when my brothers got older. I have one brother who's an attorney and another one who has a lot of rental property and things. Even though we took the ponies to parties in the past, it was never a big part of the business—it was very sporadic. But when we closed down the riding academy, I didn't want to get rid of the horses and needed some way of making money to feed 'em. I also had a young daughter coming up and wanted to spend time with her; I didn't want to work outside the home. So I decided to start taking the ponies out to kids' birthday parties—it was a way to use my ponies and spend time with my daughter and support her.

I just made up little flyers like this and hung 'em around the neighborhood (shows the flyer). I also ran ads in local papers—that's how we got started. We found people right off, and as the years have gone by, we've gotten a lot busier. People learn about me through word-of-mouth; they also see my truck going down the highway. I have one truck right now with my name and number painted on the side—it holds three ponies at a time. I have twenty-two horses total, and I've raised 'em all; I have males and females that I breed. I probably do about twenty-five parties a week. Last Saturday I did thirteen in one day—they were scattered all over the place. With the traffic the way it is, you just can't do any more than that.

So this is what I do full-time now. It's at a level where it's all I can handle, and it's stayed there the last couple years. Basically, it's me. If I get a real busy day or overly booked, I have a brother who'll come help me if I con him hard enough. My daughter also helps me—she catches the ponies, helps break 'em, things like that. Occasionally, I'll still do carnivals and store openings. I'll hire neighborhood kids to lead the ponies around. Our prices vary based on where people live, but we usually charge between $50 and $65 for a three-hour party. The downtown area is $50, and further out is $65. My main expenses are hay and gas. I think I'm probably going to keep the business about where it is. It's just getting too big to handle. Sometimes I have to turn down calls. I could do a lot more business on Saturdays and holidays. I mean, I could get another truck and pay someone else to deliver ponies, but . . .

Sometimes funny things happen. Once we took a pony to a party and didn't know she was pregnant. The people called up and said, "Something's wrong with your pony." When we went back, there was two ponies instead of one. (Laughs.) She had a colt at the party! That was a surprise to all of us. Another time, I took a pony to a party—I really don't like people taking my equipment off the ponies—and they took the saddle, the bridle, and everything off, then went in and had ice cream and cake. They didn't tie the pony up or anything, just left it standing on their lawn. This was a busy neighborhood, and as I'm going down the street, I see my pony going across the intersection. (Laughs.) I come to a dead stop, stopped traffic, and tried to stop the pony before somebody got killed. When I went back to the party, the people said, "We thought he'd just stand there." I said, "Your dogs and kids won't even just stand there!" Now I try to warn people not to do that. Anyway, the ponies really do get adjusted to the parties. They like ice cream, cake, apples, hotdogs—you know, they learn to like it. The kids love it too; I have a lot of repeats, I really do!

> You have to take responsibility and go in with the idea that you're going to make it work.

I don't know if this is the American dream, but I enjoy it. I never thought I'd be doing this now. It put us through college, paid for all our tuition and books and things—but I didn't think I'd be doing it when I got older. But it was a good opportunity for me to stay home with my daughter when she was little. It was also good for her to be around the horses—it was a good hobby.

I think people can start a business if they have an imagination and a good idea. But you have to take responsibility and go in with the idea that you're going to make it work. You can't say, "Well, if I fail, I'll try something else." I've had a lot of hard times where I wondered if this was going to work, but you just have to keep going. I think this is a problem in our society right now: kids don't know how to work anymore. I see too many kids say, "Mom, can I have ten dollars?" And the moms say, "Oh yeah," 'cause it's easier than saying, "You have to go out and mow the lawn first." I don't believe in that. I think kids need to learn responsibility— there's just no other word for it. They need to have a sense of work taught to 'em. You go down to the mall and you see these kids walking around aimlessly with no goals, just hanging out. Where are their parents? Why aren't they doing something? When I was growing up there was always chores. My parents were comfortable, but we had to work for everything. So I think we have to go back to basics and teach kids to work.

Bill Fitzgerald

Bill is the founder and CEO of Beautiful Images, a company that sells support garments to women over fifty. Before starting the company, Bill had three decades of experience in the direct marketing and specialty catalog industries. He discovered this opportunity while consulting with one of his clients. His wealth of knowledge, experience, and contacts produced incredible success from the beginning. The company achieved nearly $3 million in sales the first six months, and more than $9 million in three years. At the end of 1996 Bill sold the company to Value Vision Incorporated, a company based in Minneapolis. He says:

In 1975, I went to work as a catalog manager for Hanover House Industries. Hanover was doing around $8 million a year and had three catalogs: Hanover House, Lana Lobell, and Lakeland Nurseries. I ran the Lana Lobell division. Prior to this, I had worked for a company called National Bellas Hess for ten years. It was a very disciplined company, and I had been schooled in the rules of direct marketing. After two years at Hanover, I had taken Lana Lobell from $2 million to $17 million, and from $1 million in losses to $2 million in profits. I did it by applying the disciplines I had learned at National Bellas Hess. For example, I knew it took six months to make any changes in the mail-order business, so I started planning before I even arrived at Hanover. At the time, they were using a shotgun approach: "Let's buy as many items as we can, put them on the page, and see which ones sell." My catalog was forty-eight pages and offered 290 items. There is no way you are going to make money in the apparel business with $2 million in sales and 290 items because you can only buy forty to fifty pieces of each item. So taking the information we had about customer preferences and price points, I narrowed the catalog down to 130 items. I was now able to give each item more space and could go out and buy 400 pieces instead of forty. So we narrowed our focus, and our sales went up dramatically.

In 1977 I was made the general merchandising manager and executive vice president of the whole company. I started expanding the business with new categories of merchandise and new catalogs. For example, I put shoes in my apparel book and found out they sold really well, so we added a shoe book. We also added a gift book and other apparel catalogs. We noticed that some people were buying the more expensive items in these books, so we added books in the same categories with higher-priced merchandise. Essentially, we started competing with ourselves, but it gave us places to move customers to as their incomes increased. In other words, a woman may buy the top-of-the-line clothes at K-Mart, then start buying the bottom-of-the-line at Macey's. Well, we became both a K-Mart and a Macey's to our customers. We did the same thing with our gift catalogs: we had a low-end book, a moderate-priced book, and an expensive book. We learned that people with higher incomes would buy from the low-end books, but people with lower incomes would never buy from the high-end books. However, people at the high end of one income range would start buying the lower-priced items in the next book up. So we'd go into our database and send customers books based on their financial position.

Another thing we did was sell our merchandise through on-page advertising in newspapers and magazines. When new customers ordered our products, we added their names to our database and started sending them catalogs. So our customer lists just kept getting longer and longer. We also figured out a way to give people credit so they could buy out of any of our books. When it was all said and done, we had our own credit card—the Hanover Shop at Home Card—and twenty-seven catalogs.

When I left the company in 1989, I had been the president and CEO for the past seven years. We were doing $350 million a year, with $21 million in net income.

I semi-retired when I left the company and started doing some consulting. I found it very disheartening because people wouldn't follow my recommendations. I helped a chap start a book and got him to $30 million in two years. Then he told me he didn't need me anymore. I told him, "If you don't keep doing it this way, you're going to mess things up." He said, "No, we're going to do it our way." A year later he closed up. So I found it real disheartening to bill people for advice they wouldn't follow. I learned that the more I charged people, the more they listened. No one ever did what I said when I worked cheap. One of the clients I worked with had two companies. One was a direct-mailing company called Myron Manufacturing that sold business-to-business specialty items. It was doing about $150 million a year. The other was a company the wife and son ran called Comfortably Yours. It was doing about $15 million. One August the husband had a heart attack and a triple bypass; he'd never been sick a day in his life. He came out of all this and told his wife, "I've got five or six years to live, and I want to enjoy the money we've got. Let's unload your company, let our kids run the other one, and move to Florida." So they said to me, "Bill, we want to get rid of Comfortably Yours." I tried to buy it, but we couldn't work things out, so they asked me to liquidate the business. Along the way, they said, "By the way, you can have anything you want at the liquidated prices." What they had was a mail-order catalog of items that made your life more comfortable. It was for people over sixty. The wife, who ran the company, used to visit her mother in a rest home and discovered all these things little old ladies needed. They had little whoopie cushions that made your seat softer, dresses that buttoned down the front rather than the back, a little portable stool for women under five feet tall, some support bras, some girdles—things to make people's lives more comfortable. It was a tremendous idea and a very nice book.

I didn't want to get into a full-blown catalog, a full-blown staff, computers, overhead, and warehouses. So I told them, "I'll buy the bra and girdle part of your business—the inventory, the patterns, the markers, everything." I knew this business well because I started a catalog at

Hanover called Night and Day Intimates. It was doing $50 million in sales when I left—one book selling bras and girdles! I knew it was one of the most profitable and best repeat businesses in the mail-order industry. So I chose this part of the company rather than the dresses or foot-care items.

I started the company in May of 1994. I came up with the name Beautiful Images because they wanted Comfortably Yours to die. I started with a handful of foundation garments for women over fifty. They are basically bras and girdles that help people with specific problems. For example, a high percent of women this age have osteoporosis, so we sell a posture bra that helps them stand up straighter. Women also tend to spread out at this age, so we sell a bra called the minimizer which makes them look less busty. On the girdle side, we sell a product that offers tremendous support for people who suffer with lower-back problems. Also, many women who have had children begin experiencing mild incontinence around age fifty, so we have a product for them. Since launching the company, we have created additional items. You've seen these jog bras women run in? Well, they offer no support. So we introduced an all-cotton support bra women can wear while they exercise. We've also developed our posture bra into an underwire bra. It gives women excellent support in both the front and the back. So we create things that make women's lives more comfortable.

We manufacture all these products ourselves rather than buy them ready made. We go out and buy the piece goods, have them cut, sewn, and delivered to a fulfillment center here in Tempe. These people pick, package, and ship the products according to our orders. So basically we're the manufacturer and the distributor, which gives us much better control of our inventory. We have real flexibility with regard to sizes, colors, and quantities.

We sell our products through space advertising in magazines and newspapers. Our customers call or write in to place orders. Right now I have 5,000 new orders on my desk that just came in today. When we ship our products, we insert materials in the packaging that offer more products. Then every few months we send out a mailing to our customers. We just sent out 350,000 pieces that will produce 10,000 to 12,000 orders in the next four weeks. Because our products are expendable, women need to replace them every two or three months. If I can offer a women every-thing she needs from her cotton to her lace to her underwire, I gain a cus-tomer who will buy six or eight bras a year. We're smart enough to know that not every customer can afford everything we offer, so a couple times each year we have promotions that allow people to buy two or three prod-ucts at a reduced price.

Women who buy our products love us because it's difficult to find things to help with their problems. And even though our products are mainly functional, they are top quality and very attractive—they have nice lace and nice trimmings. They also come in a variety of sizes and colors that aren't found in the marketplace. For example, you can't find a black posture bra in the stores. But we have one! Besides, shopping in stores is not a great experience these days. People are no longer nice to you, and they can't tell you much about the products. We tell you loads about our products in our space advertisements and our direct-mail pieces. We show you photographs, tell you what each item does, and explain how to use it. This is the real advantage of the direct-mail business. If you see a product in the store, it just sits there. The kinds of products we sell need pictures and explanations. So buying them from us is a much better experience than looking for them in the stores.

> There are tremendous opportunities for people to do something like this, but there are certain disciplines you have to understand. I've been able to make it go quickly because I have extensive experience in the field.

Of course, it takes cash to do what we're doing. I capitalized part of the company myself, then had a note with the original owners, which I paid back in eighteen months. I also found an investor in Chicago to pro-vide the financial backing I needed to acquire inventory. Even though I don't use his money very often, it has strengthened my balance sheet and improved my credit rating. It's allowed me to buy 5,000 yards of material at a time rather than 1,000. So people treat me like a human being, not how the banks treat you. (Laughs.) But we've had tremendous success from the very beginning. We did $2.8 million in 1994, $5.5 million in 1995, and over $9 million in 1996. At the end of 1996, I sold the business to Value Vision Incorporated, a large company based in Minneapolis. I'm continuing to operate the business as president and CEO.

I think there are tremendous opportunities for people to do something like this, but there are certain disciplines you have to understand. I've been able to make it go quickly because I have extensive experience in the field. I know how to create projections, buy inventory, get stuff made, manage costs, and sell products through direct channels. Other people who have good ideas can do it too, although it will probably take longer. But the mail-order business is an absolute dream to get into—it's not real capital intensive, and you deal with customers on an indirect basis only. Think about that! If a women has a complaint, she's going to write me a letter. She's not going to come into my store and call me names. (Laughs.) That's one of the reasons I entered this field thirty-five years ago.

> To be successful, you only have to be right one more time than you are wrong.

In the end, I think your growth is only restricted by what your mind thinks. When I was a young man growing up on the wrong side of the tracks in Kansas City, my aspiration was to drive a truck. But I met a major in the United States Air Force who convinced me I could do anything I wanted to. I had tremendous trust and confidence in this guy. Before I met him, I was floundering along as a corporal. He taught me how to study, how to take tests, how to do this, how to do that. Pretty soon I was taking these tests and getting promoted. I walked out of there as a staff sergeant and went to college. Another guy told me not to go to college because I couldn't pass. I graduated three and a half years later with a B average. The most important lesson I learned from this major was this: to be successful, you only have to be right one more time than you are wrong—51 percent right and 49 percent wrong, and you're a winner! So you have to keep trying and not let mistakes stop you from going ahead! If you think something has real potential, plan it out and go for it. If you end up with a $2 million business, figure out how to make it $8 million. There are ways to get there. A young guy recently said to me, "Bill, you don't believe you can fail, do you?" I said, "No, I know when I can and cannot fail. And when I do enough research, work hard, and lobby with the right people, I can win every time!"

Mary Ellen Sheets

Mary Ellen Sheets is the founder and CEO of Two Men And A Truck, a local moving company in Lansing, Michigan. She has franchised her business to more than fifty people in nearly twenty states. Though not affiliated with the industry originally, she discovered the need when her two sons bought an old truck and started moving students around Michigan State University. When her sons moved away, Mary Ellen courageously seized the opportunity as her phone continued ringing with calls from people who needed moving services. Though she lacked industry experience, she did have a handful of resources—a phone, an answering machine, and enough money to buy an old truck and hire a few employees. Fortunately, the tremendous demand for local moving—a need not being met in the marketplace—led to continued growth and eventual success:

Early eighties . . . I'd been married for twenty years, and my husband left me with our three children—two boys and a daughter. My daughter was a freshman in college, and the boys were in high school. We live in East Lansing, and the two boys bought an old, used pickup truck from Michigan State University—that was their transportation. They also thought they could earn some extra money by moving people in their spare time. So we put a little ad together and ran it in a local green sheet called The Town Courier. The first line in the ad was "Two men and a truck." (Laughs.) It was the boys' idea—they thought they were men. Well, I guess they were my men.

So they would move people occasionally; I think they charged twenty-five dollars an hour back then. It was all local moving around the university. After every job, they put three dollars in a little dish in the kitchen—that paid for their advertisement—then split the rest of the money. So it was a good deal for them; they were making over ten dollars an hour doing these moving jobs. The problem was, they only worked when they felt like it. If they told someone they would move them, then didn't feel like going, they would call and say, "Oh, someone stole our truck." Actually, they were probably as responsible as any other teenage boys.

When they graduated from high school, they both went away to Northern Michigan University—about seven hours from here. After they left, people would call me every once in a while and want to know if the boys could move them. Back then I worked for the state of Michigan as a data systems analyst, and I thought, "Gol, I could have a little business here." So I bought an old truck, hired two men, and started my first real moving company—this was in May of 1985. Our first customers were carryovers from the earlier business. We also put a little ad in the paper, and more people started calling. We didn't have an ad in the Yellow Pages or anything; I just used our home number and an answering machine. One night I came home from work, and we had twelve calls! I was just flabbergasted! (Laughs.) We were barely advertising at all! It was so strange!

We only had a one-part form back then. This is awful (laughs), but we wouldn't leave any documentation at the people's houses because we were afraid they would complain or come back to us if they were unhappy with our service. (Laughs.) So we would move their things, do a good job, then disappear into the night. When I finally got a business number and an ad in the Yellow Pages, the people at Michigan Bell said, "Thank Goodness! We get so many calls from people trying to find Two Men And A Truck, and we didn't know your number." So we've done very well with the name over the years: Two Men And A Truck. The funny thing is, it's almost all women who run this company—we only have a few men. People are surprised at that.

Anyway, back then my truck broke down all the time . . . The movers I had were not high quality . . . I didn't have any insurance . . . I didn't have any workers' compensation . . . I was not incorporated . . . I was not even registered with the state—I didn't know you had to be. If you can believe this, I paid my movers an hourly wage in cash every day, so I had a daily payroll! I didn't know anything about taxes! Along with all this, the gas gauge on the truck didn't work, so every night when I came home from work, I drove it to the gas station and filled it up, because we never knew how much gas we had. So the first few years were really just like a hobby. I never took any salary out because I still worked for the state. If we made any profit I just gave it away, because I didn't want to pay taxes.

Then slowly, in a very constant way, it grew. In 1986 I went down and I bought a brand-new truck, which was probably the most nervous I've ever been in this whole business. It was a little tiny cube van—a fourteen- or fifteen-footer. We thought that it was really something to have that new truck. I'm guessing we priced our services at about thirty or thirty-five dollars an hour back then—we were very concerned about what our competition was charging. Today, that's really not a concern of ours; we're much more into customer service. (Laughs.) People call us because of our services now, not because of low prices.

So slowly every year, we added another truck and another truck; the business just had very nice, steady growth. I learned how to do the payroll and all the taxes. Then we hired a bookkeeper. I also joined the Chamber of Commerce, which I was very nervous to do because I'm really shy. But I thought, "Well, at least we'll get our name out, and it'll make us seem like a real business." Now I'm on the board of the chamber—I have been on it for quite a few years. (Laughs.) We also belong to the state chamber and the national chamber. So my confidence has grown as our business has grown—very much.

About five years ago, a friend of mine who taught at M.S.U. asked if I would come talk to her class about owning a small business. When I got there, they had a panel of people. One woman had franchised her business—it's called Pet Nanny. They go into people's homes and take care of their animals. She talked to me afterwards and said, "You should really franchise your business." I said, "Gol, I don't know. All we do is move people. I don't really have anything I can franchise." She got right in my face and said, "All I do is feed dogs!" (Laughs hard.) So she gave me the name of her attorney, and I went to see him. He looked at me like I was a Martian when I told him about my business. But we met two or three times, and he agreed to help me franchise the company.

Michigan has, I believe, a hundred and fifty-three franchising regulations we had to meet before we could start. We also had to write an operations guide. So it took quite a while to get all that done. Then in 1989 I started going to franchise shows—we did four that first year. One of them was in Kansas City—it was sponsored by the S.B.A. They featured us in their film about franchising—it was McDonald's, Maaco, and Two Men And A Truck. So that was pretty neat. During this time, money was coming out of my pocket, and I had no income! (Laughs.) It's kind of hard, you know, when you have to advertise and everything. But finally we sold a franchise here and a franchise there. Then one day my attorney called and said, "Well, you've just sold your tenth franchise. That means you're going to make it." He never told me I wasn't going to make it before! (Laughs.) But that was when we passed the ten-franchise mark.

Most of the early franchises were here in Michigan, but not all. Usually our best territory is a county. Our goal is to grant a franchise that covers a population of five hundred thousand. We've found that's a nice-size population; we can advertise and cover the area real well. It's not too big, not too small, and the franchisee can make a good living. We started out charging $9,500, then $11,500, then $15,500, then $17,500. Now we're at $20,000. In the past it's been a 4-percent royalty fee; in the future it will be 6 percent with a 1-percent advertising fee. Franchisees get the name, manuals, any ads we do—which are all done by professional people—and the use of our logo. Our logo is the same little stick man I drew on the original moving sheet for my sons when they first started moving people—it's federally protected now. We also have a company store called Two Men And A Truck. We sell sixty different items—they all have that name and logo on them. We have shirts, hats, baseball caps, gym bags, cups, watches. Franchisees can buy the items and give or sell them to customers.

Up until a few years ago I ran everything myself. I went around and visited all the franchisees . . . I did all the bookkeeping . . . We have a monthly newsletter . . . We have annual meetings. I did it all, plus I ran my own moving company here in town which had grown considerably. Then I got a phone call from the Michigan State Senate—they asked me to come down and talk to them. So I did, and they wanted me to run for the Senate! I've never been in politics in my life—this is a riot! So I'm like all nervous about it, but I felt very honored. I talked to my family and said, "If I do this, will you come and run the business?" At the time, my daughter was a pharmaceutical rep in the Detroit area. She quit her job and came back to run Two Men And A Truck International, which is our franchising company. One of my sons came back to run the other company, Two Men And A Truck Greater Lansing, which is the moving company. And I proceeded to run for the senate. I set up a campaign office, got furniture, hired people, got all my slogans made and everything. I spent about two months out schmoozing with people. Then I woke up one morning, looked in the mirror, and said, "Boy this is not for you! (Laughs.) This is not you!" So I called them and said, "Gol, I'm really sorry, but I don't want to do this anymore." (Laughs.)

So I dropped out of the race, and here I am again—only my children have now stepped in. The first year they were here, we kind of just sat. Then I got a grant from the state of Michigan. They sent a franchise expert here from Detroit to work with our company and see if he could help us. Boy, he changed our whole way of thinking—we are thinking like the big guys now. We have sponsors and all these things people pay us for—things we used to pay them for! (Laughs.) It is a whole new ballgame for us; it's been really interesting. This guy was a vice president with Deloitte & Touche—had been for twenty-two years. He quit his job, came here with us, then bought a franchise. He still works here one day a week but has other clients, too.

So just a few years ago in the franchise company, we had only myself—now we have fifteen employees. For us it's a huge jump. We've gone from a budget of zero to where we're now advertising in Entrepreneur and Inc.—big ads! We have over fifty franchises in nearly twenty states. In 1990 the few franchisees we had grossed almost nothing. Now they gross nearly $30 million in sales. So the franchising business is really starting to go—we're working real hard and we're ready to boom. Our moving business in Lansing also gets a little bigger each year. We now have eleven trucks and thirty-five employees in a tri-county area with about 430,000 people. I still don't think we've topped out.

Anyway, I can't tell you how much our franchisees earn because it's against the law for us to make earnings claims. But if they have one truck and are charging the average $50 to $60 an hour and working forty hours a week, that truck will gross about $100,000 a year. How much they net kind of depends on how they run their company: Are they a hands-on person? Do they run it out of their home? Do they have a big, fancy office? Costs are mostly labor and insurance. We do require them to have two trucks now to start. We weren't like that in the beginning, but we find the longer we're in business, the more high-caliber people come to us. They have the financial backing to get started much quicker, and they can be pretty much independent in a couple of months. They really don't need a lot of inventory. Gol, all you need is a phone and a truck! (Laughs.) They can lease or buy the trucks, or get them used. Some of our sponsors are truck dealers, of course, and we have a hotline they can call to find trucks. It's only to advise them, though. What they do is their personal choice.

When I look back I can't believe this all happened. (Laughs.) I'm just totally flabbergasted by it! I never really planned on all this—never! I just thought I'd work for the state the rest of my life. I'm really proud of the fact that as a single parent I put all three of my children through college— that was my main goal. But now they all work here. It's just so wonderful that our whole family is involved in this business.

I definitely think this is the American dream. I'll tell you, this country is wonderful! It really is! One person can still make a difference. You can vote and you can run for office, if you want to. (Laughs.) Can other people do what I've done? Sure they can. It doesn't take a genius or anything. You just have to chip away at it, day after day after day. It's interesting, though—we see a lot of people who think someone else should take care of them. People are not being raised to think of opportunities to provide service or products, or even provide a living for themselves. When new franchisees come here, they want to do it so bad—they are so close. But you know, it's that little thing in their stomach—that little knot. For some, the risk is just a little too much.

My advice to students is, first, do something you really enjoy, because this isn't a dress rehearsal. You only have one go at it, so don't spend a lot of time in a job you don't like. Second, if people around you are negative with your choice and try to talk you out of it, just get away from them! Be nice, but don't talk to them about it. And third, just keep plugging away. I call it "mouse burgering." You take a little piece here and a little piece there, then one day you look back and you've really done a lot. I can remember way back when a lady wrote me this three-page letter that said, "You moved me and your men didn't plug in my freezer. Below is a list of all the things that were spoiled, and you're going to pay for them." I was in tears! It cost eight hundred dollars, and I didn't have eight hundred dollars. (Laughs.) I thought, "This is the end of my business right here!" Well, we don't do things like that anymore; we know how to handle problems when they occur.

> Do something you really enjoy, because this isn't a dress rehearsal.

I also think it's important to be community-minded. I love volunteer work. I like doing things for people. I see this company as a way to provide funds and manpower to worthwhile community projects. It's such a win-win situation. For example, a lot of our movers don't come from backgrounds of volunteer work. But they're out on the truck doing free moves or discounted moves for all these organizations—they're getting paid, but they're part of it. So they take pride in a company that does right for the people in this town. We've tried to carry it a step further. We have federally protected the phrase "Movers Who Care." So we're "Two Men And A Truck—Movers Who Care." Now we encourage all our franchisees to do good things for people in the community and pay them back. It just makes me feel so good to go beyond myself and help a lot of people.

Anyway, the moving industry is a sluggy, old, depressing industry—it really is. We get a lot of moving magazines from across the country, and you open them up and see all these frowning guys saying, "Business is terrible," "Deregulation has hurt us," "The gas taxes . . ."—blah blah blah blah. We're not like that. We see this as a huge opportunity. Only 20 percent of the people that move hire a professional mover. The rest move themselves. So our biggest competitor is our customers themselves. We always tell them, "Hey, it's cheaper to hire us than to buy beer and pizza for your friends." (Laughs.) It just begins there. We pride ourselves in our service, the politeness of our people, their training—and everything's clean and neat. It's been a huge opportunity for us. People say, "Gol, you just found a niche." But I think, "A niche? This isn't a niche! This is like the Grand Canyon!" (Laughs.) You know, most local moving companies are like Mom and Pops, but we've been able to network this all across the country so we all look alike. Hopefully when people see our truck, they do think it's just two men and a truck.

> This isn't a niche! This is like the Grand Canyon!

TIPS FOR SEIZING THE OPPORTUNITY

1. **START WITH A GOOD IDEA.**
   Make sure you've discovered a legitimate need, one that is not being met or one you can meet better. Your idea needs to make people's lives easier, more enjoyable, or more productive by providing a better product, a better price, better service, more options, or better solutions to problems.

2. **OCCUPY A CREDIBLE POSITION.**
   Be sure you are adequately positioned in the industry because of your training, skills, experience, credibility, certification, associations, networks, and so on.

3. **GET THE REQUIRED RESOURCES.**
   Make sure you have what you need to get started quickly—equipment, tools, systems, technology, partners, facilities, access to money, helpers, a truck, a studio—whatever it takes.

4. **IDENTIFY THE EAGER CUSTOMERS.**
    Find a handful of anxious customers who need and will buy the product right now! *If possible, secure relationships before or at least at the time you launch your venture.*

Chapter • 3

FINDING
A MENTOR

When Becky Brevitz graduated from college, she went to work for a
real estate management and development company. She started
"pet sitting" for people at work who were going out of town. Before long
her phone started ringing. "You don't know me, but I know you babysat
for so-and-so's pets." Sensing an opportunity, she called her father for
advice. When she told him she wanted to quit her job and start a pet-
sitting service, he replied, "Seriously, Becky, are you getting fired from
your job?" He then asked her to come visit him in Battlecreek, Michigan,
to explore the opportunity. He took her to dinner at the country club and
asked a lot of questions. At the end of the evening, he took out his check-
book, wrote her a check for $1,000, and encouraged her to go for it! With
this seed money, Becky launched a company that visits and feeds cats,
dogs, fish, birds, rodents, lizards, monkeys—almost any type of pet—
while the owners are away. Today, Pet Nanny of America has nearly
thirty franchised locations in more than a dozen states. The company has
been profitable from the first year.

Most of the entrepreneurs I interviewed had at least one significant
mentor who played a role in their decision to start a business—some
had several. Without this gentle nudge, many of our business founders

would not have launched their new venture. I observed two types of mentors in my interviews. The first was the lifetime mentor—someone who convinced our entrepreneurs they could do whatever they wanted in life if they wanted it bad enough. The second was the business mentor—someone who encouraged them to "go for it" and facilitated the launch in some way: advice, contacts, customers, money. Many of the entrepreneurs I interviewed had both types of mentors. And sometimes, one mentor fulfilled both roles—as was the case with Becky Brevitz. Regardless of how it happens, good mentors seem to be critical to getting new ventures off the ground.

THE LIFETIME MENTOR

Mentor \ 'men-tor \ noun : a trusted counselor or guide; also a tutor or coach

Mentors play an important role in our lives. They might be family members, teachers, friends, partners, or religious leaders. Strong mentors influence our beliefs, values, aspirations, and drive—our basic gestalt for living. Not only do they shape our thought processes, but they also set an example of action by leading the way themselves. The more healthy and positive mentors we have in life, the better.

Many of the entrepreneurs I interviewed were affected early in life by powerful mentors. While these mentors may not have directly influenced the decision to start a business, they definitely cultivated a predisposition to do so; they fostered independence, responsibility, and a "can-do" attitude. This environment makes it much easier to entertain the notion of launching a new venture than a critical or toxic upbringing. Becky Brevitz, whom you just met, describes the impact of her family background on her thinking:

> *All I had ever seen was independent business people. My father was in business, my grandfather was in business, and my mother came from a family of dairy farmers. My mindset was, how do I make money? It didn't ever occur to me to find someone to latch*

on to to give me money. All that occurred to me was, I've got to make my own money.

In like manner, Tony Conza, founder of Blimpie Sandwiches, talks about the influence his father had on his beliefs and bias toward action:

My dad was a real inspiration to me, not because he taught me about business—he never owned a business. But he did something that was probably more difficult than anything I've ever done. My grandparents came from Italy, and my parents grew up very poor in New York. My mom and dad always wanted their own home but could never afford one. My dad figured the only way he could ever have a house was to build it. So he worked a few jobs and saved enough money to buy the materials. Then over a period of three years, working weekends and vacations, he built this home. My dad died a few years ago, but my mother still lives there. It demonstrated to me that nothing is impossible if you really want it. So I would say more than anyone else, my dad was my mentor.

So lifetime mentors encourage a mind set and pave the way by example. In the stories I collected, the lifetime mentors are typically parents, but sometimes they are siblings, teachers, or coaches. Here are a few examples from a long list: Alvina Quam, a jewelry maker from Zuni, New Mexico, learned her trade from three generations of mentors—her parents, her grandparents, and even her great-grandfather. Paul Brewer, founder of Paul Brewer's Magical Entertainment, learned the magic business from Gene Rose, "the guy who mass-produced the rubber chicken." John Solomon Sandridge, founder of LuvLife Collectibles, was inspired by his parents—they both loved art and encouraged him to pursue it. Judi Sheppard Missett, founder of Jazzercise, was mentored by Gus Giordano, the director of Jazz Dance Chicago. In the three stories at the end of this chapter, notice how Ric Burns was influenced by a university professor, Sally Gutierrez by her businessman father, and Jon Kittelsen by both his parents—they helped him with everything from product design to business strategy from day one.

But what do you do if you haven't had positive mentors in your life? Or perhaps worse, your family environment has been negative and crippling? Personally, I'm optimistic that attitudes conducive to business startups can be learned. Here's where the second type of mentor comes into play. The business mentor helps you with the decision to launch, then guides you through the shoals and reefs of new venturing. I believe that anyone who wants to succeed and finds the right mentor has a good chance, particularly if the other keys to success are present in abundance. In other words, you can't always choose your lifetime mentors, but you do have influence over the business mentors you choose.

THE BUSINESS MENTOR

Mentoring programs are becoming popular in a variety of settings. In business, seasoned executives are teaching the ropes to younger, high-potential managers. In education, teachers are learning to be mentors of youth rather than supervisors of children. In government, successful citizens are helping the less fortunate get off welfare, put their lives in order, and become more independent. In most cases, people who have mentors do much better than those who lack this support. This is particularly true when the relationship is entered into willingly and is mutually rewarding to both parties, and the mentor has genuine interest in the one being mentored. From my interviews, it's clear that mentors also play a huge role in the business start-up process. Here's how it works. First, while participating in some industry, potential entrepreneurs observe a need or a better way to meet a need. Second, they realize they are well positioned to do something about it; they have the training, skills, contacts, and potential customers. Third, enter the mentor! Someone the entrepreneurs have confidence in now enters the scene and provides the required encouragement, support, and hoorays. Often, this person is the only positive voice in a sea of skeptics, and in some cases even has to talk the future entrepreneur into taking the plunge. Because of the mentor's unique credibility and resources, the entrepreneur-to-be chooses to believe him or her rather than the doubters. This process helps further explain the glorious accident. Since many of our entrepreneurs were only teetering with the start-up decision when an influential mentor pushed them over the edge, surprise at the outcome seems like a logical reaction.

Our stories are replete with examples of strong business mentors. Recall how Frieda Caplan had no intention of starting her own produce business until her friends at Southern Pacific Railway offered encouragement and, most important, the location. Ken Smith, founder of Southwest Traders, a large specialty-food distributor in southern California, was led into business by his brother. Carol Columbus-Green, founder of Laracris Corporation in Chicago, launched her line of women's shapewear thanks to strong encouragement and financial support from her husband, Richard. June Morris, founder of Morris Air, didn't think she could start a business until her husband, Mitch, gave her the nudge; he provided space in the corner of his building, then served as a "breakfast table" consultant.

In the three stories that follow, notice how our roles models had great business mentors in addition to significant lifetime mentors. Ric Burns followed his brother Ken into the documentary film industry; Ken reinvented the genre, set the standard, and paved the way for Ric. Sally Gutierrez was encouraged to start her business by her employer at the Hallmark Card Store; she also got colossal support from several key customers early on. And Jon Kittelsen may not have started and succeeded in his business, EZ-Gard Industries, without a high-school guidance counselor; his DECA advisor, John McDermott; and his partner, Jon Miner.

CHOOSING A MENTOR

Business mentoring works best under certain conditions. First, your mentor needs to know you well. Obviously, a mentor who understands your strengths and weaknesses is in the best position to help. If the two of you aren't fairly close, you may be pushed into areas that aren't appropriate for you—and being falsely encouraged doesn't help. Also, you don't want to miss out on opportunities for which you are uniquely suited because your mentor hasn't seen your abilities. This is why parents, spouses, siblings, teachers, partners—people with whom you have some history—often make the best mentors.

Second, your mentor needs to be enthusiastic about your business opportunity. He or she should be excited about the idea, the products, the services, and your ability to pull it off. Ideally, your mentor should feel the same degree of passion for the deal that you do. While this may seem unrealistic, it does happen. As we mentioned above, some mentors feel more zeal for the opportunity initially than the aspiring entrepreneur does. This enthusiasm is important when times get tough, which they always do. As you slug it out in the business arena, you want your mentor to be the last person standing. If you lose faith in the venture and your mentor does too, the deal is all but over. So if your mentor comes along grudgingly, you've got a strike against you.

Third, your mentor needs to understand basic business principles. He or she doesn't need to know your particular industry—although it helps. More important, your mentor needs to know what questions to ask and how to get the answers. Also, the more he or she understands product development, marketing, business finance, and basic operations, the better. The best business mentors are probably people who have started and operated a successful company of their own—"been there, done that."

Fourth, your mentor should have as many contacts as possible: people in the industry, people in related industries, people with complimentary services, people with money, people with similar interests, people with ideas, and so forth. Business is all about relationships, and if your mentor can quickly link you with people to fill in the gaps in your experience, move the products forward, and help you find customers, the better off you'll be. This will increase your chances of both early success and long-term survival.

While finding a mentor who knows you well, has passion for your opportunity, understands basic business, and has critical contacts is a tall order, he or she is out there. Many people who have succeeded in business enjoy helping their younger cohorts do the same thing. There is nothing quite like starting a company and making it work—it gets into your blood! Mentors who help aspiring entrepreneurs get to experience the rush all over again, but without the responsibility. The fact that over 90 percent of the business founders I contacted agreed to participate in this project suggests there is an abundance of support out there. I know I take great pleasure in helping young entrepreneurs struggle with ideas, launch their ventures, and eventually enjoy success. People who have "been there, done that" also make good investors if they like the opportunity. So hope for the best, then choose the best mentor you can. And if you find that magical relationship, you'll be miles ahead of the game.

OUR ROLE MODELS

Ric Burns

Ric is the founder of Steeplechase Films, a company that produces documentaries on significant and engaging topics from American history. He first collaborated with his brother and mentor Ken on the history of the American Civil War. Since then, Ric has produced "Coney Island," "The Donner Party," and "The Way West." He is currently working on a ten-hour film for public television on the history of New York City. He says:

I went to college for about twelve years in one way or another. I started at the University of Michigan, then transferred to Columbia College, then went to Cambridge University and back to Columbia to work on a Ph.D. I was really obsessed with English literature. I thought for a long time I was going to become a scholar and professor of English. But somewhere around 1984, I began to wake up and ask myself the all-important question: Do I really want to spend my life writing a handful of articles and four or five books about literary theory? And while my interest in those things was extremely high, my answer to that question was a resounding "No!"

In the bottom of my heart, I was still looking for what I really wanted to do.

I was very fortunate to have an extremely talented older brother, Ken, who by the mid 1980s had already launched his own career as a documentary filmmaker. I went from looking over his shoulder and being sort of curious about what he was doing to becoming more and more interested in his films. I helped him write proposals and scripts for some of them until the mid '80s, when I actually worked as an associate producer on a biography he did about Huey Long. It was really out of that experience that my attitude toward filmmaking went from being a jubilant consumer to understanding the extraordinary pleasure and compelling nature of this craft. So I was very, very fortunate to have a family member as talented as Ken who provided the opportunity.

About this time, Ken was looking around for someone to collaborate with on a project, which at the time was only a glimmer in his eye: the history of the American Civil War. All the films he had done up to that point touched on aspects of American history which had been profoundly affected by the Civil War. He understood what almost any student of history comes to understand sooner or later: that the Civil War was one of the great defining moments in American History. The propelling idea for him in that film was to treat the war as a seminal event: all of American history went into the Civil War, and all of American history can be seen coming out of it. And so we started from that.

We knew very little about the Civil War—sat down in 1984–85 to read and begin to write proposals. I think it was good that we weren't historians but rather filmmakers. What we confronted initially from the historical community were two things. On the one hand, people expressed a concern that the project had already been done. "Why would you want to revisit the American Civil War? There's nothing new about it!" On the other hand, some in the historical community thought it would take an enormous hubris, not to say foolishness, to undertake a project of that magnitude. "How could kids essentially who aren't even scholars have the audacity to take on a subject that large?" Actually, I think you need to be naive to take on anything large because you have to see these projects from the outside. You have to tackle the topic as if it were a mountain you have every right to try to climb. And maybe you're going to fall off, maybe you're not going to the top, but certainly it's there and you have the right to try. I think the Civil War is an important subject for all Americans to tackle at some point in life. If you don't confront the facts and meaning of that event from American history, you're essentially leading your life with a patch over one eye. There is no possible way you can understand the history of racial relations, the way America was propelled into the industrial age, or a host of other events in this country without understanding the Civil War.

So we wanted to tell a coherent story, we wanted to tell a comprehensive story, and we wanted to tell it in a narrative and engaging way. It took us five years to do it, a little bit longer than it took to fight the war itself. I think the central idea in the film is that it's possible to understand people from different times and different places. The risk Ken has always been willing to take is to assume that people in history are just like us. For example, let's assume that we could have been there, that we could have known those people—that they had essentially the same feelings, appetites, foibles, fears, and hopes that we might have had in the same situation. I think that's what people found when they looked at the Civil War: the warmth of assuming that it's only an accident of history that we couldn't have known Ulysses S. Grant. He could have been one of our contemporaries. We discover that his humanity is good and bad, which comes forward all the more powerfully if we just assume he is like us—which he is, of course.

From this perspective, figures from history suddenly lose that quaint, foreign, distant effect. Suddenly they are much more real. They are flesh-and-blood people who put their pants on one leg at a time, people who didn't know what the outcome of their own lives was, who lived from morning to noon to night in exactly the same irreversible direction that we lead our own lives. They were struggling to make up their own minds in real times. That's what it is to be a human being in history. I mean, even these characters of such enormous size in the eyes of posterity—Robert E. Lee or Abraham Lincoln or Ulysses S. Grant or William Sherman—were extraordinary but also absolutely ordinary. They struggled, they experienced depression, they failed again and again and again. Their sense of honor was both their greatest attribute and their greatest limitation. They were just straightforward human beings, and to miss that is to miss who they were, and therefore to miss the main emotional identification that it's possible to have in this dimension we live in today. So that's what we tried to accomplish with the Civil War.

Anyway, no one has ever had a mentor without leaving the mentor. In a relationship with someone who is that enabling to you, the final act of empowerment is to take on the role yourself. So after five years of working with my older brother Ken, I not only learned enormous amounts about making films, but I developed the desire to be in control of them. So by the time we had finished five years of what both Ken and I feel were extraordinary and fruitful years of collaboration, there was no way I could do anything but go off and make my own films. I actually started just before the Civil War was over. I've always been obsessed with the history of New York and particularly drawn to a postage-stamp-size corner of that history which happened at Coney Island. At the end of the nineteenth, beginning of the twentieth century, Coney Island was a unique, incandescent laboratory for all the things America was becoming at the time. It was a combination of the Grand Canyon, Cape Canaveral, Disneyland, and Times Square all rolled into one. So I decided to make a film on that and worked nights and weekends to create a hundred-page document for a film about Coney Island.

I think what compels other people to give you the chance to do your own work—to risk a half a million dollars to make an hour of documentary film for public television—is really the passion and commitment you have to an idea. It's not your connections or the opportunities you've already had; it's really passion and commitment structured in some initial way. That's the irreducible capital of a project. When people who make funding decisions see that, even if you have no experience whatsoever, if they're smart, they know they are in the presence of something worth funding. So the passion of your commitment and the plausibility of the structure you've devised speak more than anything else. I think this is really why our first project succeeded.

After Coney Island was the Donner Party. My partner, Lisa Ades, had been doing research for a large project on the history of the West and came across accounts of the Donner Party. And I have to say that like the Coney Island project, the Donner Party reached out and absolutely bit us on the ankle. So we put aside the history of the West and devoted all of our energy to telling this extraordinarily dark yet shining fable about a party of eighty-two settlers from Illinois and adjoining states that became snowbound in the High Sierras during the winter of 1846 and '47. They built crude shelters of logs and rocks; they ate their animals, twigs, their shoes, and finally, their own dead. Only forty-seven survived. So in the earliest days of the pioneer movement, these people who had projected the largest dreams and ambitions for themselves, and partly for that reason, came to such an extraordinarily ill-fated conclusion.

The passion of your commitment and the plausibility of the structure you've devised speak more than anything else.

Once we finished that project in 1992, we picked up in earnest the work for which the Donner Party was essentially a prologue: a six-hour film on the history of the expansion west from 1845 to 1893, which we called "The Way West." It was really about the clash of cultures between Native Americans and European Americans that had been going on for centuries, the final chapters of which became inevitable with the gold rush. Eventually, there was no more room for Native Americans to retreat to; there was no way they could keep out of the way of this surging, technologically sophisticated culture. So we really wanted to show the inevitable and tragic course of that conflict from the 1840s down to the 1890s. Like the Donner Party and all the work I've been most compelled by, there's an ironic and even tragic quality at the core of this story. It seems there's something alive in American culture which connects our brightest dreams with some of our most destructive forces and worst disasters. In the projects I've taken up over the years, I've been interested in interrogating the relationship between the dream and the nightmare. Certainly my films *Coney Island, The Donner Party,* and *The Way West* are all branches off that same tree.

The Way West was finished and broadcasted in 1995. We now have a ten-hour project on the history of New York, from the early 17th century to today. It will be finished for broadcast in 1999. It does something that has never been done before, which is to treat a city—in this case the greatest city in the world—as the hero of its own narrative unfolding over three and a half centuries. How did it get to be what it is? How did it invent itself as the premiere metropolis of the new American Empire? How did it become the capital of our culture's becoming? The place where somebody non-American came to become American? A place to cast off an old identity? A place where Americans came to reinvent themselves to succeed in ways they wish to succeed? New York really has been a caldron of American culture in a particularly fierce, creative, and sometimes frightening way for a couple hundred years. The film we're working on is going to tell the story of how that came about.

Anyway, I think the modest successes I've enjoyed on the frontiers of documentary filmmaking are really the result of several things. I've already mentioned the mentoring role of my brother Ken. Actually, I've been

> Success in any career really comes from that passionate commitment and determination to take a project to its conclusion.

fortunate to have two mentors in my life. The other person, who I followed around in academics, is an extraordinary and brilliant scholar named Edward Said. He's a Palestinian and a professor of English and comparative literature at Columbia University. He's one of the greatest literary critics of his generation and the reason I worked on a Ph.D. at Columbia. In terms of my style of thinking and my attitude towards intellectual work, Edward really taught me the most. My brother Ken's role was that of forging the way, which he had done since we were little children. He is a very powerful, self-directed sort of person who reinvented the genre of historical documentaries in the 1980s. His dedication to leaving no stone unturned in an attempt to create the most perfect possible treatment of a subject is absolutely incredible. And I think that's what mentors do more than anything else: set an example of unflinching and unstinting commitment to excellence—that it's the only moral and vocational standard that's plausible. I mean, it's very exciting and very challenging and very frightening to be led in that direction.

In addition to great mentors, I think success in any career really comes from that passionate commitment and determination to take a project to its conclusion. As I said earlier, it's not about where you were educated or who your connections are or anything else. Rather, it happens because you say, "I'm going to do this come hell or high water." Then almost inevitably, people see that irresistible force begin to move and say, "Let's get out of the way and let this happen." And some of us fail, absolutely! But the fact remains, everybody who succeeds does so because they make a 125-percent commitment to making something happen. With true commitment, people and projects are brought into in critical relation to each other, and they actually glow. You see it in their actions, you hear it in their voice. And the same thing that compels them becomes part of their ability to make it compelling to you. You're drawn to it like a moth to a flame. And that enthusiasm becomes the central fuel that propels the project forward. It grows like a series of concentric circles. For me, the testimony of how absolutely obsessed I am with filmmaking tells me I'm doing something that is right for me. There's really not a day that goes by that I don't feel enormous gratitude that I was so fortunate to find work which I willingly and happily get up at 4:30 in the morning to do.

Sally Gutierrez

Sally Gutierrez is one tough lady! In 1975 she won a court battle against the New Mexico Activities Association and became the first girl in the nation to play on a boy's high-school football team. Her coach, Richard Moore, said, "They rocked her and socked her and hit her hard. Hers is a story of 'just do it.' Get out in life and do it." That's exactly what Sally did when her husband left her with two small children—she created Spic and Span Cleaning Technicians in Spokane, Washington. With the help of several important mentors, she grew her business to seventy-five resi-

dential and commercial accounts before selling the company to two of her employees. Here's her story:

I studied early childhood education when I was in college in Spokane. I wanted to teach preschool and kindergarten. While I was in school, I worked at the Hallmark card shop in the North Town Mall. During this time, my husband left me with our two kids, and I was wondering what I was going to do financially. I ended up going on welfare for a while and hated it. It was just so degrading! When you're on welfare, you get the money whether you work or not. If you get a job, they take everything you make out of your check, so there's no incentive to work. Also, I could get full child care if I didn't work. Having a job, I could only get partial help. It just didn't make any sense to me! I was like, "Why do I need full child care if I'm not working? I need child care now, while I am working!"

So I wrote a letter to the head of the welfare department and said, "Why don't you guys encourage us to work? Why don't you help us with child care? Instead of taking our money away, why don't you give us an incentive to get off?" But they wouldn't do anything. It's like they wanted me to be on welfare or somethin', so I was bound and determined to get off of it. I felt like I had more to offer my kids than that.

In the meantime I got to know the Hallmark shop owners really well, Joanne and Cork Keller. They liked the way I worked and the way I cleaned their store. Cleaning had always been a fetish for me since I was little because my dad had two truck stops and I was constantly cleaning the garages. It was one of the first jobs I had after high school. He taught us to work hard and always be honest in everything we did—even when we were not being watched. So when I went to work for the Kellers it just came naturally.

After a while, Mrs. Keller asked me if I wanted to work at her house. Well, I was honored to do it because she had chosen me above all the other people who worked there. She really helped me in two ways: first, I really needed the extra money, and second, because she loved the way I cleaned her house, she told all her friends about me. So her friends began asking if I would be interested in cleaning for them, and I said, "Sure I would." I started cleaning a couple houses, then three or four. After a while, I had more houses than I could handle in a week. At the time, I was still going to school during the day and working at the card store at night and on weekends. Even though I was really busy, I thought the cleaning was great! I was charging $6.50 an hour—double what I was making at the card store—so I had the ambition to keep doing it.

Things were still really tough financially. I couldn't ever get the kids' father to pay child support—he was just a deadbeat dad. So I was always fretting about how I was going to make ends meet. I went through a down period and started praying about it because I really believe in God a lot. One day while I was in my kitchen cooking, I was listening to this Christian tape. It was an entrepreneur talking to some people who were struggling to get by. He was saying, "Start where you are! Start with what you have! What traits can you offer the community? What skills can you sell? Is it a product? Is it a service?" And it just came to me: I loved cleaning and I loved serving people, so I figured I could offer this business to the community to benefit them, and also benefit me financially. Part of my decision was that I was getting and keeping a strong clientele; that was the neatest part of it. I never lost my original clientele throughout the eleven years I was in business.

When I went and registered my business with the state, I called it "Spic and Span Janitorial." The name came to me that same day I was in the kitchen listening to the tape. I love the product Spic and Span! It has TSP in it; I mean, it's a great cleaning product! I looked under my kitchen sink and was looking at that box and thought, "Gosh, that's the name right there." But I thought I might get in trouble for using it, so I tried to put it a little differently. I ended up using "Spic and Span Janitorial" for a long time. A couple of years later I changed it to "Spic and Span Cleaning Technicians" because I started hiring people.

Early on, I went and discussed my idea with Cork and Joanne Keller, and with Dr. Gene and Jeanne Beaver—the people I first started cleaning for. They were wonderful, positive people, and we'd become very good friends. They were both involved in Amway and were trying to get me to start a distributing business, but I just didn't feel right about it. I'm not a door-to-door salesperson, you know; I could never do that. Anyway, they were very supportive of my idea and put the word out in the Amway community. Before long, I was cleaning for lots of doctors, lawyers, and business owners who were doing Amway as kind of a side hobby—it was really a "high" clientele that could afford to pay well.

When I first started out, I did all the work myself. As I got more customers, I hired my first person, Janine McCarroll. She was the daughter of a lady who used to babysit for me. She was just out of high school and a really shy girl. She didn't have the confidence, I guess you would say, to go out and get a job. But we worked really well together. I would do the kitchens and bathrooms 'cause those were my favorites. They're also the hardest part of the job, and she didn't really want to do them. She would do the vacuuming, dusting, straightening, and organizing. I figured out how long it used to take me to do the job by myself, then cut that time in half. So if it took me eight hours alone, it was going to take us four. Then I charged people double my normal hourly rate. So I was charging $13 an hour for both of us to clean. I started Janine out at $3.50, then raised her to $3.75, and just kept raising her up.

After a few years, I started charging by the house. I would figure out the price based on the number of bedrooms and baths, and whether they had kids or not. Homes with kids were always a lot harder to clean because there were toys and clothes and extra things to pick up. Also, if the homeowner had lots of knickknacks I would figure that into the price because it would take forever to dust. We would pick up each item, clean it, dust off the shelf, and put it back down. We took the time to be real careful because a lot of those things were very fragile. So after a while I had a formula. The average house we cleaned was between 3,000 to 4,000 square feet, like Dr. Beaver's. We charged him $72 per day to clean his house, which we did every two weeks. If they had special company coming or something, they would have us come in once a week. It took us three to four hours to clean their house.

After a while, I created a chart of all the basic cleaning we did, things like kitchens, bathrooms, vacuuming, dusting, front entrance doors, back sliders, things they used everyday. We also did their basic laundry—bedroom sheets, linen towels, kitchen towels—as part of our general cleaning. They loved that! My chart also included the prices of special projects we would do, things like cleaning the oven, cleaning out garages, stripping and waxing floors, shampooing carpets, washing windows inside and out. If we finished our general cleaning early, we would go the extra mile and do something special for them, like clean the chandeliers. They get real dirty and take a lot of time to clean. So we always tried to find something extra to do. We had a pretty good system.

To get new business, I put a big ad in the phone book, but I got most of my customers through word of mouth. I would clean one house and they would refer me to other houses. One of the referrals I got from Joanne and Cork Keller was the Hanning family, Marshall and Grace Hanning. They owned Mercer Trucking Company. It's a big outfit—I think they go to all fifty states. Grace is a very, very picky lady who likes things just so. Well, she and her husband loved the way I cleaned, and we became really good friends. One day, Marshall asked me if I'd consider cleaning his office at night. I wasn't sure I wanted to work nights because my kids were home and I was already working full time. But he told me how much he was willing to pay, and it was more than I thought it was worth—he was quite generous. So I started doing his offices, and he loved the way I cleaned them; and all the employees really liked the way everything was put back exactly the way it was found on the desk. We were just very thorough. By now I had eighteen residential clients and three employees, plus myself. So we always worked in teams of two.

Marshall Hanning inspired me in many ways, especially with his knowledge of the business world. He would sit down with me and give me business ideas. He was really the one who got me into commercial cleaning. I was scared to death to do it, but he kept pushing me: "You can do it, you can do it." After a while, he introduced me to several of his business associates in other trucking companies. It's hard work when you're cleaning those trucking companies; it's not light office cleaning. So I guess I got into the commercial business the hard way. But it got easier as we went along because I learned to get the easier buildings. That was when I decided to go big time into commercial cleaning.

After Marshall helped me get the first few accounts, I started bidding on contracts. I'd go out cold turkey and knock on doors. It was real hard for me, but I got used to it. I mean, I'd go out and show 'em what I had to offer, and I found most people to be quite receptive. I would talk with the general managers and have them show me what they wanted cleaned. Then I would ask them what their pet peeves were so we could make sure we took care of them: things like not throwing out the garbage, not putting things back where they had been, throwing away things they had no business throwing away. Then I would explain to the managers what we would do and ask them to give us a thirty-day trial period to see what they thought of our cleaning.

At the time I knew nothing about bidding by the foot—that's how most companies did it. I really had no idea what I was doing. So I would figure out all my costs, how much profit I wanted to make, add a little percentage on for me, and give them a ballpark figure. It was really trial and error. I earned a couple of accounts where I bid too low but ended up finding ways to still give a high-quality job. I always wanted to do a top job for everyone. I would say to my employees, "I don't care if it takes you longer. I don't care if I have to pay you a little bit more. So what if you get out of there faster? I want the job done right!" It seemed that other cleaning companies were just zippin' in and out and not doing everything, only bits and pieces. They would sweep the floors one day and not do it the next day, and they wouldn't always mop. So I came up with a list of what to do daily, weekly, every two weeks, and monthly. In an office, for example, windows don't have to be cleaned every day, but the entrance window does because that's what customers see first when they walk in the door. I mostly did it by intuition and feeling things out.

My commercial business grew just like the residential business—mostly by word of mouth. And the more jobs I got, the more employees I hired. At our peak, I had eighteen employees, fifty-three residential accounts, and twenty-two commercial accounts. I also started a window business, so we were doing windows on the side. We were shampooing carpets, too. These things were part of my business, but they were also businesses in themselves. So I was really busy working full time day and night. I hardly ever saw my kids (laughs), but I figured it was going to benefit us in a couple of years. At the time, I actually had big plans of expanding Spic and Span Cleaning Technicians nationwide like Service Master. I had the plans written out but never got to that point.

In 1990 my father had a stroke. He and I were very, very close. He had eighteen kids; six of them were boys, but for some reason I became his extra tomboy. (Laughs.) I'm sure some of it was because I played football in high school and helped at the gas station. So when he had the stroke, I was quite devastated. It left him completely paralyzed on the right side. My dad had always been very independent, and this was devastating to his ego and emotional state. He got to the point where he didn't want nobody to help him, not the doctors, not the nurses. He was just slowly dying, and I was real scared. He was in New Mexico at the time, and I was in Spokane. I just prayed to God for the chance to help him before he died. I ended up flying him to Spokane so I could take care of him. I got therapy coming to the house, and pretty soon he was learning to walk and make sounds you could kind of understand. And he was beginning to have a drive to live again.

> You've got to go the extra mile, even if you don't get paid for it.

During this time, I had other people run the business, but it never ran as well as when I ran it. It was just real hard to keep up with things and take care of my dad, too. But I always felt he was much more important than the business. Then in August of '91 he wanted to go back home and visit the family. I took him back and told him I would come get him again in October. Well, in October, I was super busy in the business and couldn't get away. I wrote him a letter and told him, "Look, it's probably going to be another month before I can come back and get you." He died before I went back for him. (Becomes very emotional.) People in town told me he just gave up when he received my letter . . . I just don't think he was ready to die . . . I'm sorry . . . I haven't cried like this in a long time . . .

So anyways . . . 1992 was really a tough time for me—I kind of fell apart. It was really hard to get over what had happened. I kept thinking there was maybe somethin' I could've done. I felt like I shoulda gone back for him when I said I would. So there was a lot of emotional stuff tied in with my business . . . (Gets very emotional.) This is really the reason I decided to sell the company . . . It probably wasn't a good move, but I wanted to be close to family again, to fill the gap. So I sold the business to two of my employees, Janine and Cheryl McCarroll. Janine was my first employee, and Cheryl joined me soon after. Those two girls stayed with me throughout the duration, so I wanted them to have it; they had worked hard and knew what the business was all about. Their dad, who owned a trucking company, actually bought it for them. After they took over, I moved to New Mexico.

I think realizing the American dream takes a lot of persistence and determination. Without that, I couldn't have done what I did. I couldn't have done it without my father's input either—I think that helped me the most. Because I was raised in a business, I already knew it was important to please the customer. I mean, that's a biggie in the service industry. You've got to go the extra mile, even if you don't get paid for it—it builds strong rapport with your customers. So find out what their pet peeves are, then go far above and beyond what they expect. And don't brag about what you're going to do, just do it! Actions speak louder than words.

Jon Kittelsen

Jon's first product sprang from an accident he had in a high-school hockey game. With support from a large cast of mentors, he developed a business plan, created a company, and expanded his product line. Today, EZ-Gard Industries produces the finest athletic mouth guards in the world. Jon's products are worn by the likes of Jerry Rice, Rocket Ismail, and a host of professional athletes in football, baseball, and hockey. He says:

I was diagnosed as dyslexic way back in 1973, which was a traumatic thing to have happen when you're in first grade. I was a popular kid in kindergarten; then all of a sudden I couldn't read or spell or do arithmetic. Dyslexia was extremely new, and I was one of the first, so psychologists from around the United States came and ran tests on me. As a result, I was taken out of the mainstream and put in a special class. At that time, the only other kids in special classes were mentally retarded. That was quite a blow the first day. But I became very good friends with several handicapped kids and developed a very compassionate personality. I also developed real thick skin, because kids can be awfully mean at a young age. I was teased and ridiculed like you can't believe!

In high school I took a vocational test to tell me where I was headed in life. It said I would either be a salesman or a musician. I figured, okay, I like both of these options. My counselor ended up pushing me into a class called DECA—Distributive Education Clubs of America. It was a marketing and merchandising class that was offered as an elective. I didn't want to do it because the kids that belonged to DECA had to wear these blue blazers and ride a bus over to another school. To make a long story short, I made a deal with my counselor: I would take the class, but I didn't have to wear the blue blazer. So I rode the bus over there the first day, and they showed us a film called "How to Bring a Product to Life." It was a real-life story about a kid from Minnesota who sold millions of these painter-type hats. Right there I knew I wanted to start a business. It changed my life!

That same year, I played for the junior varsity hockey team. Growing up in Minnesota, my best friend, Steve Rudie, and I had played hockey our whole lives. I was not a great player, but I really gave 100 percent and motivated the other kids. One day we were playing our arch rivals, Kellogg, which was where I had this DECA class. We won the game, and I happened to score the winning goal. Actually, it was the only goal I scored all year, so it was perfect timing! The varsity coach had been watching and came into the locker room after the game. He threw a couple of varsity sweaters our way, one to me and one to Steve, and said, "You guys are going to be our penalty-killing unit tonight." That was what I was good at, knocking people down. I certainly wasn't cheap, but I was real tough. We couldn't believe it! We had just played the J.V. game, and now we were going to play varsity. There were 5,000 people in the stands. This was really exciting for a couple of sophomores.

During the game, we had to stand behind the bench 'cause there was nowhere to sit, but it was still cool to be there. The first period went by, and we didn't get a shift. The second period went by, and we didn't get a shift. Then with a couple of minutes left in the game, we got a penalty, so it was a penalty-killing situation. The coach said, "Kittelsen, Rudy—come on boys, you're over." So we went over the boards and faced off in our zone. We had about a minute shift, and right at the end of it I got hit real hard. My helmet unsnapped and came up, and my mouth guard flew out of my mouth—I had cut the strap off to make it more comfortable. I glanced all around looking for it, but I was still seeing stars. So I skated back to the box and started hopping over the boards, thinking "shift change." I was surprised when the coach pushed me back out on the ice to finish the game.

At this time the score was tied, and we were still a man down. Right before the referee dropped the puck, the captain of the other team called time out and skated over to talk with his coach. Then he skated back over and said something to the referee. The referee skated over to me and asked me to open my mouth. Then he said, "Two-minute penalty, faulty equipment." I started pleading my case: "I had my mouth guard in, but I just got hit. It's clear, and it looks just like the ice. We're not going to find it!" It was no use—I went to the penalty box. So now we were down three men on five men. They shot, they scored, they won the game. Needless to say, I was the mole. Everybody was mad at me. I went home that night "woes is me." As I was taking off my equipment, I was looking at these other mouth guards I had. I was determined to make a mouth guard that would stay attached to my helmet and still be comfortable. So I went into my dad's basement workshop, took this mouth guard, and cut the big, stiff strap off it. I left the little tab in front with the slot in it. Then I started looking at different types of rope my dad had in his workshop. I found this nylon tether, cut a piece off, and melted the two ends together with a match. It formed a loop with a bead of plastic where the ends were joined. I threaded it through the tab on the mouth guard until the melted bead caught hold. Then I took the loop, wrapped it around the face guard on my helmet, and stuck the mouth guard through it. I didn't like the way the black bead of melted nylon looked, so I ran upstairs and asked my mom for some fingernail polish—I was going to paint it. (Laughs.) She held the helmet in one hand and the mouth guard in the other, pulled, and the mouth guard released. She said, "Jon, maybe that's a safety feature. It's a quick-release helmet strap." I thought, "Cool!" (Laughs.) "If you get hit too hard it will break right off, but your mouth guard will stay in and protect your teeth." So I started thinking kids would dig this. It was a new piece of sports equipment as opposed to a piece of plastic.

Later that night, I was in the bathroom washing my face and had my invention with me. My mom grinds her teeth at night and has this custom-fabricated mouth guard she wears. I saw the case sitting there, and it was the same size as my mouth guard. I stuck my mouth guard in it but couldn't shut it because the tab in front was in the way. So I took a razor blade and started cutting this slot in my mom's case. I ended up slitting my thumb to the bone and going to the hospital for twenty-seven stitches. Needless to say, when I got back home I could get the case to shut. So now I could hang the mouth guard on my helmet and snap a case over it to keep it clean. I was kind of a "neat freak" as a kid—wouldn't put anything in my mouth that wasn't clean.

The next day my sisters were watching TV and fooling around with this can of breath spray. I had my invention in one hand and dove between them and grabbed the can. I was just teasing them, but I looked at the breath spray and thought, "Wow!" I sprayed it on my mouth guard and put it in my mouth, and it tasted great. And it was alcohol-based so it killed germs. So now I had this four-piece system.

I took my invention over to a friend whose dad, Larry Charboneau, was a graphic designer. I told him I wanted to call it the "Easy Guard." He made up this logo for me, cut it out, and glued it on my case. Well, I took it to hockey practice the following Monday, and let me tell you, it was the biggest joke of the whole freakin' varsity and junior varsity teams. Here I had lost this game, and now I was the laughingstock. (Laughs.) But a few guys said, "Hey man, that's really cool. Make me one." So I made seven or eight for the guys that wanted them, and they wore them. Then when I'd go through the line shaking hands at the end of a hockey game, guys would say, "Where'd you get that mouth guard?" It was a bright yellow string, so it was very visible. And I'd say, "I made it. Do you want one?" So I had opposing players writing down their names and numbers, and I started making these things. I was still a sophomore in high school, so I was sixteen years old.

That same year I showed the mouth guard to my DECA advisor, John McDermott, and he said "Let's turn this into a class project," which we did. So I actually developed a retail package and ended up winning the state championship in a sales contest. I continued to fiddle with it for a couple of years; then during my senior year, I developed a twelve-page business prospectus to get the product off the ground. I entered it in another division of DECA that was going all the way to the world championship. You first compete at your school level, then the district level, then the state level, then a five-state area, then the United States, then on to the world competition. There were 270,000 kids in DECA that would start out in this competition. At each level there would be less and less people. But to make a long story short, I made it to the world competition in California. Around 12,000 kids made it, and about half of them were from the U.S.

I went out there with John McDermott. He understood young people, and we got along great. I was a different kind of kid, and he let me march to my own drummer. He really nurtured me! So he and I went to California, and I saw what a major event this was. For some reason, the whole time I was there I knew I was going to win. The first day was round one, and they cut the field in half. The second day they cut it in half again, and so on. Finally, they got down to twelve finalists—it was the fourth or fifth day of the competition. All the finalists were lined up so you could see who everybody was. We were all sittin' there nervous, waiting to go into the room. They had six judges and a stand-up judge in the back. Here you are a high school student going into this hotel room to stare across the table at these six adults. And these judges are venture capitalists, bankers, investors—true professionals. So it's a little intimidating. I rifled through my presentation and then fielded questions. It was only supposed to be twelve minutes long, but I was in there for forty minutes. Everybody was saying, "Geez, when you do this I want to buy stock." So I knew by the interest level that I had won. When I walked out of the room, John McDermott was standing there smiling, and we walked straight into the bathroom. He said to me, "One year a lemon, the next year a fruit." I just looked over and said, "It's over. It's done. I won." And he said, "You know what, Jon? I believe you." When we went to the awards assembly, sure enough—they called third place and second place and first place. I won a giant trophy, and I got to have dinner with Donny Osmond and the Solid Gold Dancers. (Laughs really hard.) When I came back to Minnesota, I made the newspapers everywhere. Here I was, former troublemaker, now new town hero!

So I incorporated the business in June of 1985, which was my senior year. Then I started meeting with anybody and everybody that would talk with me: prominent businessmen, investors, professional athletes, friends of friends, anybody that could help me get this thing off the ground. My mom and dad were extremely supportive throughout this whole thing. They helped me with my business plan and were constantly motivating and pushing me. At one point, my mom actually did my correspondence because I couldn't spell. I would write chicken scratches all day long; then she would come down at night and rewrite all my letters. So I was fighting, scratching, researching the marketplace, doing surveys on mouth guards. Meanwhile, I was playing in a fairly successful rock-and-roll band—guitar player by night, young entrepreneur by day.

I finally met the guy that really made things happen. He's this wild, crazy guy who played golf with my friend's father—he's just bananas. He's the original scratch-and-smell sticker king. His company is Mello Smello, "where fun is serious business." I first met with him about another deal I was doing with some friends of mine, and it was one of the better pitches of my life. It's what eventually landed me here. Anyway, I'm sleeping in one Saturday, hung over after playing the guitar all night. It's about noon, and my business line rings, so I fumble over to it and say hello. It's Jon Miner, and he says, "So what do you do for a living." I said, "I'm a struggling entrepreneur." And he says, "How much money do you make?" And I said, "Gee Jon, I don't know if that is any of your business, but I guess I'll answer anyway. I make enough to pay my bills, and I could make a million dollars tomorrow." He laughed and thought that was great. Then he said, "Well, how would you like to sell stickers? You would do so well, and we could pay you a good salary." I said, "Jon, I don't want to sell stickers, and I don't want to work for anyone. It's as simple as that! But I have some products I've invented, and maybe we could partner up." He says, "Okay."

We set up a meeting at his house just before the Fourth of July. I bopped over there in shorts and thongs and a T-shirt and brought all my mouth-guard drawings. He met me at the door in a speedo bathing suit, drinking juice and wearing red, white, and blue sunglasses. He's a very unique, genuine person—almost larger than life. I went in and we had this great meeting . . . sat out by the pool . . . talked and talked and talked. Later, I went out to dinner with Jon and his wife, Leah, and we totally hit it off! Leah became as important to the deal as Jon was; she was an attractive, brilliant business person; they became like second parents to me. After several more talks we shook hands and agreed to a 50/50 partnership. He was going to put in $50,000 and give me a desk and a phone, and I'd become a division of Mello Smello. If the freakin' product took off, we'd work out a fair contract; if it didn't, then I'd sell stickers. (Laughs.)

So I was my own division. I got a desk and a phone, and occasionally a half hour with the art department. And I just learned. I learned about printing, and I learned about manufacturing, and I learned about molds, and I learned about making products in Korea. Then I would run out of money. But I always had just enough success to keep getting more. After a while, I went from a desk to a room and had three or four people working in my division. I managed to worm my way into Athletic Express, Herman's, several Mom and Pop stores, and a few regional chains in the Midwest. At this point, the product was just a mouth guard, a nylon tether, and a case. I think we had six different versions and a couple of sizes.

In 1991, it became clear we needed more help to grow the brand bigtime. So I put together a business plan with Jon Miner and his financial advisor, Wayne Johnson, and we pitched ten different venture capitalists. We landed a group by the name of Hanrowe Financial. They brought in $2 million for a minority equity position and took two sets on our board. The two guys were Dennis Evans and Albert Hanser. They've been incredible mentors over the years. They introduced us to a top advertising agency in Minneapolis that convinced us to try consumer focus groups. What we heard was, "Why is your mouth guard made from this cheap plastic?" "It looks like a toy." "I could bite right through it!" "How much protection am I really getting?" "Why don't you engineer this thing?" "Give me protection." "Give me a dental warranty." We heard this from high-schoolers, moms and dads, customers, and dentists.

So we set out to make the world's first engineered mouth guard. I worked closely with a prominent dentist named Dr. Paul Belvedere, who, at the time, was the team dentist for the Minnesota North Stars, the NHL hockey team. He had the idea we should put kraton into this mouth guard because it is a true shock-absorbing material. He thought we should put it on the biting surface and across the front teeth because that's where the injuries occur. If we put it between the teeth, it would reduce the risk of concussion from a blow to the chin. If you put it across the teeth, it would reduce the risk of chipping the front teeth, which are the most vulnerable in sports. So I started securing intellectual property big-time. Throughout this period, I also had help from Dr. Henry Cross III, the former worldwide technical director for Colgate-Palmolive. He invented Irish Spring soap, Palmolive dish detergent, Fab laundry detergent, and dozens of other products. Today we have fourteen patents and a dozen trademarks.

> You've got to figure out how to crawl over the wall, sneak around the corner, dig a hole underneath.

To make a long story short, we now offer three main brands. The EZ-Gard is your basic, low-end mouth guard. It's a piece of ethylene vinyl acetate—one size fits all. We've made it real user-friendly with a breakaway helmet strap and a case to keep it clean. We've sexed up the package to give both the retailer and the consumer more confidence in their purchase decision. Basically, we've just made it cooler than the other brands. The next step up is the Hammer. It's also made of ethylene vinyl acetate, but we've added a kraton bumper across the front teeth. It comes with a better dental warranty, a bigger package, and a better quick-release strap. We've built this brand with a killer name and a super logo—you know, really hitting that MTV generation. Then you jump into the Shock Doctor, the engineered mouth guard. That's where you get the majority of your accessories: custom sizing, a wishbone design that allows you to breathe better, shock-absorbing pads in the back of the mouth guard, the best dental warranty, a breakaway neck strap, a boiling and stabilization tray, and a sticker inside the package. So we've got the whole range covered. We can go to any retailer and give them everything they need, including the best products and the best price points. And boy, we're not stopping here, believe me.

We now have over twenty employees here at the office and around forty-five sales reps throughout the United States. You can find our mouth guards in Wal-Mart, K-Mart, Target, Footlocker, and all the top twenty-five major sporting-good chains. We're also the official supplier to the NFL. About 150 players use the Shock Doctor, seventy-five the Hammer, and several hundred the traditional EZ-Gard. So guys like Rocket Ismail and Jerry Rice are using our products. We also have twenty foreign distributors in countries like Canada, Europe, Australia, New Zealand, Japan, and Mexico. So we are really growing. We'll sell millions of mouth guards this year!

My advice to aspiring entrepreneurs is to never say die—a never-say-die attitude has certainly led to my success—because you constantly hit brick walls, and when you do you can't stop, you can't crumble, you can't cry on your pillow. You've got to think, okay, what happened? What lesson was learned? Was it a bad product? Was it a personality clash? I can't tell you how many times I was thrown out of offices in the early days. I was kicked out of Footlocker, the Woolworth Building, Target, K-Mart, and NFL Properties at 410 Park Avenue—all because I wouldn't take no for an answer. So you've got to analyze and start packing away what you're learning. Then you've got to figure out how to crawl over the wall, sneak around the corner, dig a hole underneath. I remember of friend of mine in high school who made a crack about my dyslexia the day after I invented my mouth guard. He said, "Kittelsen, you're so stupid! You're dyslexic! How could you ever have a company that makes mouth guards?" I just smiled and said to myself, "We'll see." I guess the challenge is what has fueled me over the years. I saw him at my ten-year reunion. I was real cordial because he knows what has happened. (Laughs.) But I'll tell you, I never could have done it without help from lots of people, particularly my family—mom, dad, my sisters, and even my two grandfathers. These are incredible people who helped me through the insanity. Dreams can become reality!

1. **SELECT A MENTOR WHO KNOWS YOU WELL.**

   Make sure your mentor understands your strengths, weaknesses, and business experience. Otherwise, you may be led down the wrong path early in the game.

2. **SELECT A MENTOR WITH ZEAL FOR THE DEAL.**

   Be sure your mentor feels the same passion for the opportunity that you do. If he or she doesn't, you won't have the support and encouragement you need when things look bleak.

3. **SELECT A MENTOR WITH BUSINESS SKILLS.**

   Make sure your mentor has more business savvy, skills, and experience than you do. You need to be coached by someone who knows the ropes.

4. **SELECT A MENTOR WHO HAS CONTACTS.**

   Find a mentor who has numerous business contacts. You need to meet people early on who can help make the venture happen: designers, manufacturers, investors, distributors, and customers.

Chapter · 4

RADIATING
ZEAL

―――――――――

M*arti McMahon has three great loves: boats, people, and entertaining. She longed to combine these passions in her own business. Her dream? To own and operate a fleet of yachts that offer gourmet dining during scenic tours of the San Francisco Harbor. She bought her first boat in Florida, then sailed it through the Panama Canal and on to San Francisco with her three young children. They survived a major storm, a month of boat repairs, fights with Mexican customs, food poisoning, and the company of her bedraggled crew. She says, "I had a captain who had been married three times, an alcoholic tutor for my kids who had an affair with the captain, a deckhand who had been married seven times, and another crew guy who ate us out of house and home. (Laughs.)" Following the two-month journey, Marti spent a year refurbishing her boat, then launched her new company, Pacific Marine Yachts. The early years were rocky: a divorce, a mother with cancer, and loan rejections from thirteen banks. "During all this time," she says, "the dream I had kept me going." Today, Marti has four yachts anchored at Pier 39, twenty-five full-time employees. and seventy part-time employees. She has the capacity for 700 passengers on her largest yacht, the* San Francisco Spirit, *and can feed up to 2,500 guests per day. Her company does around $6 million in annual sales.*

Zeal, passion, love, energy, excitement, enthusiasm—all terms I heard and witnessed over and over in my interviews. Not a single success story was without a large measure of zeal! So after the first three keys are in place—industry knowledge, a true business opportunity, and a helpful mentor—zeal is the next critical component to triumphant entrepreneuring. The fact is, if you don't love what you do, you aren't going to succeed!

THE POWER OF ZEAL

Zeal is a joyful, enthusiastic, and eager interest in the pursuit of some outcome or activity. It is accompanied by a strong drive, intense focus, and some restlessness. Every great religious leader has it; every great political leader has it; and the best business leaders have it. You have seen it in our stories so far—Joe Montgomery, Mary Ellen Sheets, Ric Burns—and you will see it in the stories that follow, particularly the three in this chapter.

Incredible passion does two things for the aspiring entrepreneur. First, it's the foundation for tenacity, the topic of our next chapter. If you really believe in your cause, you'll have the strength to put in the long hours, wrestle with the problems, do the work yourself, and keep going during adversity. The obstacles to launching a new business are just too great to surmount without a real fervor to make it work. So zeal is the underlying spark of perseverance. Second, zeal is the great orator that persuades others to believe—it's captivating and infectious. As Ric Burns so eloquently explained, "You're drawn to it like a moth to a flame. And that enthusiasm becomes the central fuel that propels the project forward. It grows like a series of concentric circles." And so zeal inspires other people to get involved, loan you money, patronize your services, give you a chance, and join your team. Simply put, you cannot light a fire under someone else unless you are aglow yourself.

I see the power of zeal in business almost daily. Those who have it get the jobs, win the accounts, make the deals, and facilitate the growth. In our company, we always tried to hire people who had real enthusiasm for our products and services. Those who loved our healthy frozen desserts won out every time over applicants who could have cared less whether they served hamburgers or chicken or pizza. The same was true for our vendors and suppliers. Those who won our business were the ones who were most excited about their products and our account. Brent Matthews, owner of Taylor Freeze of Utah, is a great example. Initially, he supplied our company with the best soft-serve freezers in the market. Because he loved our business, he later brought in other equipment lines just to meet our needs. Before long, we had a turnkey arrangement. For years, Brent supplied and installed nearly every piece of equipment we needed to open our stores. Of course, we were equally enthusiastic about the relationship—it allowed us to concentrate on what we did best.

So zeal is the fire that gets entrepreneurs over the bumps of the start-up phase. It's also the catalyst that brings the pieces and players together. Personally, I believe the business world belongs to those with energy and enthusiasm. The zealous always rise to the top! Of course, in entrepreneuring, it's important that as many of our ten keys as possible are present—and the more the better. All the zeal in the world won't help a pipe dream materialize, particularly if it's launched by an uninformed founder. But someone with all the key factors *but* zeal has a lower probability for success than a person who lacks several keys but has a monstrous amount of zeal. It's just that important! You will meet a few entrepreneurs in this book who, working against unfathomable odds, made it on pure passion and perseverance. So zeal is a powerful and critical key to success.

THE SOURCES OF ZEAL

From my interviews with our entrepreneurs, zeal appears to come from two sources. First is the product or service itself. As you've seen so far, Joe Montgomery loves bicycles, Diane Dimeo loves horses, and Ric Burns loves documentary filmmaking. You'll also learn that Judi Sheppard Missett loves to dance, Chuck Harris loves show business,

John Solomon Sandridge loves art, and Robin Petgrave loves helicopters. All these entrepreneurs were able to turn their passion into a thriving company. But the development and growth of the business was almost secondary to the love for the activity.

The second source of zeal is a burning drive to succeed in business, which is fueled by the desire for independence, accomplishment, and excellence. In this case, an interest in the products or services is secondary to the passion for success. Sean Nguyen, for example, had no special love for electronic components but really wanted to start a company to help his family members find work. The electronics field just happened to be the first industry he learned about when he came to America. Likewise, Debrah Lee Charatan, founder of Charatan Realty, felt no special passion for commercial buildings in New York City but really wanted to succeed in an industry that was dominated by men at the time. Dave Burbidge, founder of Burbidge Disposal, actually disliked being in the garbage industry but had an incredible drive to own a successful business. During his first few years, he wore sunglasses and a baseball cap so no one would recognize him in his truck. And finally, after making millions of dollars for other people as an executive in the catalog industry, Bill Fitzgerald wanted to do it on his own. His business, Beautiful Images, is a thriving success, even though he has no burning love for women's support garments.

This remarkable desire for success was the most common source of zeal I observed in my interviews, and it will probably continue to be so as more and more people want to start businesses but have no particular passion for a product or service. Of course, the best of all worlds is when an aspiring entrepreneur has both types of zeal: a love for the product or service *and* a passion for success in business. Several of the entrepreneurs I interviewed fall into this category. Matthew Naythons is a great example. He loves medicine, photography, and creating companies. He first went to medical school, then worked in emergency rooms around the world while taking pictures for Time Magazine. In this capacity, he photographed the Pope in Poland, the Jonestown mass suicide in Guyana, the Sandinista victory march into Managua, and a wake for Anwar Sadat following his assassination in Egypt. Since then, Matthew's love for business has led to several companies that conceive and produce first-class photo journalism books, some of which deal with the field of medicine—*The Power to Heal* and *The Face of Mercy.* So Matthew Naythons has successfully merged his passion for creating companies with his passion for specific products and services.

CULTIVATING ZEAL

Many people think zeal is a personality trait: you either have it or you don't. If you have it, you have a chance for success; if you don't, you won't ever start or you'll fail along the way. While I agree that zeal is linked to personality more than our other keys to success, I do believe it can be cultivated. Over the years, I have worked with numerous executives who have lost their jobs in layoffs. While many are discouraged about starting a business initially, they warm up to the idea after looking at their options and realizing that no corporation will ever guarantee them lifetime employment. The first seedling of zeal is planted. Next, they learn more about the factors of success and realize they do measure up pretty well—they have industry knowledge, a legitimate opportunity, a great mentor, and so on. Now their zeal shoots up dramatically! Before long, they're convinced that starting a business is their best opportunity, and they move forward with enthusiasm and confidence.

So you can enhance your zeal by following a few simple steps. First, look at all your alternatives to see how starting a business measures up. Second, see how you stand on the ten keys to success reviewed in this book. (The epilogue will help you do this.) Third, learn to clearly communicate your "zeal for the deal." While this step may sound odd, I know many entrepreneurs who are fired up about an opportunity but don't know how to articulate the reasons for their enthusiasm. Consequently, other people know they are excited but aren't sure exactly why. Thus, every entrepreneur can benefit from writing down and rehearsing answers to the following questions:

- What exactly is my product?
- How is it different or unique?
- Why would customers get excited about it?
- Why would anyone buy it over existing products?
- How will I find customers and get the product to them?
- What is the real potential for this idea?

In other words, be prepared to quickly tell people why your product is the latest and greatest, and why customers will want to buy it over everything else out there. When you can do this well, sparks of zeal will begin to ignite.

Here are three exceedingly zealous role models. Judi Missett's fervor for dance has led to a worldwide organization. Tony Conza had the passion, lost it, and then got it back—which led to Blimpie's explosive growth during the '90s. And Chuck Harris has incredible passion for entertaining. When agents could no longer sell him, he learned to sell himself. Then he used his skills to develop and sell other aspiring entertainers. Notice how he creates a "log line" to get customers to "bite." This is what you need to do to passionately communicate your idea to others.

OUR ROLE MODELS

Judi Sheppard Missett

Judi is the founder and president of Jazzercise, the largest exercise/dance company in the world. Judi's choreographed exercises are taught by 5,000 instructors in 20,000 classes a week, both nationally and internationally. Over the past ten years, Jazzercise has served more than twenty million people. Judi's love of dance, exercise, and serving others are the forces behind her extraordinary success, as you'll see in her story:

I started working in the theater when I was fourteen years old. I was part of the road company of West Side Story and continued with that through high school. I then went to Northwestern University and majored in theater and radio/TV, specializing in dance. I was lucky 'cause I got an agent right off my freshman year. In addition to singing and dancing and modeling, I went all over the United States with different road companies. I also danced professionally with Jazz Dance Chicago, a company which is still very prominent today. Gus Giordano, the director of the company, was really a mentor to me.

After graduating from Northwestern, I continued performing with Gus's company and teaching in his studio. I noticed there were a lot of people in my classes, particularly women, who would come a couple of times, but then I wouldn't see them again. Apparently they weren't feeling too successful, so I wasn't being successful as a teacher. That really disturbed me! I guess I had the idea that my students were taking jazz dance classes to become professional performers. But that was not why they were coming. They were there because they took dance lessons when they were younger and wanted to experience it again—it was fun, it brought back good memories. Or they were coming because they wanted to go from a size twelve to an eight and they thought dancing would be a fun way to do it.

Back then, the choices for exercise were either a calisthenics class, which was pretty boring and designed for men, or a dance class, which could be rigid and disciplined—that was what I was teaching. I began to see that people wanted a third choice—basically a combination of those two things. So I designed a new class and put the word out. What I did was turn my students away from the mirror, and I became their mirror. I focused everything I did on the success of the student. I choreographed movements that were easy to follow and gave out lots of positive encouragement. I wanted them to walk out the door feeling exhilarated and successful—the way I felt as a dancer onstage. And I wanted to give them that experience without the rigidity and discipline required of a professional.

Well, I had about fifteen students in the first class. The next week I had thirty. Then I had sixty, then the room wouldn't hold any more people. They just loved it! Everyone felt energized and successful and happy—and all that came into play when we did the last routine. It was like a big finale, so they felt like they'd just completed a performance. What it did was expose a great many people to the world of dance who otherwise wouldn't step inside a dance studio.

A few years later, my husband and I moved to Southern California. That was a turning point for me because I decided to do more teaching. I certainly have a huge performer's ego, but it was being gratified through teaching. And because Southern California is the mecca of health and fitness, people welcomed me with open arms—it was basically whatever I wanted to do. Everywhere I went, people said, "Sounds great, how about ten o'clock?" "How about this room over here?" "Hey, fine, how about six o'clock?"

So I started teaching mostly in community centers: recreation departments, YMCAs, churches, and some dance studios. This is still part of our philosophy today: to take the program to the people in every community. What I would do was list my class in their listing of programs, and it must have sounded interesting because tons of people would show up. And they were never disappointed! Then they would bring friends, and the classes would become packed. It was incredible! I mean, people would come and stand in line at the Carlsbad Parks and Recs department at five in the morning to get on this list to take my class. So I did this for about five years. I was driving about a thousand miles a week around Southern California, teaching about twenty-five classes. During this time, I really learned the value of publicity. When I started a new class in a different town, I would go to the local newspaper and give them a photo and a story about the class. Almost without question they would run it, and tons of people showed up. (Laughs.)

In 1974 one of my students said, "I think you should call this Jazzercise because it combines jazz dance and exercise—that would be a cool name." I agreed with her and immediately filed for the state and federal trademarks. Even though I never thought of myself as a business person, I thought it was the smart thing to do. (Laughs.) It turned out to be a very good decision. So I think you have to have common sense and pay attention to your instincts, which is what I did here.

Anyway, for those five years I was pretty much a one-woman show . . . on the road with my records, my record player, my car, and me (laughs)—and a lot of babysitting toys. Early on, I realized the value of child care—it made it easier for people with children to attend my classes. I would find somebody in the community to tend them, or I'd trade out tending for classes; you know, someone would watch the kids in the morning, then take my evening class, or vice versa. In the summer I'd find high-school students to watch the kids, and my students would just pay them. I think it was something like a quarter or fifty cents a child at the time, which was very affordable. So I had baby toys and everything else I was dragging around with me.

In 1977 I realized I wasn't going to be able to keep up the pace; I knew I needed to train some people to help me. I had a whole bunch of "groupies" with backgrounds in dance or P.E. who followed me every-where. (Laughs.) I picked five of them who had been with me most of those five years. Now, being an organized person, I had notes available at my fingertips for all the choreography I'd ever done. A woman in my class who had a degree in business said she'd be happy to help type them up. Three husbands and another degree later she's still with me. (Laughs.) Her name is Margaret Stanton, and she's the executive vice president of our company.

So I distributed the notes to the five women I'd picked to help, and we discussed how the classes should be taught. I then assigned them some of my classes and held my breath. I began getting phone calls from my students the week I sent these gals out. I was thinking, "Oh no, they're going to hate so-and-so," but that wasn't the case. They loved Nikki, they loved Maureen, they loved Judy—they thought they were all great! They were sorry I wasn't going to teach their class anymore, but they understood. So it started working for me! I thought, "Well, isn't this interesting . . ."

When I started using these gals, I had to decide what the business arrangement would be. I could have made them employees and paid them ten dollars a class or something like that. But I wanted them to do most of the work and reap the benefits of their efforts; you know, the old American dream: the harder you work, the more you can make. We sat around and discussed it and decided I would take a small percentage of the money for getting things started and doing the choreography. So basi-cally they became independent contractors. By the end of 1977, these five girls turned into ten.

This went on for a while; then two interesting things happened. First, San Diego is a military town, so a lot of the women who became instructors for me in '78 and '79 were either in the service themselves or married to service people. When they moved away, nationally and internationally, they wanted to keep teaching. The second thing that happened, as luck would have it, the home recorder came on the market. I saw video as the means to keep the quality of the program high, because it's very difficult to translate and perform choreography from a written page only. So videotapes enabled instructors who had moved away and could no longer attend the workshops in Carlsbad to actually see the choreography firsthand. So I kept adding instructors, creating new materials, and shipping out videos.

Up until 1981, all my instructors were still independent contractors. By that time, I had gotten a lot of business advice from accountants and attorneys, all of whom came to me through my students. So I have my own wonderful network of information. (Laughs.) Anyway, I started thinking I might have legal problems, tax problems, and (groans) all of that stuff if I kept doing what I was doing. As I mentioned, one option was to make my instructors employees, but I didn't want the old American dream to go down the tubes for a thousand people who were used to making up to $300 a class. I knew that wouldn't do! So I decided to officially franchise the business, which was not one of my happier choices. In most cases it's been fine; I mean, we're always in the top twenty of the Franchise 500. But franchising has some downsides, too.

Anyway, instructors now pay a franchise fee of $650. For that, they get the materials and the training, so it's one of the least-expensive franchises out there. First they get the materials to study, then they come in for an intensive three-day workshop. They have to pass physiology/anatomy tests and a practical where they teach the routines. We also educate them in marketing and business practices. Everybody used to come to Carlsbad for training, but now we train all over the world. Then they get continuing education: newsletters, videotapes, and new materials. We give them about thirty new choreographed routines every ten weeks. For this service, they pay a royalty which is about 20 percent of their sales.

Over the years, Jazzercise has really grown through our classes. We've never advertised for instructors. Our best instructors always come from within a class. They experience it firsthand, it touches them in some way, and they decide they want to teach. Right now we have about 5,000 instructors and franchisees who teach around 20,000 classes a week, both nationally and internationally. Over the past ten years we've reached over twenty million people. Our annual sales are about $50 million—that's the money generated by the classes.

Along the way, I've created two other businesses that are both very successful. Like Jazzercise, they just kind of evolved as the opportunities presented themselves. I never took out a loan for anything—the money was just always there to do the next step. I know some people start with an idea, create a plan, raise money, and are phenomenally successful. But I didn't do that. In fact, I have many friends and acquaintances in business that have done it the way I did. They started with something they loved, they saw the cues and messages along the way, then they took advantage of the opportunities.

One of our other companies is called Jazzertogs, a mail-order business that sells active wear, videos I've done, all kinds of weights, and other accessories for working out. It started when I did the Dinah Shore Show years ago. I put the word Jazzercise on my leotard so people would see it across the nation. Well, after the show all my students were clamoring, "Why can't we have those?" And I thought, "I don't know, why can't you?" So my friend who is an artist designed a logo, and we bought a bunch of leotards and T-shirts and silkscreened 'em. In two days they were all sold out, which gave us the capital to do more. So that was a sign for me: "Gee, this is a whole 'nother thing I could do!" And it's evolved into a nice subdivision of our company.

The other business we have is JMTV, which is our video production company. It all started with the videotape my husband and I did at our rented house in Vista, California. (Laughs.) We got a camera and two tape decks and

> You really have to believe in what you do; if you don't believe down to the core, you won't work hard enough to be successful.

filmed all my new choreography in the backyard. My husband did all the editing—sometimes he'd stay up all night! As we got more money, we bought more video recorders, until we had about twenty in our living room. So from that beginning we started JMTV, which has grown tremendously. The company produces all of my videos, and my husband oversees the distribution.

I think the American dream is still alive, but it's harder than it used to be. So you really have to believe in what you're doing or you won't succeed. I started dancing when I was two and a half and knew from an early age I would spend my life in dance. It was always something I felt deep in my soul. I never had to ask myself, "Oh, what am I going to do? I don't know what I like." I feel extremely fortunate I found something that was right for me from day one. So I think you really have to believe in what you do; if you don't believe down to the core, you won't work hard enough to be successful. I can't say enough about this! Being passionate about what you do is the key!

> I never let anyone tell me no if I really believe in something, because I know I can make it work.

A second thing is you have to be able to change. You have to make change a part of your life—you have to love it, embrace it, and take chances. You have to love climbing up the tree, getting on the top branch, maybe falling off, then climbing back up again. Because if you get up there and you're strong enough, you're going to be able to fly away with the birds. And that's what taking a chance is all about.

Number three: I think it's real important to maintain balance in your personal life and your professional life. If you work all the time, your personal life goes down the toilet, and you don't have the energizing recharge you need to do the hard work. The opposite is also true. If you spend too much time playing and trying to nourish the "personal" you, the business goes down the tubes. If you love what you do, that generally won't happen, but you do have to obtain the required balance. People who are really driven sometimes forget to take personal time and lose their perspective. So take time for yourself—not for your spouse, not for your kids, just you.

Sit on a rock in the middle of the desert or by a waterfall in the mountains or by a flowerbed for just ten minutes each day. It will give you the nourishment and energy you need to succeed.

To summarize: This was never something I sat down and said, "Oh, I'm going to build a business." It was done for love. It certainly wasn't done to make a lot of money or develop a company. It evolved, but it wasn't what I started out to do. I was motivated by the fun and the great gratification of helping people improve, feel good about themselves, laugh like kids again, and let out some of their stress and frustration. And I really believe money follows goods ideas—it's not the other way around. If you go into something for financial gain only, you're either not going to succeed or it'll be short term. I've never been motivated by the money. Even today, if you ask members of our management team, they'll tell you, "Judy never thinks about the money." (Laughs.) You know, that's not always a good thing, but when I have a good idea, I really go for it. I never let anyone tell me no if I really believe in something, because I know I can make it work.

Tony Conza

Tony is the founder and CEO of Blimpie International, one of the fastest-growing companies in the restaurant industry. Although he started the business in 1964, the company's rebirth and remarkable growth have occurred in the '90s. Today there are nearly 2,000 Blimpie sandwich shops across America. Tony attributes his enormous triumph to a re-kindled flame of passion:

A couple of high school buddies and I met at a party one night and started talking about going into business. We talked about this sandwich shop we had heard of on the Jersey seashore that had a reputation. We decided to take a ride down there and visit this shop. Not only did we love the sandwich, we were fascinated by the way it was made in front of the customer. On the drive back to northern New Jersey, we decided to open our own sandwich shop. We had one little problem: no one had any money. (Laughs.) But we managed to convince a friend to loan us two thousand dollars, and with paintbrushes, hammers, nails, and used equipment, we put together the first Blimpie location in Hoboken, New Jersey.

Before we opened the store, we had to make a decision about what to call the sandwich. Today everyone knows it as a sub, but back then the word sub wasn't well known. We found out they were called hoagies in Philadelphia, but the people in Hoboken, New Jersey, didn't know what a hoagie was, either. We figured if we were going to teach people a new word, it might as well be our own—one no one else could use. So one night we took a dictionary and went through the A's, then the B's, and got to the word Blimp. We thought it sounded kind of like the sandwich looked. (Laughs.) We added "ie" and that was our market research.

The first store opened up with a menu of nine cold sandwiches, which really hasn't changed that much over the years. It was just the three of us and one employee. Right off, people flocked into the store and loved the sandwich. Our first day of business we did $295, which was a lot of money in 1964 dollars. It was kind of overwhelming to us because we didn't have any business experience. I was a college dropout myself, so it was really trial and error from the start.

When the first store opened, I was working on Wall Street for E. F. Hutton. I didn't take the risk of quitting my job immediately. For about three months I worked on Wall Street during the day and at the store at night. The store was doing so much business that after a while we said, "This is great! We need to do more of these." We all decided to quit our jobs and open up two more stores—one for each of us to run. Borrowing some more money, we didn't pay the meat guy and didn't pay the bread guy, so we could pay the plumber and the electrician to build two more stores. Forget bank funding! That was not even an option. So on borrowed money, cash flow, and momentum, we opened two more stores in Jersey City. Again, customers came flocking in and loved the sandwich. Then something else started happening. People we knew, and even some strangers, started saying, "Wow, this looks like a great concept! How do we get our own Blimpie store?" In 1964, franchising wasn't very well known. There were certainly the McDonald's and Dunkin' Donuts of the world, but the general population was not familiar with franchising, including us. (Laughs.) We went to a lawyer we knew and said, "We need a franchise agreement," and he quickly put something together. We awarded our first franchise for six hundred dollars—now they are eighteen thousand. About the same time, we decided to go for the big time and open a store in New York City. So again on borrowed money, cash flow, and momentum, we opened a location in New York. All these original stores are still operating by the way, and they've done well.

After the New York location was opened, reality came home to roost. What happened was that we were paying attention to what we call in the restaurant business "the front of the house." This is how your product tastes, how you treat your customers, your advertising strategy. We were obviously doing a pretty good job of these things because we were selling a lot of product. However, we weren't paying any attention to the "back of the house," like what things cost, distribution, inventory, things like that. So even though we were selling a lot of sandwiches, we weren't making any money, and all the debt began to pile up and crush us. Some steps had to be taken.

The first thing that happened was one of the partners decided to leave the business. We gave him one of the locations in exchange for his stock in the parent organization. The next thing we did was sell off the stores we owned as franchises. That enabled us to bring cash into the company and pay down a lot of debt. However, we learned a pretty good lesson from that because it also totally cut off our cash flow. At the time, we had about ten franchised locations. Our revenues were much smaller now, and we no longer had access to the cash. All these franchisees expected support, but there was no money! This all happened during the first few years, so our problems just mounted.

I hate to go into the sad story, but I ended up selling my cars and cashing in all my insurance policies. I remember one time my partner and I were driving from Jersey to New York City. The toll for the Lincoln Tunnel was fifty cents at the time—it's four bucks now. I pulled up to the toll booth, reached in my pocket, and didn't have any money. I asked my partner, Peter, if he would give me fifty cents, and he said, "I don't have any money either." (Laughs.) So we had to pull off the road. Things were pretty tough! What kept us going was the fact that our problems had to do with our own ignorance and management mistakes, not the concept itself. People were buying our sandwiches and loved the Blimpie concept. And more and more people wanted to become Blimpie franchisees. So we just kind of endured until we got enough stores out there and enough revenue to become real people again. (Laughs.) I mean, I used to do everything: I did all the secretarial work, I typed all the leases, I handled all the problems. We just couldn't afford any help.

During this time, our franchises were selling for a thousand dollars. In the '70s we raised it to five thousand. The royalty was always 6 percent. So we kept franchising and growing our cash flow. However, the progress from then to now was not a straight line up. In the early 1980s we did a small public offering and used the half a million dollars we raised to diversify the company—like the Blimpie concept wasn't enough for us. (Laughs.) We started opening these full-service Mexican restaurants and bars. The worst thing that happened was the first one was successful. We made a lot of money, so we said, "Hey, let's do what we've always done: open more of these." So we started devoting all our time and money to other concepts and forgot about developing Blimpie. And the next restaurants we opened were not as successful as the first one. At the time we had about 200 Blimpie locations—all were franchises except maybe five.

> People sometimes think the desire to make money will give them the passion, but it's really the other way around: you get the passion for something, and the money will come.

Anyway, I specifically remember opening twenty-five new Blimpie locations in 1987. We were in the middle of developing these other restaurants and losing money on that whole operation. We had five restaurants called the "The Border Café" and a rotisserie chicken concept called "Amsterdams." We realized if we didn't change what was happening it would take the whole company down. So we decided we had to do something. At the same time, I was having this personal . . . how do I say this . . . I was feeling unfulfilled, I guess you could say. It was like, we had 200 Blimpie stores operating but we were more successful back in the early days.

We definitely made a mistake with those restaurants, but there was still something else missing. I was feeling like something was lost. I thought about it and thought about it and, in fact, took a three-week vacation. I had never taken a vacation this long in my life. I had a cousin living in Tanzania and went to visit her. It was like really out there—no television, no newspaper. It gave me a lot of time to think and reflect on what was happening. And I realized I had lost the passion for the business—the passion for success. My first thought was, "Maybe I ought to get out of this business, sell it and do something else." Then I started thinking, "I'm too young to retire, and if I do something else I'm going to have to get the passion for that or it won't be successful." So I thought, "We have a really good concept here. Maybe I ought to just get the passion back for this business and make it happen." In the early days, even though I wasn't able to articulate it back then, it was definitely the passion and excitement that kept us going. I mean, you don't survive under the conditions we were in without having real passion to be successful.

So I had a meeting with myself (laughs) and said, "You've got to get the passion back for this." The word passion is kind of hard to describe. I read something at the time by the late grand master of the New York City ballet, George Balanchine. What he said was, "I don't want people who want to dance, I want people who need to dance." That was kind of an inspiration—it described passion to me better than anything else I'd seen. People sometimes think the desire to make money will give them the passion, but it's really the other way around: you get the passion for something, and the money will come.

So when I got back, the first thing I did was get together with the top executives in the company. I talked to them about all this stuff and said, "Look, we can make this happen. We just have to decide to make it happen." It was actually a welcome discussion, and they said. "Yeah, let's do it!" So the first thing we did was establish three goals for ourselves. The first was to have a thousand locations by 1995. The second one was to increase our earnings by at least 35 percent every year. The third goal was to increase the price of our stock by a dollar per share per year. At the time, it was really in the doghouse—something like twenty cents a share.

The next thing we did was to get all the other management people in the company together in a conference room. This happened in Atlanta, where we had just opened a regional office. We ordered in food and sat there all day and all night. We made a list of everything we needed to change, improve, eliminate, and make better—we called it 101 small improvements. Then we assigned these tasks out to people who could handle them. At that time, I realized there was no way we were going to accomplish our goals with the people we had. First of all, we didn't have enough people, and second, we didn't have the right kind of people. I made a decision to only have positive people in the company—I didn't want anybody around with a negative attitude. So we went out and began recruiting people who could make this happen. Obviously, they couldn't be the most expensive people in the market because we couldn't afford that. But we looked for the most motivated people we could find. We brought in a sales director from Norell Systems, a marketing director from Hardee's, and a training director who had been with Domino's. Replacing people was tough, but it was necessary. When you make new demands on team members, some of them either can't or don't want to play anymore.

For me personally, I had to make a move from being a manager to being a leader. That's not the easiest thing to articulate, but I had to create a vision of the future and set an example for people to follow. I had to buy the hearts of people, not just treat them like employees. This was an important part of our rebirth. What I did was start a weekly communication with our staff—I called it "Pres Sez." The concept behind it was, gee I wish I could sit down with everybody in the company for fifteen minutes every week to see how things are going, share my thoughts, and talk about how the company's doing. You know, "What are your plans for next week?" "How are things in your personal life?" Obviously, I couldn't do that with every employee, so I started this written communication to let people in on my thoughts. I included information about the Blimpie vision, the need for passion, how we should work, what results we should produce, how we should treat our franchisees, and so on. In turn, I asked the employees to write a one-page summary of what they did last week and what they were going to do next week. I made it clear this was not a time sheet—I just wanted to know what was going on. I don't think many CEOs communicate with their staff like this. In fact, I was talking with Frank Biloti, the CEO of America's Favorite Chicken in Atlanta. I told him about my Pres Sez communication, and next thing I know, Frank is doing this weekly thing called "Frankly Speaking." (Laughs.)

Anyway, during this time, I set a goal to visit 150 of our locations in a year. In this weekly publication, I started talking about the visits I was making. Every time I'd go to a store, I'd list it in my publication. That was great! I think it let people know I really cared about the business now and wanted to make this happen. It also helped the franchisees understand we were a different company now. We really were determined to be winners!

In summary, our big push started in the late '80s. Lots of people talk about the early years of entrepreneuring, but this was a rebirth for us—it was like starting all over again. In a way, it was more difficult, because we had to take something that wasn't working and turn it around. Sometimes it felt like I was trying to push a Mack truck up a hill by myself. But I'm happy to say we accomplished every one of our goals. In 1995 Nation's Restaurant News ranked us the fastest-growing company in the restaurant business, and for two years in a row Forbes ranked us number 24 and number 25 of the 200 best small companies in America. We now have almost 2,000 locations across America. We're opening forty to fifty new stores every month. We just opened our first international locations in Europe and Latin America. Systemwide we have 107 area developers and somewhere around 20,000 employees. We're approaching $400 million in sales. Our franchising company hit $40 million in 1997 with about eighty employees. Our stock has also hit an all-time high. We've had one split and several substantial stock dividends. So it was a fabulous buy in the late '80s.

My advice to anyone who wants to succeed in business is a philosophy I call ACT. The letter *A* stands for attitude. One of the biggest reasons businesses fail is negative attitudes. Unless you decide you can make something happen and develop a passion for doing it, it's not going to happen. The *C* stands for communication. To be successful, you really need the ability to communicate with other people, both one-on-one and in small groups. I even think public speaking is important. The letter *T* stands for two things. One is tolerance, which means putting yourself in other people's shoes and treating them with respect. This applies to any business situation, but it takes on even greater importance in franchising because you have to be able to think like a franchisee and feel what a franchisee is feeling. The other part of *T* is trust. You won't accomplish anything unless people can trust you to do what you say, especially when you're the leader. Your employees, your suppliers, anyone you're involved with—the more they trust you, the more successful you'll be.

I think you determine your own fate in life. If you believe you can or cannot do something, you're right.

There's another thing that's real important: Don't let other people tell you what you can and cannot do. Before I started the business, I went to see a friend who owned a luncheonette and said, "I'm going to open up this place." He said, "What are you going to sell?" I said, "I'm going to sell sandwiches." And he said, "What else are you going to sell?" I said, "I'm not going to sell anything else, just nine sandwiches." Then he said, "You're crazy! There is no way you can make money just selling sandwiches. You've got to sell other things, too." (Laughs.) That kind of thing has happened to me over and over again, both in business and life in general. Like one time I decided to run the New York City Marathon. Two months before the marathon, I broke my big toe. I went to this doctor, and he fixed it up. Then I told him, "I just want you to know, doc, I'm going to run a marathon in two months." He said, "You're not going to run a marathon. You can't even walk right now!" So I left there very depressed. Then I started thinking about this doctor. He was kind of overweight and had probably never run a block in his life. Who was he to tell me I couldn't run this marathon? (Laughs.) I cut a hole in my shoe so the splint could hang out and got on a stationary bicycle—I started riding two hours at a time. Eventually the toe got better, and I ran the marathon. So I think you determine your own fate in life. If you believe you can or cannot do something, you're right. And when you believe, you make things happen!

Chuck Harris

Chuck Harris loves show business! He is the founder and owner of the Visual Arts Group, a company that finds, develops, and books highly unusual, highly visual, one-of-a-kind acts. Chuck discovered a market niche that no one else wanted or knew how to handle. He is really a "creator of creators." His acts have appeared on Leno, Letterman, and many other shows in America and Europe. Chuck also produces television shows and films worldwide. He says:

I don't like to talk about the two lives I have led, but it started with my dad when I was a kid. I saw him singing on stage, and it was instant love. I had never seen anything like this in my life. I saw the elation the audience was giving him, and from that moment on I wanted to be in show business—any facet I could. It's hard to describe that feeling, but it's like I was driven from the day I saw my father work. And he was really the great teacher! He taught me how to sing, how to dance—and he taught me about business. He also gave me that encouragement to be somebody different, somebody better. He always said, "Whatever you do, make sure you're the best at it. You want to drive a bus? Be the best bus driver. You want to be a doctor? Be the best doctor. Want to be a writer? Be the best."

I went on to work as an actor for many years. My stage name was Oaky Miller. I was on *The Ozzie and Harriet Show, My Three Sons,* and *Family Affair,* and I worked with Marlo Thomas on *That Girl.* I also did seventeen different films: *Divorce American Style* with Dick Van Dyke and Debbie Reynolds, *Rich Man Poor Man,* and I had a nice part in a picture with Sam Elliot called *Lifeguard.* Then all of a sudden it stopped. I must have been about forty-three when the phone stopped ringing. I wasn't the new breed of hip comedian; I didn't talk dirty on stage, and I didn't do the really bright, esoteric things. So I didn't know what to do. Literally, for five years, I didn't make enough money to pay my rent, and I had a very low rent, too. I mean, it was unbelievable!

Then one day I got on the phone, and I started trying to book myself. My father's name was Chuck, so I started calling people as Chuck Harris and trying to book me, Oaky Miller. I would say, "Hey, let me tell you something, he's great, he's this, he's that." I found that what the agents couldn't do for me, I could do for myself. Now I started getting work again. I came back from the dead. Then I did it for a friend of mine and took a commission from him. Then I did it for somebody else. All of a sudden Oaky Miller faded, and Chuck became more dominant. People were calling me who didn't even know I was once Oaky Miller and asking me to represent them. And they were making good money because I was good at what I did.

Around this time I started booking magicians, ventriloquists—people that were a little bit . . . different. Then I found that I had an eye for finding that very, very strange act. A guy came to me by the name of Hillel Gitter, who physically put his entire body into a balloon and did a very unusual dance. It was a party trick, basically. I saw that and thought it was great! I said, "Why don't you add this? Why don't you shoot balloons out of the top of the balloon like rockets? Why don't you put your head out of the balloon so just your hair comes out because your hair is funny?" We created some conceptual ideas that he took further, but I was guiding him, and that's what a manager really does. I put this guy in a show called *Victor, Victoria*. He's in Minneapolis now, then he's got Chicago, but they're going to end up on Broadway with Julie Andrews. So I took a plain, basic, unusual variety act, and I legitimized it! Now, not only is this kid happier than a pig in mud, he's thrilled to death that he is going to be on Broadway with, I might add, fourth billing in the show!

Shortly after the balloon guy, I found Christopher, who at the time danced with puppets and did lip synch to the Jackson Five. He was recommended to me by a friend of mine at William Morris named Dick Howard. I said, "If you guys don't want him, why would I want him?" I didn't realize my friend was guiding me into something. He thought the act was good, but it wasn't a money act for him. I mean, what do you get for an act like this? We figured 500 bucks. They deal with people who get $5,000, $10,000, $20,000, $50,000 a night. So I went to see the act, and I saw the greatest act I'd ever seen. I fell in love with this kid who was creating something different. When I gave him my card, he said, "I don't need an agent; I can't give away 10 percent of my money because I'm making $50 a night." I said, "First of all, I take more than 10 percent—I take 15 percent and sometimes more. Second of all, I'm not an agent; I'm a manager and producer—I can create and give you conceptual ideas. And third of all, if you're making $50 a night, I don't want money on that—I'm not interested." I was figuring maybe $500 a night so I could make at least 75 bucks commission. Little did I know Christopher would be as successful or go as big as he did.

The first thing I had to do was learn how to sell Christopher. How do you describe him? I can describe a guy who juggles six clubs, ten clubs, or juggles fire. But how do I describe a guy who dances with other people that are not real but look like the Jackson Five? And this is where the creativity comes. It's almost like studying for a test. I would sit up at night and look for what they call the "log line" when they're selling a new television show—it tells what the show is about. I had to paint the picture of what Christopher did and do it in a very short period of time, because when you're pitching on the telephone, the buyer wants you to get on and get off. Here's how I used to sell it: "I've got this kid who dances with four puppets attached to long poles, two in front of him and two in back; they look just like the Jackson Five. When he moves one hand, all five hands move. When he moves one foot, all five feet move. It's very, very unique." So I created the log line for Christopher, and then I had what I call "the bait on the hook." I put the hook in the mouth, and they say, "Well, send me a videotape." Then I reel the customer in—that's what a good salesman does. Because managers, agents, or producers, we're nothing but salesmen. And whether the product is a film that Steven Spielberg produces or an act like Christopher which I produce, we're still selling a product.

To begin with, we booked Christopher in a few small places. I didn't know how to ask for $500 for a three-minute act, but I would ask and we'd negotiate. Maybe I'd get $200, $300, or whatever. He'd go out and do a good job, people would see the act and call me up. "Oh, I saw this kid Christopher; how much is he?" If they called me I knew they liked him, so I'd say, "It's $500 a night." Then I got very, very lucky. I called a very good friend of mine, Dick Clark. Dick was doing a show called *Keep On Cruising.* And Dick said, "Look, Chuck, I'd love to put the act on because we're friends, but the show is booked solid." I said, "Dick, do me a favor. Just take a look at the kid and tell me what you think." Dick Clark calls me back and says, "You're a sneaky guy! You knew I'd love the act. Because he's so great I'm taking somebody off the show this week and putting him on!"

To be very honest with you, I really did not have that in mind. I'd like to claim I did, but I got lucky—and sometimes you get lucky. The key was, Christopher was that good! Anyway, a few days after the show, I get a call from Dick, he says, "Cheese and crackers, we've had 157 calls from people who want to book him all over the world!" I realized at that moment the power of television. Instead of putting him into a private party where I reach maybe 600 people, or putting him in a theater where I get 1,000, you go on television and reach millions of people! And that was it! I fell in love with the power of putting an act on television. I realized television makes the quirkiest, kookiest acts very legitimate.

So what happened is I followed up on those leads from Dick's show and started booking Christopher every place I could. One thing led to the other, and I kept raising the price—nobody was squawking. To make him even more legitimate, I put him on *The Children's Royal Variety Program* in England. A friend of mine was producing the show, and he loves Christopher. His name is John Fisher—a very, very powerful guy. I called John on the phone and said, "John, why don't we put Christopher on the Royal show? It's a great idea! It will be good for Chris." He said, "You know we don't pay." I said, "I'm not interested in the money." I felt I needed to put him in that bracket. So he went over there, and when Princess Margaret got up and gave him a standing ovation, I knew I was home free. I hit the grand slam!

So what Christopher has done is taken a brilliant, brilliant idea, and with a little help and guidance from me, has taken this act to the millennium of brilliance. He, to me, will always be the best visual variety act in the world. Without a doubt, he is the highest-paid performer of his kind. Christopher makes over $500,000 a year. He gets $2,500 an appearance in the U.S., plus, plus. Overseas, no less than $6,500, and up to $12,000 for three- to five-minute spots. The longest show Christopher has done was the Super Bowl. He did eight minutes 'cause it was a long way to get out and back from center stage.

So early on I realized that I was hitting on a marketplace that nobody wanted and nobody knew how to handle. The niche I found was the very best, one-of-a-kind, visual performer. For instance, Michael Davis is one of the better jugglers in the world, but Michael Davis has to depend on talk for his act. Michael Davis can play England and Australia, but he cannot play Germany, he can't play Paris, because the act depends upon talk. Now Christopher walks out and does the Michael Jackson act or the Village People act, and everybody all over the world has heard Michael Jackson or the Village People records. So it's recognizable. And the guy who gets in the balloon has no talk. Or the guy who is the great regurgitator has no talk. So I look for that most unusual, highly visual, one-of-a-kind act. Let me give you some more examples.

Allison Bly. There are several people who have done this act before. It's called the Dynamite Man or the Dynamite Lady. Allison Bly has several things above anybody else. First of all, she's a woman, and people would much rather see a woman blow herself up than a man. Even women want to see a woman blown up rather than a man. And of course, men love it! Second, Allison Bly is extremely good-looking. Why she choose this profession I would never know, and I have never asked her. Finally, Allison Bly has a great personality. So she's got all these things above all the guys that have ever done the act. She literally gets into a coffin, detonates some dynamite, and blows her body up into the air. You think she dies because it's a large blast. People run over, and she lays on the ground for another ten seconds as if she can't move. Then she gets up and shakes her head and walks away.

I also had a kid who died recently, unfortunately of AIDS. But he was half Lionel Richie and half Diana Ross. It was one of the greatest acts in the world. He would walk out on the stage, and from the side he looked like a black guy—Lionel Richie. Halfway through the song he would turn around, and he wore half a dress, half lipstick, half mascara, half a wig, and he would start singing like Diana Ross. You could absolutely die! It was the funniest, most brilliant piece of business I have ever seen next to Christopher's. I mean, it was unbelievable!

A kid by the name of Stevie Star is known as the great regurgitator. And literally, he swallows a Rubik's Cube, can turn it around in his stomach, and bring it back up. Now, don't ask me how he does it! I always accuse Stevie of having another Rubik's Cube already put together in his stomach. If that is true, it's a better trick than the first one because he would have to keep two Rubik's Cubes in his stomach at the same time, then separate one from the other. But I have videotape where you can actually see him swallow this thing, and it's not in his mouth. He can also swallow ten coins in a row, numbered from one to ten. You ask him for number six, he'll bring up number six. Ask him for number ten, he'll bring up number ten. In any order you want them! In fact, he's the only act ever to be on *The Tonight Show* for one solid week in a row! He's also been on Letterman.

> I've put myself in a situation where I am in control. And to be successful, you have to be in control.

I also have a guy who balances a car on his head, literally. We had him on the Jay Leno show too. No kidding, the car is lowered by a hydraulic crane on top of his head, and he balances it. He used to be a bricklayer in England—called a "nobber." He did nothing but take bricks up and deliver them to guys. They didn't have any hydraulic lifts or anything, so he did it by putting the bricks on his head. Of course, his neck became very strong. When I met him he was putting a guy on his head on a board. I said, "Let's do a washing machine, let's do a car, let's do whatever." He said, "Well, I can only lift 400 pounds." I said, "We'll take the engine out of a car and make the windows out of clear plastic instead of glass." It's still basically a car he's putting on his head.

There's one other act I'll tell you about who's also been on Leno. You may have seen this guy. He actually gets into a washing machine with eight pairs of handcuffs and leg irons on and picks the locks while the machine goes around. When I met him he was doing backyard parties. I said, "Geez! We've got an act here, kid!" He said, "What do you mean, an act?" I said, "We can get money." "You can get money for this?" I said, "Yeah! Who else gets into a washing machine with eight pairs of handcuffs and leg irons on! We'll put soap and water in there, you'll wear goggles, we'll make it legitimate. You'll go in there with a dirty shirt on and come out with a clean shirt!" He couldn't believe I could make money for him with this. Now he makes $8,000 a television show! I mean, this is a big, big money-making act. This guy has worked in front of millions and millions of people all over the world!

Anyway, my acts are now broken down into two categories. On the A list, I have about 300 acts. On the B list, maybe a thousand. I try to work only off the A list. Every act in the world I see, I get the phone number, fax, Social Security, everything, and program it into my computer. Now if you want a one-armed juggler, I go to a spot on my program, and I type in "one-armed juggler." If there's any in the world, they'll pop out. And the thing I like about what I'm doing now, more than what I did as a performer, is I'm in total control of my life. You know, the happiest time of my life was when I was standing on stage, but I never had control over that. I had to depend upon everybody to book me, or someone to love me, or whatever. So I've put myself in a situation where I am in control. And to be successful, you have to be in control. Now I'm helping other people create a vision and achieve their dreams. I mean, what more could a man ask for? This is now where the power comes, where the creativity comes. I don't have to be on stage anymore.

TIPS FOR RADIATING ZEAL

1. **MAKE SURE YOU REALLY HAVE IT.**

   Do a sincere "gut check" before launching your venture. Is it what you really want to do? Are all the key factors in place? Are you willing to achieve success at all costs? If you find you are not ready, then wait. Starting a business is too tough without a burning passion.

2. **LEARN HOW TO COMMUNICATE IT.**

   Create a "log line" for your business. Be able to quickly tell others why your idea is great, why people will buy it, and why you are the right one to implement it.

3. **SURROUND YOURSELF WITH PEOPLE WHO HAVE IT.**

   Zeal expands geometrically from a radiant group. Also, one negative person can bring down the whole team. So make sure you bring in associates who have the same level of passion you do.

Chapter • 5

WORKING
WITH TENACITY

John Solomon Sandridge loves art! During his early career he made a
living painting signs, billboards, and commissioned portraits. He began
researching successful companies because he wanted to start his own business. He learned that Coca-Cola had not used African-Americans in their
advertising until the 1950s. He painted a portrait of himself in front of a
Coca-Cola sign wearing a suit and hat common at the turn of the century. He sent it off to the company requesting permission to reproduce it
in a print. After several meetings with corporate executives, he was
granted a license to use the Coca-Cola theme in limited-edition prints of
early black America. His new company, LuvLife Collectibles, next
approached JC Penney about carrying the line. The home office said they
already had enough African-American art in their stores. But John's philosophy is "never take no for a no. It may be no today but not tomorrow."
So LuvLife approached a JC Penney store in Chattanooga and convinced
the manager to buy some prints. When the art quickly sold out, the home
office was now interested. LuvLife's products proved so popular that the
company won the JC Penney National Minority Vendor Regional Award
in 1992. Today, John's products are sold in major chains and specialty
shops throughout the country. According to John, "If a little black boy out

of the projects can do it, anybody can do it. If you know what you want and you pursue it, putting God first, success is totally guaranteed. It's that simple!"

No pattern appeared more often in the stories I collected than outright tenacity. And it's absolutely critical to the success of any new venture! All these entrepreneurs had numerous chances to call it quits along the way—but they didn't. They worked exhausting hours, did most of the work themselves during the start-up phase, and took full responsibility for the success of their new enterprise. Without a sizable dose of tenacity, new ventures just don't survive.

PUTTING IN THE HOURS

Starting your own business has many advantages: you're the boss, you write your own schedule, you develop new skills and talents, you earn more money over time, and you build equity. But there is one big difference over employment: You work longer hours than you ever did working for someone else. Because you own the company, you're married to it: you eat it, drink it, breathe it, and sleep it—at least when you can sleep. And often you fret about it during long restless nights.

Nearly all the entrepreneurs I interviewed worked around the clock during the start-up phase of their business. Jim Dolfi, owner of Town Car Limousine in Orlando, Florida, represents the group well:

Working for somebody else means you can go home and forget the problems. Owning your own business means twenty-four hours a day. I think you have to realize what you're getting into. It just takes a lot of determination. I can get a call at 11:00 at night, rearrange my schedule for a 6:30 pickup in the morning, then be on the road until 4:00 A.M. You've just got to be willing to forfeit some fun to get the job done.

When we started our business, I was consulting full time, so Mary managed the day-to-day operation. She was our first store manager, regional manager, bookkeeper, marketing director, and delivery person. She would actually meet forty-foot trucks, unload products in a parking lot, then shuttle them to our first five stores—all with our young children in tow. I put in my hours in the evenings and weekends. I recall many fifteen-hour days at store openings, having already worked a full week in my practice. Then came the late-night problems. On one occasion, we got a call from a mall security office saying our employees had locked themselves in our store. Apparently the manager took the key home and told the employees to simply close the gate when they were through cleaning. Well, they closed the gate *first*, then cleaned. Mary went down around midnight to let them out. When she arrived, they looked like anxious inmates awaiting release from their cell. This was one of many unexpected visits to our properties at strange hours. But we loved what we where doing! We were selling healthy products, we were creating jobs, we were providing superb service, we were building a reputation, we were making a contribution. And best of all, it was our business! As time went on, we realized the benefits of ownership. But if you don't want to work day and night, and you don't like the weight of responsibility, and you don't feel enthusiasm for solving problems, then working for someone else may be a more attractive option.

DOING REAL WORK

Not only did our entrepreneurs work exhausting hours, but they also did most of the work themselves during the start-up phase. They called on customers, assembled products, drove trucks, sailed boats, worked in stores, served customers, cleaned floors, went to the bank, and so on. While this may seem inefficient in this age of available capital and management, it provides some distinct advantages. First, it keeps initial costs down. This makes precious dollars available for other things and reduces the financial toll on the entrepreneur if the venture doesn't work. Second, it allows the entrepreneur to learn every aspect of the business from the ground up. This pays high dividends during the hiring, training, and growth phase of the company. Third, it creates a marvelous intimacy between the entrepreneur and his or her customers. This facilitates rapid changes in products and services as customers' needs are revealed in daily interaction.

Lorraine Miller, founder and president of Cactus & Tropicals in Salt Lake City, describes her experience of doing the real work of the business:

> I'd get up at six in the morning and race out to the wholesale florist, fill up my little Volkswagen van with plants, and bring 'em back to my shop. Then I'd say to myself, "If I can just sell $20 a day, I'll make it." This didn't pay me a salary, but it covered my costs—I only paid $375 for the whole building. (Laughs.) Since I lived upstairs, if I saw someone looking in the store windows at night, I'd run down, open the door, and let 'em in. I used to cry myself to sleep at night 'cause I'd be so tired. I remember at one point, my dad gifted all my brothers and sisters and their children a trip to Hawaii, and I didn't go because I would have had to close for a week. I didn't have any employees. That went on for about two and a half years.

Today, Cactus & Tropicals is a thriving business with many employees, dozens of products, multiple facilities, and thousands of customers. In 1994 Lorraine won the National Small Business Person of the Year Award from the Small Business Administration. President Clinton presented the award. At the time, Lorraine was only the third woman to win this honor. Much of Lorraine's success resulted from keeping costs down early, learning the business from the ground up, and staying close enough to customers to know what they wanted to buy.

This "do it yourself" approach runs counter to the common strategy of bringing money and workers together, then directing the new enterprise from the sidelines. Personally, I am amazed at how many business owners and company executives take a backseat to their basic operation. I feel the greatest weakness of corporate America is that top decision makers are far too removed from the real work of the business—and hence the customers! When lower-level employees know more about customers' needs and reactions than top executives, the organization is in trouble, especially in today's breakneck environment. Yet this describes many large bureaucracies in America. I once approached the senior vice president of a bank about a line of credit for our business. He visited one of our stores to check out the operation, and I happened to be there serving customers. He later mentioned his concern that the president of a growing company had to work at the store level. He assumed we were either very short on cash or unable to staff our business—and possibly both. I was dumbfounded! Shouldn't it be perfectly normal for corporate executives to participate in the real work of their business? I made it a common practice to work alongside our associates. The time I spent serving customers, restocking shelves, mopping floors, and interacting with team members provided great insights for developing and leading our organization. Most of the entrepreneurs I interviewed started this practice early, then maintained it as their companies grew.

TAKING RESPONSIBILITY

In the 1996 Summer Olympics, Michael Johnson did something no other track and field athlete had ever done. He won Gold Medals in both the 200 meter and 400 meter events. Conventional wisdom said it couldn't be done: "You can't switch from the pure power of the 200 to the steady strategy of the 400 in the same meet." For this reason, the Olympic schedule didn't even accommodate the attempt—the final round of one race overlapped the preliminary rounds of the other. Being a top-ranked athlete in both events, Michael lobbied the International Amateur Athletic Federation to change the schedule in Atlanta. They said no. Michael didn't blame them for spoiling his dream, he didn't become angry and lash out, and he didn't give up! He decided to show them he could win both events at the same meet. He accomplished this objective twice—at the U.S. Championships in Sacramento *and* the World Championships in Sweden. The IAAF changed the Olympic schedule.

John Solomon Sandridge did the same thing to get his work in

JC Penney. When the corporate office said no, he approached the store in Chattanooga to prove that his prints would sell. When they did, the corporate office listened. Not taking no for an answer, then figuring out how to make things happen occurs over and over in our stories. Our entrepreneurs are masters at hiking over mountains, scaling around barriers, and crawling under hurdles. It's an attitude of personal responsibility that fuels these feats. Paul Brewer, a full-time magician I interviewed, discusses the role of responsibility in his performances:

> *I have a number of principles that drive my business. One of them is that I am 100 percent accountable. A prime example is the audience. At one point I was doing 150 birthday parties a week. Some would go great and some would go terrible. If you walk away and say, "That was the worst audience," then you have no recourse. But if you walk out of that room and say, "I didn't give that audience what they needed," then you have a million options. If you are 100 percent accountable, you can find a way to give them what they want so they will come back for more.*

This belief in "control over outcomes" gives entrepreneurs many options in the face of adversity and empowers them to persist until their objectives are achieved. Unfortunately, we live in a society where numerous forces are spawning victim status for Americans. In recent years, the marketing ploys of personal-injury law firms have increased dramatically. You can't watch daytime or late-night TV without hearing the call for victims to come forth so blame can be placed. Then too, the helping professions continue to "discover" and often market new disorders that excuse undesirable and antisocial behavior. Furthermore, governments aid the onslaught by introducing social programs that end up serving far more people than the founders ever dreamed possible. Charles Sykes documents the history of this trend in America in his witty and insightful book *A Nation of Victims*.

The fact is, there are more opportunities than ever before to divorce ourselves from the consequences of our actions. But where does the truth lie? Are we responsible for all the circumstances of our lives, or do we control very few of them? Does the truth lie somewhere between these two extremes? Regardless of where reality draws the line, the entrepreneurs in this book take full responsibility for their lives, their businesses, and the outcomes of their actions. They simply don't play the blame game! Those who buy into victim philosophy likely rob themselves of the personal power needed to bring a startup to fruition. If you don't believe you control your destiny, you just aren't suited for entrepreneuring.

Here are three incredible role models who made it on pure tenacity. Their extraordinary successes resulted from arduous hours, hanging in there, slugging it out, and never giving up. Lan England and Lorie Line now thrive in industries that initially denied them access. And Gail Frankel is a gallant example of constantly plowing forward in spite of unfavorable odds.

OUR ROLE MODELS

Lan England

Lan is the creator of The Great American Bathroom Book, *a collection of short summaries of literary classics. His four volumes combined have sold nearly two million copies. His outlandish perseverance got these books on the shelves. Lan is a dyed-in-the wool entrepreneur. He has owned an automotive parts business, a company that serviced air filtration systems for diesels, a printing business, and several successful companies in the health-care industry. Here's his story:*

I've always loved entrepreneuring. I remember in ninth grade I formed a company called the Evergreen Better Box Builders. We built toolboxes, had an assembly line, and everything. We sold stock in the company and had a 100 percent return within a month and a half. (Laughs.) At the end of the year, the school gave me a big award for doing it because I had taken a lot of kids that didn't like shop—and were otherwise into marijuana—and put them on the production line. It was then that I knew I really wanted to entrepreneur. Before that, I thought I would go into something stable like dentistry, then play on the side. I ended up playing on the side and never changed.

Over the years, I've pretty much been a pathfinder and primary stage implementor—those are my strengths. A pathfinder is someone who goes into the marketplace and looks for brand new ideas that might meet a need. Primary-stage implementation involves setting up the initial machinery to put the product or service into the hand of the user. But that's where my strengths stop. I don't consider myself a good day-to-day manager. It's much more invigorating for me to stay in the creative mode. I know the rules for managing, and I guess I could be good if I needed to, but I really don't enjoy it very much. (Laughs.)

One of the more interesting businesses I started was a health-care company. It's the largest company of its kind in the country. It's one of those things where you focus on a niche and say, "Is there really a need here?" Then you play with it a little bit, find there is, and go with it. I developed this company around the idea of accurate coding. Physicians use a five-digit code called a CBT that explains the procedures they perform. There are 10,000 of these codes, and they're changing every year. If they don't use them right, they don't get reimbursed; they can also be fined heavily by the government, especially in Medicare cases. So we had consultants, seminars, and all kinds of things nationwide as part of this company.

When I sold the business in '88, there was one tiny piece missing. It's an industry that's never had any certification or recognition available to coders. The people that do this are most often folks in back offices or family members of doctors. "Hey, take care of putting these codes on these bills. You can do it; just open this book and go for it." But it's not that easy. I asked the company I sold my business to if they were interested in doing something with this, but they thought it should be a nonprofit entity. So I formed a nonprofit company in Chicago called the American Academy of Procedural Coders. Its sole mission is to train, certify, and give recognition to these procedural coders nationwide. The AMA now works with us, and the Office of the Inspector General has us certify their personnel—they're the ones who send out people to do insurance audits. So it's kind of become the CPA of coding; it's called the CPC, and you put it behind your name.

I was in the process of selling the consulting company and starting this new one when the idea for The Great American Bathroom Book came to me. I was on a long flight from Atlanta and had my day planner with me. I had read everything in it, everything on the plane, and was really quite bored. I thought, "What I'd really love to have in my day planner would be pages from libraries of thoughts, ideas, or great books"—material that would refresh my memory about literature I had read or get me excited about literature I hadn't read yet. So I got home and jotted down some ideas and put them in a manila folder. At any given time, I'll have forty or fifty manila folders in the drawer that have ideas in them. As additional thoughts come, I'll drop notes in the folders. It's an inexpensive way to do due diligence because the good ideas rise to the top and the bad ones just stay put.

Anyway, I guess about a year and a half passed, and a friend of mine called. He was a former schoolteacher who had gone back east to work for his father-in-law. He was back in town looking for employment opportunities. He said, "Lan, I know you are always hiring folks; do you have any ideas?" I said, "You know, Steve, I have an idea I think would be a lot of fun to develop. Why don't we create two-page summaries of all-time great works that people can put in their day planners? They won't take up a lot of space, and they'll give people a taste of what good literature is all about."

So we started building a library for what we called "Compact Classics." We thought we could finish the project in ten to twelve months. As I recall, it took eighteen months. Steve was the final editor, but we had about twenty-five contributing editors we hired to assist us. We sought out people who loved literature. We posted notices on campuses, put ads in the paper, different things like that to find them. They ranged from Ph.D.s to a prison inmate. He was a fabulous reader, but we could only talk to him on Saturdays. (Laughs.) They were from all walks of life because the books were from all walks. It had to be a passion with them, because they didn't get rich doing it. Anyway, the contributing editors would cut the books down to 2,500 words. From there, Steve would reduce them to about 1,800 words. I think the first volume summarized 130 books.

Even though we started with the day planner idea, I decided to publish the summaries as a book. I called it Compact Classics and was stubborn enough to put my own cover on. It was a rather ugly two-tone burgundy. We thought we had a real winner! We printed 5,000 copies in-house on our own printing presses and started shopping 'em to bookstores. We got a few stores to take it, but it just didn't sell—it was dead! I later learned that selling 5,000 copies of any title in the publishing industry is considered a success. Had I known that starting this project, I would have said, "Absolutely not!" So I was ready to drop it. Instead of having a success, we had a lemon. But that's the kind of consulting I love to do in the real world. I like to go into something that's got problems and try to fix 'em.

At that point, I talked with some of our staff and said, "Go to the bookstores that have our book, stand around, and tell me what's happening." Sometimes they'd be there a whole day and no one would pick up the book. Other times, one or two people would look at it. And when people picked it up, they bought it almost every time. So we knew we had something the consumer liked. What we didn't know was how to get them to pick it up. So we had a couple of brainstorming sessions and decided to call it something obnoxious, just so people would be curious. We came up with *The Great American Bathroom Book,* and the more we thought about it, the more we liked it! So the last assignment I gave them was, "Go look on the bookshelves and tell me what sticks out the most." You know, there are some gorgeous books out there with all kinds of foil and colors. But they all came back and said, "The ones that stick out are kind of bland—white with very obvious points to them—not the beautiful ones with all the colors."

So we chose a basic white laminated cover with some foil embossing. We kept it really distinguishable and clean. We printed another 10,000 copies with the new cover and went back to market. We found that no book distributors wanted to carry our book because we were too small. What we heard was, "Wait a minute, you're a one-book house? We don't want to buy from a one-book house. We want to buy from a company that's putting out lots of books so we can go down their pick list." See, what happens in publishing is bookstores like B. Dalton and Walden's buy from book distributors who buy from the publishers. And the distributors don't buy from the publishers unless there's a demand in the bookstores.

So being a small company and only having one book, we had to create a demand. We put together a telemarketing room and had about a dozen telemarketers call nearly every bookstore in America and beg them to take a few copies. By the way, you don't sell books that way—not directly to bookstores. We did everything backwards in this whole play, and that's what's been fun about it. It's also having some tenacity, hanging in there, and not giving up.

In order to get bookstores interested, we had a contest. We sent out a flyer asking them to create a display for our book, take a picture of it, and send it to us. The prize for the winner was a Caribbean cruise for two. We had some wonderful displays. One store used an entire window that was fifty feet long. It had a bathtub, a toilet, and all kinds of things you'd find in an old-fashioned bathroom. The manager went out on a limb to do it, but it really paid good dividends. They were moving books as fast as they could. We also called radio stations and set up appointments for live interviews. The name is unique enough that it makes a real good radio interview. Steve has done so many of these now that he's pretty colorful. He uses a lot of the synonyms for bathroom terms.

> You have to be willing to hang in there. Sometimes it's just hanging in there a minute longer than the next guy that makes all the difference.

Anyway, customers started asking the bookstores for the book. Then the bookstores went to the distributors and said, "Have you ever heard of this *Great American Bathroom Book*? Can you get a few copies for us?" So we created demand, and the distributors were now willing to place orders with us. From then on, it really started to grow. Once it started growing, we published it out of house because we can only do about

10,000 copies. Our typical print run ranges from 50,000 to 100,000 books. Several major distributors have ordered 100,000 copies at a time.

So the book has done really well. We've tried to put out a new volume every fall—we've done four now. We've established a name and have lots of repeat business. People buy volume 1 one year, volume 2 the next year, and so on. It's interesting that volume 1 is still the best seller. The only reason it hasn't been on the *New York Times* bestseller list is because it's a synopsis of other works and therefore not considered an original. But it's done great! It's even used as a textbook at Stanford, Harvard, Texas A & M, and several other big-name schools. We thought the academic world would really shun it because the summaries are short. You know, "You can't do that to these wonderful works." But they love it! Anyway, our total for all the volumes is almost two million copies in four years. It certainly went up geometrically after we got the distributors buying.

> I went four months having food delivered on my porch so my family could eat. An old man in the neighborhood would deliver it in a box. I don't know how he knew, but he figured out we were not in good shape. What's really interesting is that ten months later I was a millionaire.

I think the book still has lots of room for growth. We've now produced it on CD-ROM so it comes up on a computer screen and you can search through the library. We are also producing it on tape and CD audio. The guys doing it are wonderful readers. It takes between two and three minutes to listen to each book, so it's perfect for driving to and from work. Another one of our ideas was to approach the travel industry. You know the headsets they give you on airplanes? Well, I'm negotiating on a repeating tape that will play a dozen or so summaries on one of their channels. At the end, it will have a number they can call to order the books. We also have a hotel that produced a really nice felt-cover version of the book. They put it on people's pillows at night so they'll have something to read before going to bed. So we're working on a lot of ideas.

I really do think this is the American dream, but you've got to be willing to take risks, have tenacity, and stay in there. One of the rules of entrepreneuring is identifying the need, then going after it. The trouble is, we all perceive needs through our own experiences, and sometimes we're way off. This is a problem with a lot of would-be entrepreneurs. They have this great idea for a widget, but it only serves them or a small market. They haven't done enough homework. And of course, proper packaging, proper marketing, proper all of those things are so important. Then you have to be willing to hang in there. Sometimes it's just hanging in there a minute longer than the next guy that makes all the difference. You have to be willing to sacrifice all over the place, and it takes its toll. I went four months having food delivered on my porch so my family could eat. An old man in the neighborhood would deliver it in a box. I don't know how he knew, but he figured out we were not in good shape. What's really interesting is that ten months later I was a millionaire. You know, that's the swing of it all. If you don't have a gut for it, don't do it.

In the end, it's really up to you. You have to be responsible to make it happen. *The Great American Bathroom Book* is a good example. If we hadn't changed the marketing angle and kept trying, we would have had a sad story and a large loss. But by being responsible to the product, pushing hard, and hanging in there, we pulled it off. That doesn't mean it always happens. Lot of times that's what drives someone to the poor farm, too. (Laughs.) But it's been fun to see this one succeed. I walked into a bookstore over the holidays, and there was temporary help at the counter. I asked one of the girls, "By chance do you carry *The Great American Bathroom Book*?" She said, "I'm not sure where it is, but I know we do. It's the only thing my mother wants for Christmas." So she was temporary help, but she knew they had it, and it was the only thing her mother wanted for Christmas. This book's kind of a crazy story!

Gail Frankel

Gail is the founder of Kel-Gar, a company in Dallas that creates juvenile products for travel and the bathtub. Gail's innovations—the Stroll'r Hold'r, Tubbly Bubbly, Hoop & Hold, and others—are sold in Toys R Us, Walmart, Target, and Sears. Having limited knowledge of the industry initially, Gail stayed with it, figured things out, and accomplished the near impossible:

I was a stay-at-home mom. I had worked as a speech therapist in the school system for quite a few years but decided it was no longer fulfilling and took some time off. Had our first child and subsequently our second child. And like many moms in suburbia, I spent time in the malls—not so much to shop but as a place to get together, a place to see other moms, a place to have your kids run around. I usually had one child in the stroller and the other one walking beside it. I had my purse, a diaper bag, and various toys and things. My older son always had a half-drunk cup of lemonade, which, of course, he didn't want to throw out. (Laughs.) So I never had enough hands, and I kept thinking, "There's got to be a better way to hold this stuff on the stroller." At the time, the baskets on strollers were teeny–they didn't even have enough room for a diaper bag.

I had never thought of myself as creative, but several designs for products literally came to me. They were essentially "napkin sketches." I envisioned two products in the beginning: a three-hook holder, which looked a lot like our current Stroll'r Hold'r, and a cup holder. After conceiving these products, I did what most consumers do. I went to my neighborhood Toys R Us and to other mass merchant and specialty juvenile stores to find them. And guess what? I couldn't find anything to hold stuff on a stroller. So the more I thought about it, the more I became convinced this was a niche no one was filling.

I hadn't seriously thought of going into business for myself before this. I knew people who dreamed about starting their own company, and I thought it was wonderful, but it wasn't something I wanted to do when I grew up. But as I stayed home with my boys, which I really loved, part of me wanted something more to do. Part of the puzzlement for me was that I wasn't sure what I wanted to do when I grew up. (Laughs.) So now I had this great idea for a product, and the question was, am I going to do it or not? And I really wanted to do it! I felt a lot of energy! So I turned to my husband and said, "You know, I would really like to do this." And he said, "Sounds great!" Now quite frankly, had he said, "No," or, "Don't waste your time," or, "Blah, blah, blah," and I hadn't had his support, I'm not sure I would have taken it to the next level. Luckily, I never had to face that situation.

So the next thing I did was find somebody to sketch out what I envisioned the products looking like. I could see different embodiments in my head, but when God gave out drawing ability, I was last in line. (Laughs.) So I needed someone to translate what I saw. I remembered a friend of ours telling me about a guy at Texas Instruments who could sketch things, so I called him and got the gentleman's name. He was a young guy who was willing to moonlight and sketch up these beginning drawings, and we worked up many different embodiments of what I thought a stroller holder should look like. He also told me, "This looks like a plastic product, so it's going to be injection molded, and you're going to need an engineer." It was like walking this path where the second step appeared only after taking the first step.

So I knew I had to find an engineer to create more specific drawings for injection molding. I visited with a couple and found a guy I really liked. He used to work at TI but was now doing consulting. He and I clicked right off—I could see he understood what I wanted to do. So I spent many months sitting by John, watching him make changes on his CAD system as we talked about the product. You have to understand, at that point I was still a full-time mom, so I was catching a couple of hours during the week here and there.

After a while we had several drawings I could get quotes on, but I still had questions about what would work, what wouldn't work. Someone suggested I prototype one or two versions of the product to see what I liked, what I didn't like. And trying to find a prototype person—it's not like they're listed under P in the Yellow Pages. (Laughs.) You find one or two people and realize they aren't quite right or they cost too much. Then you find a couple you like, but they have to work you into their schedules because you're this itty-bitty person, not a big company that gives them work on a consistent basis. I finally found a gentleman I still work with, and we developed several versions of the product. For instance, we had a cup with a hook underneath it, but it just didn't look good. We also had a cup with a strap, but it didn't hold real tight. Finally, we put the cup on the bottom hook, and it looked pretty good to me. Prototypes aren't hugely expensive, but they can run a thousand dollars or more apiece. My husband and I had some money saved up, so we just used whatever we needed.

Another acquaintance of mine knew someone who worked in marketing and had done focus groups. So I found out what a focus group was. (Laughs.) I thought, "Well, I trust my gut on this, but it probably won't hurt," so we arranged the meeting. The marketing guy said, "It's really not a good idea for you to be there." And I said, "Why can't I pretend I'm your helper so I can hear and see the reactions?" So that's what we did. We had some women come in, and they really liked the product. Two things made the group worth the money I spent. The first was that many of the women came to the meeting with large-handled purses. The three hooks I had on the Stroll'r Hold'r were small, even though they were strong. Still, to the eye, it didn't look like they could hold the straps comfortably. Their suggestion was to make the back hook large enough to hold purses. I thought, "Okay, that's not a bad suggestion." The other suggestion was to make the product white so it would go with anything. That was a surprise to me because I though everyone would want gray. I can remember like yesterday leaving the focus group and going right to my engineer, 'cause we were close. I sat there at the computer with him while he literally cut off the back hook and made it larger. It was wonderful!

So now I had a final version of the product. I knew my next step was to get quotes from injection-molding houses. At that point, I just assumed I would make the product locally. It never occurred to me to make it somewhere else in the USA, and certainly not overseas. So I sent my drawings out to injection-molding houses in the Dallas/Fort Worth area, got my quotes, went and talked with them, and settled on a company I still use today. I remember writing the check for the down payment on the mold and initial inventory. My hand was shaking when I wrote it. The deal was half up front, which I want to say was twenty thousand, but it was a number with a lot of zeros. (Laughs.) I had never written a check that large in my life!

At that same point, I knew I had to get packaging for the product. So many things were happening on parallel paths. I called up the wife of a friend of mine who had done some marketing, and she said, "I don't think I can help you, Gail, but I have a friend who owns a couple of toy stores in New York and one down in Houston. Why don't you give him a call? He's down in Houston right now." So she gives me the guy's number, and he's staying at his mother's house. (Laughs.) He was nice as can be but said, "I can't help you because it's a juvenile product, not a toy product. I suggest you call up the Juvenile Product Manufacturers' Association. And by the way, their show's in November, and I think it's in Dallas."

At that point, it was really close to when the show was. (Laughs.) But I thought, "Wouldn't it be great to secure something there." So I contacted JPMA and learned they had very few booths left for the show. They told me to FedEx a catalog sheet or some kind of description of the product, and they would then mail me an application. At the time, I was working on my Kel-Gar logo and a catalog sheet. You give those to the buyers in your industry to describe your product, both in words and in pictures. So I FedExed my information to them with a FedEx package inside so they could FedEx back the application without wasting any time. Then I FedExed back the money and got one of the last remaining booths for the 1988 show.

I have a friend I do business with, and when nice things happen to me, he'll go, "Gail, there's no such thing as lucky. You're just ready and the right time comes." Well, obviously I wanted that booth and was very determined. (Laughs.) Actually, I figured if worse came to worst, living here in Dallas where the show was, I could always take one if someone defaulted. But now I had to get the product ready and for the show: photograph the Stroll'r Hold'r, get the packaging ready, and so on. I remember it like yesterday. I had one prototype with the bigger hook, and the old prototype we showed the focus group with the small hook. So we literally sliced off the small hook in the back and screwed in a larger hook. (Laughs.) I think we painted the screws white so they would kind of blend in. But you need to understand, I was determined to do this product with or without the impetus of the show. Foolishly or not (laughs), I had already paid my money for the product, we were already tooling up the final version, and we were already setting up a photo shoot. So it all just kind of worked.

Anyway, I'd never been to a show before. I mean, I got this huge, huge, huge notebook of stuff, an exhibitor's manual, and I'm thinking, How do you set up the booth? How do you figure out the pricing? Beats the heck out of me! (Laughs.) Don't ask me how I figured it all out! Actually, I had a cousin send me a price sheet, an order form, and other things she used in her gifts and dinnerware business. Also, one of my closest friends, Sheila, who has done every show with me since that year, said, "Yeah, I'll help you with the show." (Laughs.)

And, oh my gosh, it was incredible! I wheeled in my stroller and decorated it. I also borrowed a little grocery cart because the product goes on grocery carts. I brought in my son's tricycle just to fill up the space! (Laughs.) I brought in a table and my prototypes. And, literally, the night before the show, the molder had samples of the product. But as I've learned the hard way, initial pieces from a mold usually aren't the final. The mold still needs to be finessed and worked through. And while these pieces looked real good, they wouldn't come apart. (Laughs.) The cup wouldn't separate from the hooks, which it's supposed to do. But I can remember backing up in my station wagon, loading up a carton of product, filling up the grocery cart, and putting a couple samples on it. So just before the show we had the product, the price sheet, catalog sheets, photographs, and a mocked-up box.

The first day of the show was like a zoo! We were in a big, open area called "The Great Hall." We weren't high enough on their list to warrant one of the enclosed glass offices, nor could we have afforded one at that point. But we were just bombarded with people; had wonderful press come by; had lots of buyers come by. People were saying, "Wow! This looks great!" "This is really needed!" "You're going to do real well with this!" I remember one guy saying, "It's a great product; don't ever sell it!"

Somebody else came by and said, "Hey, do you want to sell it?" It's not like I had an offer in writing, but there was just a lot of excitement over the product. We also had real interest from industry magazines like Baby Talk and American Baby Magazine, which ended up featuring the product. Best of all, we started taking orders that first day. I remember at almost five o'clock, a company out in California ordered a gross of them. I thought it was the hugest order. (Laughs.) And remember, at that point, I didn't know anything about pricing the product, repping the product, the percentage for reps, or anything. I was such a novice at so many things, but for some reason it all worked out. It just seemed like I was in the right place at the right time.

One of the mistakes I love to tell on myself is about the boxing. Now in hindsight, I probably should have studied the industry much more than I did. There are so many things I could have done to make my job easier. I just kind of did it by the school of hard knocks. But I didn't have a whole lot of time. I remember literally taking my boys to the engineer's office and plugging in a Sesame Street video, which gave me thirty minutes. (Laughs.) That's terrible to admit, but it's true. And God bless those who helped! There really aren't a lot of people who would be open to that type of thing. But anyway, I came up with the brilliant idea of having this triangular-shaped package. It's hard to explain, but the roof sloped down, and it was really beautiful! I had already photographed it and made separations, and it was sitting at the box makers ready for my initial run. For the show, they mocked up a sample box from the film.

During the show, a man walked up to my booth who had been repping juvenile products for years and years and years—a heavy hitter who sold to Toys R Us. After a few minutes he said, "Really good product. Terrible box." Of course, I said, "What do you mean?" He said, "How are you going to stack it?" I went, "What?" (Laughs.) He gave me his name and said, "When you get your act together (laughs), we'd be interested in taking it to Toys R Us for you." So I had a hard decision to make. Do I stay with my beautiful package that I loved, or do I listen to someone who's had experience? You have to understand, I'd already spent a couple thousand dollars shooting and separating the art. I mean, I was ready to go. But this guy was in the industry, and what he said carried weight. So I could ignore him and go on my merry way because I wanted my own look, or I could choose to listen to him even though it would cost me money. Well, I pulled the plug and created a new box. That's something I feel I've been blessed with in business: the ability to admit I don't know everything and listen to what other people say. And sometimes I follow their recommendations 100 percent, and sometimes I make changes to their recommendations. But I think it's really important to listen, especially for someone like myself who didn't come from Mattel Toys.

So the Stroll'r Hold'r was our first product, and we've been shipping it since 1989. We named our second product the Tubbly-Bubbly. It's a soft elephant that fits over the faucet so children don't hurt their heads. It's also a liquid bubble-bath dispenser. You put the bubble bath in the nose; it mixes with the water and is dispensed in the tub. We now have a whole line of products around that cute elephant face because it's really taken off. One of them is the Tub Rug. It's a really soft bathmat with the elephant face on it. The elephant is blowing three bubbles, which are filled with heat-sensitive ink. If the water becomes too hot, the ink starts to disappear, and the words "too hot" appear in the largest bubble. So it's basically a mat plus an extra safety device parents can use—along with their wrists, I might add. (Laughs.) We also have another new product called the Hoop & Hold. It's a tub toy holder and a basketball game all in one. It has a basketball backboard, an inflatable ball, and a net with a zippered bottom. You can load your tub toys in the net. When you want to play basketball, just unzip the net, take out the inflatable ball, and shoot!

So being innovative in bath and travel products is what Kel-Gar is all about. We own all our ideas and the molds, then employ other companies to make and warehouse our products. This allows me to do what I do best: create innovative products, put a new twist on things, and grow the business. I really don't want to be a "me too" company. I'm not going to get into a bidding war over a pacifier, for example. And I'm happy to say our products are now found in the top juvenile catalogs and the major

> When people put up roadblocks, you have to figure out how to get around them.

mass-merchant chains: Walmart, Target, Toys R Us, JC Penney, Sears. We're increasing our distribution channels all the time. We now have representatives across the country who sell directly to the stores. Back in 1988 I had to practically beg reps to take on our one-product line. Now that we're larger and more stable, we get unsolicited calls from product representatives all the time. Our reps are all independent contractors. They'll represent Kel-Gar plus any number of juvenile companies in certain territories. Our sales are around $5 million.

I really do feel I'm living the American dream. And I think others can do it, too! You just have to be a barracuda and bite into something and not let go. When people put up roadblocks, you have to figure out how to get around them. There were so many times I wouldn't take no for an answer. I think that's what you have to have. It's like a fire in your belly. I'm sure other people have their own words for it, but I was persistent—I wouldn't give up. Although, if I had it to do over again, I'd learn a lot more about the industry before going forward. I'd walk it, feel it, smell it. I'd go to trade shows, talk to product reps, and read the trade magazines. There's so much information you can gain. I also think you need to surround yourself with positive people. After I finished the Stroll'r Hold'r and was seriously thinking about doing the Tubbly Bubbly, a friend of mine said, "Why do you want to have a second product?" I'm not saying to discard all your old friends, but it's important to have a support group around you.

Anyway, I never thought I'd be doing this. Never! (Laughs.) This is going to sound strange, like I'm writing my biography or something. But as a kid my parents taught me I could do anything. And I may not be president of the United States, at least not yet. But I am president of Kel-Gar. The important thing is that my mind was open to the possibility. And now I get a thrill every time I see someone using one of my products. It's almost like having another child. Each product has its own gestation period: I conceive it, create it, name it, and it becomes a living, breathing thing. And some take a lot longer than it took me to have my kids. (Laughs.) Then to actually see people using them fills me with an unbelievable joy! We were traveling home on a plane a couple of weeks ago, and this woman was trying to find a place to put her stroller—it had a Stroll'r Hold'r on it. My husband was so funny. He was saying to the flight attendant, "Don't close the lid on the Stroll'r Hold'r. My wife invented it." (Laughs.) It was great! So it all started with me in the mall looking at the backs of strollers. Well, I still look at the backs of strollers 'cause I love to see my product there.

Lorie Line

Lorie Line started her career playing the piano in Dayton's Department Store in Minneapolis. After numerous requests for an album, she hit the studio and recorded her most requested songs. Failing to get the attention of the major record companies, she "took her music to the streets." Her company, Time Line Productions, eventually achieved nationwide distribution as more and more consumers began requesting her works. Today, with fourteen albums and a public television special to her credit, she's one of the hottest female pianists in America. Here is her story:

When I was five years old I found a toy piano in a garbage can on my way to kindergarten—it was a little Fisher Price type toy. My teacher noticed I had a gift and could play anything by ear—simple melody lines, nursery tunes, things like that. The problem was, the only thing I wanted to do was play that piano every single day. So my teacher called my parents and said, "Hey, she's great on the piano, and you should give her lessons, but you've got to make her keep this thing at home because she's not playing with the other kids." So my parents made a deal with me: I only got to take the piano to school on a limited basis, and they promised me lessons and a real piano when I was six.

I remember waiting on the curb watching the water roll down the gutter when the truck drove up on my sixth birthday. My parents put the piano in the living room and hired a young girl to teach me. I was very disappointed because I wanted a real teacher. But they said, "Well, let's see how you do," because they didn't have a ton of money. So they paid her a little bit to entertain me each week. That lasted about six months, and I said, "I want a real teacher." I ended up getting this girl's teacher to teach me. (Laughs.) Her name was Mrs. Day, and she was great! But Mrs. Day retired after a few years and gave all her students to this other teacher. And for some reason, she and I had a personality conflict. Isn't that funny? How can you have a personality conflict with a nine-year-old? But she didn't like me at all. I think I was probably very strong willed and wanted to play things my own way. Also, she may have felt some jealousy because I had such a good ear. If she played something one time, I could play it back to her. It may not have been exactly how she played it, but she didn't care for what I did. So I was in tears a lot.

I entered my first competition that year. It was a twelve-year-old division and I was nine, but I entered it anyway. And I won! I've still got the certificate sitting on my wall right in front of me. So I got a small taste of success. Later that year, I decided to enter a statewide contest. It was a variety show with bands and dancers and various things. There was going to be an award for the piano division and a grand award for the whole night. I asked my teacher if she would help me prepare for it, and she told me no. I said, "Why not?" And she goes, "I don't believe in those contests, and there's no way you'll win." I said, "Well, I really want to do it just for the experience." But she said no. So I worked really hard on my own and prepared a couple of pieces for the contest. I ended up winning the piano division and the grand prize that night! So I got another taste of winning at an early age.

The next day we had a workshop at my teacher's house. She presented scholarships to two of her students, and of course, I didn't get one. She only briefly mentioned the award I had won the night before. I was just crushed that she didn't recognize my hard work with one of the scholarships. I got into the car and cried all the way home. So my mom said, "We're not messin' around anymore." And that very day she called another teacher in town who only took seventeen-year-olds who were gettin' ready to go to college on scholarships. I vividly remember the call! She said, "My daughter is Lorie Porter and she plays the piano." Then she said, "Oh good, you do know her." She went on to say, "Lorie loves the piano, and we want her to study with someone who will nurture her. Would you be willing to take her?" And she said, "I would love to teach Lorie." Of course, I was thrilled because I was really little. So Alleta Gray took me under her wing and nurtured me musically more than anybody ever had. I showed up every week for nearly ten years and became like a daughter to her. It was a really affectionate relationship. She passed away after I went on to college.

While I was going to school I had to support myself, so I always had a job. I started out typing and ended up as the director of marketing for a construction company. Basically, what I did was help them get projects. I painted a pretty picture of the company to make them look like they could really do a great job. (Laughs.) I actually did this for a couple of companies. They were small enough to let me see the big picture of how companies run, yet large enough that there was a variety of things to do. Anyway, I really enjoyed the business part of it, and it paid the bills.

So I graduated when I was twenty-eight, having no idea what I was going to do with a degree in piano performance and a background in business and marketing. What a combination! Who would have ever thought! Anyway, right before I graduated, I met this guy on a plane. He knew my sisters, and I thought he was different. I sat across the aisle from him, and we talked all the way home. My mom was traveling with me, and I said to her, "I'm going to marry that guy!" His name was Tim Line, and of course, he never called or asked me out. But I looked him up in the phone book so I knew where he lived.

About three months later I saw him workin' out at the club. I was like, "Oh, what am I going to do! Here's the man I'm going to marry!" (Laughs.) So I walked up to him, and he said, "Hi Mary, how are you?" I said, "Nope, my name's not Mary, it's Lorie." I was crushed! (Laughs.) I'm going to marry this guy, and he didn't even know my name. So anyway, I said, "I know your name, and you live about a mile away from me." And he said, "How do you know?" I said, "I looked you up in the phone book after we met." And he said, "Oh, you must want to go out with me." I started laughin' and said, "Yeah, I do." And I thought, "This is going to happen!" And sure enough, it did. Four months later we got engaged. Four months after that we got married.

We moved to Minnesota the day after we got married. Tim worked for Jostens, the class ring company, and they transferred him to Minneapolis. Oh man! Where is Minnesota? I had to go look on the map to see where Minneapolis was! Living in Reno I knew what cold was, but this was completely different—it was a real adjustment. I started working in the construction field again 'cause what I had been doing was very unique. I worked for this huge company here in Minneapolis and hated it! They were all old-time thinkers who had never had a woman as the director of marketing. Here I was twenty-eight years old, and they're all looking at me shaking their heads. I was miserable the whole time!

About a year and a half later we were walking by the piano at Dayton's, a really beautiful department store here, and Tim said, "Now that's what you should be doing. You could do the two things you love most under one roof: play the piano and shop!" (Laughs.) Then more seriously he said, "Really, you should audition." So I went and auditioned and got the job! I ended up playin' every night seven to nine, then big hours on Saturday and Sunday. I didn't give up my day job because I wanted to make sure this was right for me. They paid me twenty dollars an hour, so it wasn't great—forty dollars a night. I mean, I could spend that in half an hour! It was really just therapy for me because I hated my day job so much. But at night I loved life! I will never forget my first day, which was a Saturday shift. I played for five hours from the top of my head, no music. My adrenaline was up so much I had a migraine by the time I walked out. But I remember thinking, "This is what I was meant to do!" So I was very happy there, and people responded to me. They walked up and said, "Who are you. Do you have an album?" I was laughing and going, "I just do this part-time; I actually have a real job." (Laughs.) But so many people came up and asked if I had an album that I started takin' their names and numbers. I said, "If I ever do one, I'll let you know." And I got a ton of names, something like five hundred.

One day my husband and I were talking, and he said, "You really should do an album. Let's find out how you do it, see if we can afford it, then see what happens." Well, how do you make an album? I had no idea! So I looked on the back of a George Winston album, which is solo piano, to see who the engineer was—his name was Russell Bond, and he lived in San Francisco. I called him up and said, "Do you still engineer albums?" And he said, "Yeah." So I said, "Good. How long would it take me to record ten pieces." He said, "Well, about two or three days." I said, "Great. When can I come in?" So I booked a flight to San Francisco and made all the arrangements. Before I left I called him and said, "How will I know who you are?" And he said, "I'll be the barefoot guy at the airport." And I thought, "Oh, man." You know, I come from a very nice background.

So anyway, he shows up at the airport, and he's wearin' earth shoes. So I thought, "Okay, this is a little better then I expected." And we go out to the parking lot, and he's got a black Ferrari. We get in and drive off to the studio. I'm thinking, "Now this is livin'! I can handle a black Ferrari." So we spent three days recording, and it was awesome! We did ten songs, seven cover tunes and three originals. It was all very easy listening: "Terms of Endearment," "St. Elmo's Fire," "Send in the Clowns." I just did the most requested songs from Dayton's. I figured people would turn the album over, see what was on it, and buy it. Of course, all the arrangements were mine. Anyway, what I remember most about that experience was going back to the hotel at night and laying in bed thinking I was doing something that would make a contribution.

The way we financed this album was that Tim, bless his heart, cashed in his 401K—he had $2,500 in it. Russell Bond was ninety dollars an hour, which included the studio time, so the whole thing was like 1,300 bucks. When I got on the plane, I had the masters in hand. I was tearful 'cause I had done something in three days that would definitely change my life. When I got home, we had a local duplicating place make a thousand tapes and five hundred CDs. When they printed the first CD, they called me up and said, "Ma'am, what's the name of the production company? You've got to have a company name on the CD." Of course, I'm goin', "Well . . ." So I called up Tim to do a little brainstorming, and he said, "Why don't we do something with that typo we're always getting in the mail?" We get a lot of letters that say "Time Line" instead of "Tim Line." So we named the company "Time Line Productions."

The next thing I did was go see the manager at Dayton's. I took a few tapes and CDs and a business plan that was bound in leather. (Laughs.) It was really just a marketing strategy for selling the tapes: where they would go in the store, how to display them, my sales projections. See, I couldn't just haul merchandise into Dayton's; I had to become a vendor. They had to buy the tapes, put their little sticker on 'em, and sell 'em. So I sat down with the manager and said, "Here's what I want to do, and here's my business plan. I think customers will buy a lot of these." I had a whole big thing put together. She looks at me and says, "You're right, I think this would go really far. I'm going to send you down to the vice president's office at the Dayton/Hudson Corporation." Gulp! I was like . . . okay.

So she sent me to Dennis Toffolo's office, a big player in my life because he looked at me and said, "This is a hit, it will go!" He bought a hundred tapes and a hundred CDs against the wishes of many people at Dayton/Hudson Corporation. But Dennis kinda winked at me and said, "Just be a little careful; don't make a big deal about this. Let's just see how it goes." And oh, man, the first day the tapes and CDs hit the store I was so nervous. I'd made a significant investment gettin' this whole thing going—2,500 bucks—and had a few more bills due in thirty to sixty days for the artwork. I stacked the tapes and CDs on the edge of the piano, sat down, and started to play. After my first piece I sold one! I thought, "Yes! This is going to work!" Well, before that first day was over, I'd sold forty!

About this time, I quit my job in corporate America. I said, "I don't care if I'm poor, I'm going to do this!" What I did was quickly up my hours at Dayton's. I continued to play evenings and weekends but took on Monday and Wednesday afternoons. So I went from twenty-one to twenty-eight hours a week. The discouraging part was that I only sold albums when I was playin' the piano. It was tough because I was becoming more popular in the community and also playing at a lot of events and private parties. I didn't feel like I could shlep my stuff in and be a merchant at those things. I was too classy for that. So I was trying to be in all places at once and still keep my hours up at Dayton's.

So Tim and I started thinking, "How can we do this?" The record companies! I called some of them up, and they laughed at me. "What's your name? Lorie who? No, we only take major artists. You've got to have a track record first." "Okay, well how do you do that?" So we started calling little Ma and Pa gift stores—it's a huge business out there. They play your tape, put a sign up that says "Now Playing . . . ," people hear it and buy the album. So we lived on the phones trying to get some distribution.

The first company to try me out was called "Lifedance," out of Portland. They did a consignment for the first order. A while later I got a check for $325. It was the best $325 I'd seen, because I knew if I could sell through one channel, there were ten more of these guys out there. And if I could do it ten times, it would be $3,250. So, I started saying, "Hey, Lifedance is carrying me, and they're doing pretty well. Would you like to try it?" Now that I had a track record, other companies started picking me up. Pretty soon I had ten distributors around the country. And yep, I started making 3,000 bucks a month. At this point, I was working my product all day and still playin' the piano at night.

Along the way I made a few more albums. It was my third album that really kicked in. It was a holiday album called "Sharing the Season." It really did great! So I started thinking, "I really need to get some help." I wanted somebody who understood the business right off the bat, so I hired the person at Dayton's who was buyin' all my stuff and putting it in the stores. What we did next was take my music to the streets. We had a database of customers, so we started scheduling concerts in towns where people were buying my stuff. Consumers started walking into the major retailers saying, "Where's Lorie Line?" One day the CEO of Musicland walked into the Mall of America and asked the manager, "What's the hottest thing selling today?" And the manager said, "We aren't selling the hottest thing because we don't carry it. Everybody that walks through the door wants Lorie Line." So the CEO said, "Why don't we carry her?" And the manager said, "None of the buyers are buying it." He said, "I'll change that!" So I get a call from this guy, and he says, "My name is Jack Eugster; I'm the CEO of Musicland. I understand you've got a hot-selling item." I said, "I sure do!" He said, "I'd like to set up an account and put you in Musicland." I'm now in eight hundred Musiclands, all the Best Buys, and some Target Stores—all because we reached the consumer!

Along the way, my husband quit his job; that's the fun part. One day I said, "Golly Tim, we're doing over a million dollars in business. Why are you going to work?" He saw how much fun I was having and didn't like his job in corporate America anymore. When we went to parties, every-

> If somebody tells you no, you're talking to the wrong person.

body wanted to talk about Lorie Line, not class rings. (Laughs.) So he quit his job a few years ago and became our general manager. He does all the tour management, which is a huge, huge job. He rents the halls, buys the media, runs the advertising, contracts with the musicians, and does all the legal work. So he's basically the nineties version of "Reuben Kincaid" of the Partridge Family. He also manages our direct-mail marketing. We now have over 40,000 people on our list, so we have a substantial group of fans.

Our approach to business is very, very unique in this industry. I don't know of any other company that does what we do. Our philosophy is to do everything in-house. I'm the artist, I'm the arranger, I'm the producer. I have no manager, I have no agent. Because our costs are down and our profits up, I'm able to hire twelve world-class musicians to travel with me. We do seventy "knock-em-dead" concerts a year. We also sell direct to the retailers, so they make more money and we do too. It's Tim's job to make sure the product is in the chute when we do concerts in all cities. We're selling fourteen albums now. We also have a live CD, a live cassette, and a video from our public television special. It aired in August of 1996 on 251 stations. Thirty million people saw it, so it really boosted our sales. We'll do about $4.5 million in sales this year.

> I think the biggest problem people have in business is they either take itsy-bitsy steps and don't see the big picture, or they see the big picture but don't know how to take the itsy-bitsy steps to get there. It's a combination of the two.

I'm definitely living the American dream, and I think others can too. I do a lot of presentations these days, and I tell people, "Decide what you want to do, calculate the risks, figure out what you could lose, then take a chance!" It's actually a fairly safe thing to do when you consider the alternatives. Then if somebody tells you no, you're talking to the wrong person.

Many, many times I was told no, but I kept thinking, "I'm talkin' to the wrong guy here, because this is a great idea."

I think the biggest problem people have in business is they either take itsy-bitsy steps and don't see the big picture, or they see the big picture but don't know how to take the itsy-bitsy steps to get there. It's a combination of the two. I'm definitely a musician first, but I'll tell ya what, I'm at the office every single day by nine o'clock taking the itsy-bitsy steps. Because, looking at the big picture, I've got shows comin' up, and I'd better have product to sell, and it'd better sound good, and it'd better look good, and it'd better be who I am. So I have to be at this office every day taking those itsy-bitsy steps to make sure the big picture happens and my dream is fulfilled.

TIPS FOR WORKING WITH TENACITY

1. **LAY OUT A LONG WORK SCHEDULE.**

   New venturing requires a major time commitment, especially in the early days. Plan to work long hours each week and schedule the time. It's much easier to plan long weeks, and then quit early when possible, than it is to schedule short weeks and end up wrestling alligators long after hours. If you aren't realistic about the time commitment, you'll end up disliking your work.

2. **KEEP YOUR COOL WHEN YOU GET A NO.**

   When someone tells you no, you're talking with the wrong person. Brainstorm all your alternatives, then go back and try a new angle. Remember, it's your responsibility to convince them, not the other way around.

3. **WORK ON THE FIELD, NOT ON THE SIDELINES.**

   Stay involved in the real work of the business. Most important, talk with customers daily. Make sure you know more than anyone else in your organization about what people need and want. Make changes accordingly.

4. **KEEP ON SCRAMBLING.**

   If you know the industry, have a legitimate opportunity, and love what you're doing, just keep on scrambling. Eventually you'll figure out how to make things happen. So don't give up!

Chapter · 6

GIVING MIND-
BOGGLING SERVICE

Carol Stenquist and her husband bought a medical supply company in 1983. In addition to wheelchairs, beds, and braces, these companies often sell products to women who have had mastectomies. Carol quickly realized that women hate to buy these products from this type of store—they are usually staffed by men, the ambience is cold and impersonal, and the inventory is limited. Within a few years, Carol created a separate company to address this disheartening need. She offered a warm and caring environment, personal counseling, private fitting rooms, and a broader line of products—prostheses, bras, swimwear, turbans, hairpieces. She met women during their lunch hours and on Saturdays, offered some services for free, and never turned anyone away—even those who couldn't pay at the time. Today, "Carol's Personal Boutique"—one of the few businesses in America to provide this unique service—is meeting the needs of thousands of grateful women.

For the past decade, management gurus have touted the power of superb customer service as a business strategy. While service may be improving in America, in my opinion few companies successfully define service in a way that sends customers out the door raving about their experience. Like Carol Stenquist, most of the entrepreneurs I interviewed *have* found a way to treat customers much better than other companies in their industry. Extraordinary service is not only critical to getting a venture off the ground, but it's also absolutely imperative for growing and stabilizing a fragile new business. In other words, aspiring entrepreneurs must first find a way to give customers much more than they expect, then create systems for perpetuating this mind-boggling service on an ongoing basis.

IT'S ALL ABOUT
OVERSHOOTING EXPECTATIONS

Expectations can be a burr under the saddle of human happiness. When we expect too much from life, we're often disappointed, angry, and frustrated. At the other extreme, when we expect nothing, we are occasionally surprised by joy. I experienced the power of this phenomenon while attending the world handicapped games in Seoul, Korea. The participants had lost eyes, arms, legs, and hearing—their bodies were racked with disorder. Yet they were the happiest group of people I have ever met. As I interviewed some of the athletes, I discovered their secret: After their injury or diagnosis, they dropped all aspirations for a "normal" life. As a result, their subsequent successes, which far exceeded their loftiest expectations, produced an ongoing state of happiness.

Expectations also form an important baseline in the world of customer service. There is no question that customers enter a business with a preconceived notion of how they should be treated. If their expectations are *not* met, they are dissatisfied—they complain, tell their friends, and don't go back. If their standards *are* met, things are okay—they're not jumping for joy, but they are basically satisfied. Interestingly enough, satisfied customers are not always loyal customers; they often patronize competitors' businesses as well. Thus, being satisfied may be the same as being neutral. So what does it take to produce raving customers and long-term loyalty? *Mind-boggling service!* That's when you overshoot customers' expectations, giving them much more than their cognitive sets were programmed to receive—and the higher the better. When customers receive service beyond their furthest imagination, they rave about it, tell all their friends, come back again and again, become a strong advocate for the company, and even feel guilty if they ever go to a competitor's business. Women who go to Carol's Personal Boutique, for example, never go back to medical supply companies or the typical retail stores that sell post-mastectomy products.

The trick is to figure out how to overshoot the expectations of the fussiest customers; if you win that group over, you automatically get everyone else. The entrepreneurs in this book understand this concept well. Over and over again, I saw incredible prices, money-back guarantees, extra services for free, broader selection, faster delivery times, and superb customer support. For instance, Sally Gutierrez, the founder of Spic and Span Cleaning, always tries to clean one item for the customer over and above what was contracted for on each visit. Mary Naylor, founder of Capitol Concierge, offers an entire array of services and products that are unavailable to customers in a single retail location: flowers, gifts, restaurant reservations, catering, theater tickets, dry cleaning, sedan service, rare books, prescriptions, and even pet food for tarantulas. And David Spafford, cofounder of Megahertz, a company that manufactures modems for laptop computers, built his entire company around maximizing customer satisfaction. He wanted people to say, "I'll buy Megahertz over Brand X every time!" According to David, "You need to offer a total package which represents at least the top three decision preferences of your customer. For our product that's ease of use, technical support, and price. Then you need to throw in the kitchen sink as well." Megahertz offered a three-year warranty when the industry standard was one year. When the industry moved to three-year warranties, Megahertz went to five years.

Scheming up ways to blow customers' minds is not always easy, but I believe it can be done in any business. When we started our company, we racked our brains to think of ways to provide service people would talk about for a long time. This was a tall task since all we do is serve frozen dessert products to customers over a counter. What could we do to *really* turn people on? While contemplating the challenge, we wondered what would happen if we opened a store for free one day. We knew *that* would create excitement but weren't sure we could afford it. After analyzing our costs, we realized it was much less expensive than other types of advertising—you can't even buy one TV ad for what we expected to spend. So we circulated flyers, hung up banners, told all our customers, and opened a store for free on a Friday. To our delight, several thousand people showed up to try our products—the store was absolutely mobbed! The end result: sales went up nearly 50 percent from previous months!

We continued this mind-boggling event with great success every time we opened new stores. We also used it at other times to thank customers, build goodwill, and boost sales. A few years ago we had trademark troubles in a region and had to change the name on our stores; we were all concerned about the ramifications. How could we ensure that customers would not be disappointed with the change? How could we let them know we were still the same company? How could we affect the change without losing sales? The free day was the answer! Only this time it would happen in sixteen stores on the same day in a city of one million people. It turned out to be one of the most successful campaigns in the history of our company. A week before the event, a local newspaper—intrigued by the idea of a free day—did a front-page story on our company and the name change. The night of the event, a local TV station, sensing a frenzy, showed up to broadcast live from one of the locations during the chaos. As it turned out, we served nearly 40,000 people free products, explained our name change in a positive way, shocked people with our generosity, and built goodwill within the community. A week later, a letter in the newspaper echoed the sentiments of our customers:

> *I took my family expecting a small portion in a cone similar to those in the grocery store taste sample. I was surprised and delighted to find that they were giving their regular product in their regular containers. The personnel assigned to work that evening were willing to make special orders and still kept the line*

moving quickly, truly a well-orchestrated procedure. Thank you, Golden Swirl, for your generous gesture.

The best news of all, sales went up following the event! Exceeding expectations seemed to further endear customers to our business. Afterward, I told our team we were going to change our name every two years as a sales-building strategy; it was just a joke. But experiences like this are essential in the early days of a business; it's the only way to win a handful of customers over from competing entities and get the new venture rolling. Having a great product but lousy service usually leads to early failure. The stories I collected are full of examples of extraordinary service, and it's not just being nicer to customers than the next guy: its going way beyond what customers expect to receive. Aspiring entrepreneurs need to ask the question over and over again: "What can I do to give customers more than they are getting elsewhere?" And it's best to get the answer directly from the customer. If *you* think you're giving legendary service but your customers *don't*, it won't help the new venture succeed.

THE SERVICE IS IN THE SYSTEM

During the service craze of the past decade, I attended, taught, and learned about numerous workshops on customer service. I watched with interest as many employees went back to their companies psyched to serve, only to fizzle out within a few weeks. Several factors may explain this phenomenon. First, as a company grows, it's difficult for the founding entrepreneur to be everywhere at once, and since employees don't always have the owner's enthusiasm for service, the personal touch is soon lost. Second, the systems, policies, and procedures in organizations emphasize certain priorities and often don't support—and sometimes even negate—superb customer service. In other words, the mechanisms that govern who gets hired, how they are trained, what priorities are emphasized, how people are evaluated, what gets rewarded, how customers are treated, and so on, may not promote extraordinary service as the top priority. This is particularly true in large corporations where various policies and systems are created by people other than those who directly lead the service team. In this type of "disjointed" environment, the systems prevail in the end and function to maintain status-quo behavior.

In the early days of our business, Mary and I were everywhere all the time; we knew all our managers, most of our employees, and many of our customers. As we grew from five to thirteen to twenty stores, it was clear that our emphasis on superb service was slipping. The solution was in the system! First, we asked customers what we needed to do to have them rave about the service they received in our stores. From their responses we created a "Profile of Mind-Boggling Service." It outlined simple things to do with every customer: greet them the minute they enter the store, smile, help them through the ordering process, always offer free samples, thank them for coming, and so on. Next, we used this profile to drive every human resource system in the company: we *hired* according to the profile, we *trained* according to the profile, we *evaluated* according to the profile, and we *rewarded* according to the profile. To elaborate, we designed an entire staffing program that emphasized hiring employees who had effectively performed our service profile in previous jobs. Our training program then emphasized the profile as the number-one priority in the company. We next developed an evaluation program that gave team members feedback from customers and managers on how well they enacted the profile. Finally, and most important, we based our reward system—pay raises, bonuses, promotions, recognition—on how well the service profile was performed. This approach is illustrated in the model on the next page.

So how well did the system work? It was an ongoing challenge because it was implemented through hundreds of teenagers. Nonetheless, I believe our service was much better over the years than many of our competitors in the fast-food industry. We saw some remarkable feats from teenagers! One of the rewards we provided was a $150 cash bonus to employees caught in acts of superb service. We then highlighted their stories in a newsletter to show team members what "mind-boggling service" meant to us. Over the years we had

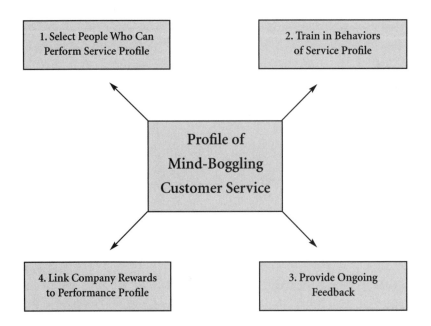

employees visit customers in hospitals, drive products fifty miles to school reunions, help the elderly and handicapped to their cars, stay open late to meet customers, come in on their days off to make products, and on and on. Here is an award-winning story from a sixteen-year-old:

> *It was Saturday night and the store was pretty busy. About fif-teen minutes before we closed, a lady came in and explained that she had ordered two pies earlier that day and was there to pick them up. I looked in the freezer and they weren't there. I decided to check the cooler just in case, and sure enough, they were melted all over. We didn't have any more pie crusts, so I couldn't make her new pies. I told her if she would leave her name and address, I would somehow get them to her the next day before her 3:00 P.M. party. I took quarts of the flavors she wanted home with me, bought two graham-cracker pie crusts at the grocery store, then made her pies and froze them in my freezer overnight. The next day I took them to her house.*

Of course, it was another teenage employee that put the frozen pies in the cooler and caused the problem in the first place, but I'm sure you get the point: The service is in the system! And our system was the most powerful I have seen for producing exceptional acts of service from a minimum-wage workforce. Everyone in our company knew that service was our top priority, and it was reinforced by all the human-resource systems—hiring, training, evaluating, and rewarding. It didn't always work the way I wanted it to, but I would have hated to see our customer service without this program.

The pattern that evolved in our company is seen over and over in the stories from our entrepreneurs. First, the business founder provides extraordinary service to win a handful of customers during the launch phase. Next, because these early customers are the lifeblood of survival, systems are created to perpetuate phenomenal service with every customer as the business grows. In the most successful companies, all of the systems, policies, and procedures operate in perfect harmony to sustain a level of service that is unheard of in the industry.

In the stories that follow, notice how all three entrepreneurs go beyond industry standards in providing customer service. David Tibbitts offers free vacation-planning help to everyone that calls his 800 line, even though the person may not book a river trip with his company; he genuinely wants each customer to have a superb time in Jackson Hole, not just on the river. You'll also marvel at Jason Olim's incredible service system. By negotiating agreements with music warehouses, then offering their products on the Internet, his company provides more CDs, more information, and greater convenience to customers than anyone else in the retail music business. Most important, customers get the same extraordinary service every time they shop at CDNow, because they interact with the system itself. And Dave Burbidge has his drivers get out of their garbage trucks and clean the entire area around the customer's dumpster at each stop; other companies simply dump the container and drive on. In addition, his Christmas clean-up program "knocks customers' socks off" and guarantees they stay with him long-term.

OUR ROLE MODELS

David Tibbitts

David Tibbitts is the founder of Jackson Hole Whitewater, a company located in Jackson Hole, Wyoming. Each summer, his company allows thousands of vacationers to enjoy the spectacular scenery and raging white water of the powerful Snake River. Dave has kept his company small by choice in order to offer a personal touch on every trip. His goal: to have every customer say, "Our white-water trip was the highlight of our vacation!" Even though Jackson Hole Whitewater is a relative new-comer to the river-running scene, it has been voted the number-one com-pany on the Snake River by the locals. Here's how Dave describes his experience:

I was born in 1945 and adopted by my step-father when I was twelve. He bought some property in Beverly Hills and opened up a dog kennel that had capacity to board 150 animals. He felt there was a good market there with all the movie stars that had dogs. So I ended up talking with people like Henry Fonda, Lucille Ball, Dustin Hoffman, and Jane Fonda on a weekly basis. I got to know them well because we were taking care of their babies—their dogs were just like their children—I mean, Henry Fonda had five Lhasa Apsos he would drop off every Monday. But they were really nice people, and it was fun to see them drive up in their Rolls Royces and Ferraris. As time went on, I decided I wanted to have money, and I knew I would have to work hard because no one was going to give it to me. My father also worked very hard, and a lot of that rubbed off on me.

When I was twenty-one I bought my first house for $19,900—it was a four bedroom with a swimming pool. I had a '63 Corvette at that time, which I sold for the down payment—2,500 bucks. All my friends laughed and said, "Why would you sell this beautiful car?" Well, it was a very dif-ficult decision because I was twenty-one years old and the car was impec-cable. But I thought, "If I still had the car, then I wouldn't have the house," which really started me on the road to purchasing other properties. I later sold that house for $36,000 and bought another house in Canoga Park. Then I wound up buying a much bigger home on a half-acre with a pool.

My father eventually sold his kennel in Beverly Hills and rented the property next door from a man named Bertel—he was a blacksmith. He approached my dad one day and said, "Ray, do you want to buy this property for your dog-grooming business?" And my dad said, "No, I'm sixty-five years old!" Then he said to me, "David, why don't you buy it?" I said, "Dad, I don't have $110,000 to buy this piece of property." But I wound up buying it anyway. At the time I had a 1969 Porsche—a little Targa—that I sold for $8,000. Then I borrowed $6,000 from my dad and $6,000 from my father-in-law, which gave me twenty grand for the down payment. I rented the little house in front to my dad for $300 a month—he converted it into a little dog shop. In the rear were apartments; the building was so old it actually had glass doorknobs and toilets with high tanks and chains that you pull. It's probably a hundred years old today.

In 1978 I came up here to Jackson Hole on a vacation with my wife. I said to her, "You know, this is the most beautiful land I've ever seen in my life, and I want a piece of it!" So I wound up purchasing two three-and-a-half acre parcels on Teton Village Road; it's absolutely gorgeous property! While we were driving back to California I said to my wife, "Honey, when we get to be eighty years old and retire, I want to build a home on that property." And she looked over and she says, "Why do you want to wait until you're eighty years old to move to Jackson?" And I said, "You know, I don't; let's go back to Beverly Hills and put the apartment building up for sale." Well, it took about six months, but we finally sold it for half a million dollars. I got $120,000 down and annual balloon payments which I used to pay for the properties up here.

So I put together my initial capital through real-estate transactions. But I'll tell you, it wasn't easy money. During the seven years I had the building I lived on the edge. It was so old it literally had old steel pipes running through the apartments that were constantly springing leaks. I'd get calls at two in the morning and have to drive twenty-six miles at like high speeds (laughs) to stop these leaks. I had to use hose clamps and inner tubes to patch the pinholes because I couldn't afford to replace the plumbing. One time I had a fire on my roof, and the fire marshal said, "You know something, buddy? Your whole building needs to be rewired." And I begged him with tears in my eyes, "Sir, please, I have no money; I can barely make these payments, and my wife is pregnant. If you make me rewire, I will lose my building." He finally said, "OK, I will come over on Saturday on my own time and show you what I want you to fix up that is dangerous." So I repaired this and I repaired that, but it was not easy money. Absolutely not!

Anyway, we moved to Jackson, and I heard that this business called Teton Expeditions might be coming up for sale, so I contacted the man. He was located in Alpine, which is about twenty-five miles south of Jackson. It was a very casual whitewater rafting company which took about 1,500 people a year down the Snake River—they were mostly people from this guy's church. He was tired of the commute and tired of not making much money. So I said to him, "I'd be interested in purchasing the two permits from you. How much do you want?" He told me $65,000. See, there are no more permits available for the Snake River, and there never will be, ever! So permits are worth quite a bit. Now it didn't take a rocket scientist to take $30 and multiply it times 1,500 people. And I knew some of the companies up here were putting down 10,000 people every summer; some were putting down 20,000, and some were doing 30,000. And I'm thinking, 30,000 people times $30 is nearly a million dollars in four months. So I bought the two permits for $65,000.

I wanted to locate the business in Jackson, so I found a gentleman in his eighties who owned this land where my building's at now. I asked him if he wanted to lease me some of his property, and he said, "You know, David, I've never leased land to anybody, ever, but you just hit me at the right time." So we went out together, and I showed him what I wanted. And he said, "Go get that rock and put it down there, put another rock over there, another rock there, and the last rock there," and we laid out all four corners of the building. Then I said to him, "Now what do you want for this piece of property?" He said, "Give me $500 a month." Then he stuck out his hand and said, "All you need from me is a handshake." And I said, "Roxsdale, I believe you."

About the same time, I was talking to a friend of mine in town and told him I was planning to move the white-water business I had just bought up to Jackson. He said, "I'm tearing down these old buildings here at this Executive Inn, and if you want one I'll just give it to you." I said "Perfect!" So now I had a piece of land that I'm paying $500 a month for and a building that was given to me for free. Actually, by the time I moved it, got permits, did all the repairs, added water, electrical, sewer, and built a deck, it cost me $40,000. I mean (groans), it really wasn't free.

Anyway, I put my sign out in front, "Jackson Hole Whitewater," and thought, "Boy, with this location and a new name, I'm going to have thousands of people flocking in my front door." But nobody came! I didn't realize that the white-water rafting business was highly competitive in this town, and that the hotel owners were sending their customers to companies that had been around for a long time. It made sense because they were sending people on a serious whitewater rafting trip, not a bus ride, so they recommended companies they could trust. They didn't realize I had hired some of the top people in this town to work for me. Consequently, I lost $60,000 my first year in business and had to refinance my home in town.

The next year I worked really hard to get my name out; I went around to as many hotels as I possibly could and did my thing. I only lost $35,000 that year. By the third year, however, I made $20,000, and we've continued to grow and make increasing amounts of money every year since then. What happened was that people went back to the hotel owners and told them they had a fantastic time with Jackson Hole Whitewater, so our reputation started growing. Last summer we put around 15,000 people down the river at $30 a trip—that's a lot of people! We were also voted the number-one white-water rafting company in Jackson in a survey called *The Best of the West,* done by our local newspaper, *The Jackson Hole Guide.* That really means a lot to me because the survey came from the local people, which includes all the hotel and motel owners. And you have to realize, we're competing with companies that have been around a lot longer than we have.

I think a lot of things have led to our success. One is I decided to specialize in white water only. We don't do scenic trips, we don't do overnighters, and our boats are geared and rigged for white water. All the other companies in town do both scenic and white water. We can tell our customers when they call, "And by the way, we are the only company in Jackson Hole, Wyoming, that does strictly white-water rafting; that's it!" That impresses them a lot! But also, we're not a threat to the companies up in Grand Teton National Park that only do scenic trips. Say Triangle X, for instance, has ten customers that want to do white water. I'm not going to steal their people in the future on scenic trips because I only do what my name says, white-water rafting. This is not true for all the other companies in town which do both. So that was a decision I made, and it's worked out really well.

Another part of my philosophy has been to remain small and efficient. I haven't purchased any additional permits. A permit gives you the right to put so many boats on the river. My permit is a two-boat permit, where Mad River, for example, has an eight-boat permit. I can legally float thirty people five times a day down the river. They can legally float 120 people five times a day. So we're continuously booked on every single trip, but they are seldom fully booked. I mean, I've given a thousand people away this year to other companies but have not received one call from any company to help because they always have room. But they have to carry the overhead to send eight boats down the river on any given trip: the staff, the buses, the drivers, the guides. Now how are you going to keep a guide happy giving him one trip a day? Our guides are out on the river all day long. I think we are the most efficiently run company on the river.

Another thing I do is treat my employees extremely well. I pay them top dollar! My bus drivers make more than other drivers on the river, my office help makes more than anyone else, and my guides make between $200 and $250 a day—that's pretty good money! I also give my people a $5 beer allowance every day after work so they can stop and buy a six-pack of Coke or whatever and enjoy a nice cold one on the way home. Then we go to dinner at a restaurant on a monthly basis, and we're always getting pizzas and beers. So we have a great time, which is important to building harmony in your company—and we certainly have that!

Treating employees well really pays off. The head person that works for me makes $14 an hour, and she's twenty-five years old. I let her live in one of my apartments absolutely free all summer. This winter she's living in my four-bedroom log home that's totally furnished with antiques and a

TV—and she's living there for free too! A couple days ago I called her up and said, "I'll be there in about fifteen minutes. Is everything fine?" She goes, "Everything's fine, but why are you coming to work today?" And I said, "What do you mean?" She said, "We don't need you here. The guides are on the river, all the bus drivers are here, everything is running perfect, and we've got all the steaks pulled for dinner." This is in the middle of July on a day when we are totally booked, and she's asking me, "What are you going to do here?"

So being efficient and treating employees great are critical, but ohhhhhhh—the most important thing by far is how we treat our customers. We just do a lot of things that other companies don't do. For instance, I have an 800 number that runs me about $1,200 a month. If you were to call me up, and you're from Nantucket or wherever, I would tell you all about my company, and then I would say, "And where are you staying?" And you would probably say, "Well, we don't know yet, we're looking for a place." Then I would say to you, "Could I make some recommendations and give you some 800 numbers?" And you would say, "Oh, that would be wonderful!" Then I'd give you numbers of hotels, I'd tell you about the rooms, and I'd give you the prices. Next I'd encourage you to ride the tram, go to the Bar J Chuck Wagon, and go out on the river with a fishing company. I have all of this information in front of me so I can help people have a great time in Jackson Hole, not just while they're floating the river.

> I had a doctor from Florida who was fifty-five years old come up to me and say, "You must be the owner." And I said, "Yeah, (laughs) how'd you know?" He said, "I could tell by your enthusiasm."

So we give people way more than they ever expect; I believe that's so very important. Other companies don't seem to want to do this. There are people up here who say, "You know why I don't have an 800 number? People call me up and ask me what the weather is doing and what they should wear and what they should bring." I say to them, "Oh yeah, me too." And that's all I say. Then they say, "Man, my phone bill was running me $1,000 a month, and I can't have that, so I don't have an 800 number anymore." And I'm going, "Fine." But I tell my people, "You answer all those questions." Because if I'm grossing a half a million dollars in four months, I could care less that my phone bill runs $6,000 for the year. You know what I mean?

It's really just common sense, and it has a big payoff. I mean, I'm booked! And you know something? I thank God for that. How fortunate can you be? I actually have people come in here on a daily basis and say to my people, "Where's David?" "Well, he's on the river." "Oh, am I going to be able to meet him?" Then when I come in they say, "Hi Dave, I'm Frank Smith, remember me? I talked with you for about thirty minutes in February, and you told me about this and you told me about that, and I hiked to Hidden Falls because of you." Then they tell me, "You know, you've made our vacation so great. You really should be a travel agent." And my answer is, "Listen. I've been on vacation before, and I know how much I would like to have someone help me plan a great time in Santa Barbara or Cancun or wherever."

Another important part of my philosophy is that the client is always right, even if they are so blatantly wrong that they showed up on the wrong day or whatever—it doesn't matter! And we never, ever, ever argue with a client. We spend as much time as it requires to take care of them and make sure they have a good time. When I first started my business, I'd get calls at 11:30 at night, and it would be five drunk guys. They'd wake me up and go, "Hey man, we wanna go rafting tomorrow. You got anything open?" And I'd say, "We sure do, sir. Hang on one second and let me get the books." Then I'd jump outta bed at 11:30 at night and book them a trip. They'd show up in the morning with hangovers, and I'd say, "Hey, you're the guys who got me outta bed last night." They'd laugh; I would make $150. So you know, service is so very important.

We're also big on spending time with our people once they arrive. I think it's so important! Last year we were sitting out front and I was barbecuing steaks for our 4:30 group. I had a doctor from Florida who was fifty-five years old come up to me and say, "You must be the owner." And

I said, "Yeah, (laughs) how'd you know?" He said, "I could tell by your enthusiasm." I said, "I'm just cooking!" And he goes, "No, you're telling jokes, you're flipping garlic bread to people, and you're just having such a good time." And I said, "Well, thanks." Then he asked, "What do you do in the winter?" I said, "Well, I have a beach house in California, and I'm going to be wintering out there next year." And he said, "You know something? I make about $600,000 a year, and I would trade you my practice, my income, my home, everything, for your lifestyle. Do you know how fortunate you are to have a business you run in Jackson Hole in the summertime where you float the river, wear Tevas and shorts, get real tan, then ski a couple of months and head on down to your home in California?" I said, "You know, I realize that, so I won't be trading you." I really do feel that I'm the most fortunate person in the world!

Jason Olim

Jason is the cofounder and president of CDNow, a Pennsylvania company that sells more than 250,000 entertainment products on the Internet. The company has every CD, every cassette, every video, and every laser disc that's available. No other music store in America carries as many products as CDNow. Incredible demand for the company's services has resulted in more than $17 million in sales after just four years in business. You can reach the company at CDNow.Com. Here's what Jason has to say:

I graduated from Brown University in 1992 with a degree in computer programming. I went to work for an electronic mail company and learned to build large-scale systems. I've always been a music lover, so I went into a lot of music stores during this time, but they never really did it for me. There was always something else I wished I could have, whether it was the ability to listen to albums or the possibility of having a music expert nearby. So I went about inventing gadgets in my own mind that would make music stores better. In fact, there was a device called the "I Station" made by a group called "In Touch." You'd walk up to it with a CD and scan in the barcode, and it would start playing something about the CD. They eventually went out of business, but that was one of my ideas. (Laughs softly.) I'm glad they did it and not me.

Anyway, when I went into these music stores, I used to take one of the music guides off the shelf, like the Penguin, and walk around reading it while I looked at albums. The guides are compendiums of reviews, so you can flip through them to see if an album is good or bad before you buy it. If you find one that's good you say, "Okay, this is great!" So one day the thought crossed my mind, "What if I went right to a music warehouse, put their database of products online, and backed it up with one of the guides?" I figured if I put a whole guide online and maybe some music magazines, I'd have a pretty compelling music store. I spent about five minutes thinking about it and said, "This is what I'm going to do!" My first thought was to make a standard program you could ship to people's homes, but the Internet made the most sense because it was "way cool" at the time. You have to remember this was February of '94, so it was before the Web—the Web didn't come out until that summer.

> I think the biggest key to our success has been creating value for our customers. You have to figure out what people want, then focus your business on delivering that.

So I decided to do this but didn't leave my old job right away—I stayed there for a few months while I developed the concept. One of the first things I did was hook up with my twin brother, Matt, who learned how to program in two weeks from reading. (Chuckles.) He picked up the original book on today's biggest program, which is C, and in two weeks he was flying. He's really a brilliant programmer! In the beginning I did 90 percent of the programming myself; just before the program went online, I was only doing about 10 percent of it. I ended up doing more and more of the business stuff, and Matt started doing more and more of the logistics, operations, and technology development. We did as much as we could as cheaply as possible. We only had to borrow a small amount of money from my father, who was great! He said, "Quit your job, have some fun, and if it doesn't work you can get another job anywhere." So my rationale was, "What do I have to lose?" Now my mother was a different story. She said, "Don't tell me about it; it makes me sick!" Leaving my nice comfortable job to do something as goofy as this turned her stomach in knots.

Basically, what Matt and I did was take a warehouse worth of products, which is much more than a music store—I mean, a typical music store has between seven and twenty thousand products. We had 145,000 products that were all available for shipping that day. We didn't own the stuff, we just went to the warehouse, bought the products, and had 'em shipped directly to our customers. The other thing we did was negotiate rights to put the All Music Guide online to support the products. We looked at a number of different guides, but the All Music Guide is the most thorough and has the best database of support. The company is also an electronically savvy firm.

So we put the store up online in August of 1994. It was just a text interface, but let me tell you, it was exhilarating! It was just me and my brother working at home on an old, beat-up computer. We went out to the news groups on the Internet and said, "Hey, check out this music store online, it's really good!" And right off, we had eight people shopping in the store at the same time. What our customers do is go into the interface and type in the name of an album or an artist or a record label or even a song they're interested in. If they type in Frank Sinatra, we show them the biggest list of Frank Sinatra albums they've ever seen—we pop it up right on the screen. Then they can click on a button and read reviews of all the albums. At that very moment, they can buy any one or all of them and pay with their credit card. We send the order to the warehouse, and they ship the product directly to the customer. The customer pays us, we pay the warehouse, and we make money on the margin. So we don't own a penny of inventory; we've never owned a penny of inventory—imagine that!

Well, in our first month of business, which was August of 1994, we sold $367 worth of CDs. In our second month, it was dramatically higher. By October of '94 we developed a Web interface. By February of '95 the

Web interface had completely overtaken the tele-interface. In our first full year of 1995, we sold two million dollars' worth of CDs. Now we're selling about a million a month and growing at a good pace every month. We have more than thirty employees right now, with an office in Philly and an office in L.A. L.A. came on board in September of '95. Our employees do marketing, customer service, programming, art, administration. We have one guy who kind of oversees the data transmission back and forth from the warehouses, but nobody has to process any orders. We now have a number of warehouses and 250,000 different products online. If we keep up our current pace, we'll do more than $17 million this year. So it's really startin' to roll!

Essentially, we're a Mom and Pop for every customer in every market niche.

I think the biggest key to our success has been creating value for our customers. You have to figure out what people want, then focus your business on delivering that. Basically, we built a better mousetrap than other companies, which is the only way to grow at this rate. If I were less value focused, I would have spent more time advertising, creating promotions, and whatnot. But that's not what we did. We focused on adding new warehouses, adding extra data, and designing a Web site which is smoother and more functional. There are people out there who build Web sites that are really rich in color and graphics and give you this 3-D movie environment (laughs), but it doesn't add value for customers. It actually detracts from the experience because it's so slow to use. So for us it's always been, how can we make it better from the customer's perspective?

Specifically, there are three things we do to provide greater value to our customers. Number one is selection. Right now we deal with five warehouses. We have got every CD, every cassette, every video, every piece of non-rare vinyl, every T-shirt, every laser disc—everything! I mean, you do not find 250,000 entertainment products available anywhere, except here!" (Laughs.) If you go into the typical music store and look up your favorite artist, they might have one or two albums. We've got every one there is, which blows people away! Our selection is so extraordinary we have an entire segment of people coming for stuff they've heard of but never seen before. So selection is the most important thing we've done for our customers.

Number two is information. We've developed what we call "decision support mechanisms," and one of the best is the listing of reviews. You can click to read about any album listed on the screen. If the review says, "This album sucks" (chuckles), you're going to say, "Well, I'm not going to buy that one; I'll buy another one." We also have biographies you can read on the artists. If you're interested in a certain band, we can tell you when their albums were released and which ones were pivotal in their career. In addition, we have discussion groups for every artist, so you can communicate with people who also like that artist. I mean, one time I wanted to buy an album from an artist I really liked. I went in there and said, "Has anyone heard this album?" Somebody responded and said, "It's kinda folksy and very different from the other ones" and told me not to buy it. (Laughs.) So you can communicate with a community of like-minded people. Also, if you like a certain type of music, like Baroque music, we can tell you which albums you should own. So we really cater to people who go into music stores and end up leaving without buying anything because they can't decide. People who don't have a good Mom and Pop record store down the street that specializes in their kind of music really appreciate it. Essentially, we're a Mom and Pop for every customer in every market niche. (Laughs.)

The third factor that makes our service better is convenience, and that sort of comes in two flavors. One flavor is you're busy and just can't get to the record store. Well, we're open twenty-four hours a day. In fact, we do our biggest volume at lunchtime. As the sun rolls around the country—noon East Coast, noon Central, and noon West Coast—you see spikes because everyone's breaking for lunch and coming to shop. We're also pretty busy right at the end of the workday, then later at night. These are often yuppie baby boomers with computer sophistication, musical taste, and money—they're the best type. It's amazing! I thought we were going to sell mostly to college kids, but they make up a disproportionately small group of our customers. So here's the other part of convenience: There are a lot of people out there who want to buy the latest John Tesh at Red

Rocks album, but they're afraid the guy behind the counter with the Mohawk is going to laugh at 'em. (Laughs.) So people can buy anonymously and feel cool about their musical style. I mean, I think about my mother; if she has to go through the rock section to get to the classical section, she's never goin' in. A lot of people simply do not like the noisy, retail environment. We've created a positive environment for everybody.

So the advantages we offer our customers are incredible selection, much more information, and real convenience. Then on top of all that, we are generally cheaper than a typical record store. If you buy one CD it's about the same, but if you buy two or more it comes out cheaper. However, we've found that no matter how much we discount the top 100 titles they have at Circuit City or Best Buy or other electronic superstores, we can't really sell those as well. But the other 249,900 sell great! So overall we're a little cheaper.

Actually, I'm shocked by what has happened. It was just a silly idea. Very few people were supportive at first. I mean, nobody had any idea this was going to happen—certainly not me. Our initial plan assumed we would hit the big time if we could ever sell a million dollars in CDs. How was I to know the Web was going to explode like this and that we would get such good positioning? I guess I've got some kind of rabbit's foot in my pocket. But we made really good decisions early on, and we've made good decisions along the way. Our team has been a real factor, too. My brother is such a genius that we've been able to do things other people haven't done. Also, we went out and found the smartest people we knew. I think it takes really smart, dedicated, and ambitious people to do something like this. I mean, my one skill (laughs) is stealing everybody else's ideas and putting them all together. But you have to have smart people in order to get good ideas.

I'll tell you, the future of the Internet is going to be tremendous. Think about this: You want to apply for a mortgage so you go down to the bank and do something with a face. But it doesn't help that much to sit there in front of a functionary when the deal has to be approved somewhere else. Well, you could probably get your mortgage online. You could also buy your car online. You could get the information you need about all the models without calling all these people and having 'em send you glossies which cost eight bucks a pop. Once you narrow down your choice, you could go to the showroom, test-drive a couple cars, and buy one. So the Internet provides a tremendous opportunity for companies to give customers more information and better service in many environments, from learning to working to shopping. I think we're going to see a humongous explosion in the next few years. I wouldn't be surprised if 90 percent of what we buy is online within ten years.

Dave Burbidge

Dave is the founder and president of Burbidge Disposal Company. Before selling the business to USA Waste in 1997, Burbidge was one of the largest independently owned garbage collection and disposal businesses in the Intermountain West. The company has a fleet of trucks and thousands of accounts. Dave's strong emphasis on service has made Burbidge Disposal a leading company in a very competitive industry. Here's the story:

In my younger years, I had worked for a couple different contractors as a laborer. I helped them stand walls, pound nails, whatever they needed. When I was in college I needed an extra job. One day I was talking to a contractor, and he told me he had a real problem finding a crew to come in and clean up homes after he finished them. All the brick had to be cleaned, the windows had to be washed, the vents had to be vacuumed out, and the appliance boxes, sheetrock, and garbage had to be picked up and hauled to the dump. So I started cleaning homes for different contractors. I hired my wife before I married her. We could do one home a weekend. Our average charge was $500.

My biggest slowdown was that I couldn't get all the garbage out to the dump fast enough. I would take ten pickup loads full every weekend. All I did was haul garbage while the gals cleaned the houses. Then one day I was going by International Harvester, a truck dealer, and I saw an old used garbage truck—it was a 1965 Ford. I thought to myself, "If I could load that up with garbage from these homes, it would sure solve my problem." When I investigated to see how many tons it would hold, I discovered it actually compacted the garbage. I thought, "Hey, this would be great because I can smash up all those big boxes!" So I bought it for $2,200. I thought it was a ton of money, but after figuring the cost of my trips, I knew I'd save a lot of money. And talk about productive! We ended up doing three or four homes on a weekend. I would pull up in the truck, load the garbage in, and go to the next house. I ended up working inside instead of going to the dump all the time. Then I'd haul a whole weekend of garbage in one trip and push it out just like a brick—it was unbelievable! It turned out to be a great deal; I made fantastic money and paid off the truck.

Then home construction came to a screeching halt. We got down to two homes a weekend, then one, then one every month. It just died! I thought I'd sell the garbage truck and bag this home deal, but then I thought to myself, I see these garbage trucks all around town picking up garbage; I can probably do that. I called all the disposal companies and checked on their services and prices, then went door-to-door calling on businesses. I went in to the first company and said, "Can I pick up your garbage?" And they said, "Someone does already." So I said, "That's too bad, but maybe I can offer a better price or better service." After a few rejections I altered my sales pitch. "I'm in the neighborhood, and I'd like to do your garbage. I'm sure I can give you a great deal." Before long, I picked up three or four accounts and had a little route. I would do it in the morning before school.

The real dilemma came when I got my first large account with a real-estate company. I'd been working them for a while, and they finally said, "We'll try you at one complex." Well, one complex took twenty-one containers. I came home sick and told my wife, "I got this great new account, but I don't know how I'm going to pay for all the dumpsters." Fortunately, some of the accounts I had didn't need dumpsters—I'd just back the truck up to a dock and load up boxes. My wife was working, and I had a scholarship to the university. Not needing much to live, we put all our money into the business. I also talked a bank into giving me a six-month promissory note. When six months came up, I paid off the note and asked them for more money.

After a while I had a bunch of dumpsters all over town, and my old 1965 Ford. During this time, I really thought this garbage deal was just a temporary thing to get me through school. I never wanted to be a garbage man; I thought that would be incredibly embarrassing for myself and my family. When I was a little kid, my mom always used to give me the big warning: "If you don't go to school and get good grades, you'll end up being a garbage man." That was a real fear. Out on the route, I always hoped no one would see me. I left my house at three in the morning and had the truck back at seven. If it got the least bit light, I'd put my sunglasses on and pull my baseball cap down over my face.

I always thought I'd work for a bank or in the area of finance. However, I felt I could really be successful building the garbage company. I thought if you own a business, why not put your own name on the truck? I guess I could have called it "Intermountain" or "Rocky Mountain," but hey, what's better than your own name? I think there is a pride factor involved, and you take better care of your customers. When someone sees me, they say, "That's Dave Burbidge; Dave Burbidge picks up my garbage." Today with all the trucks I have running around town, half my customers still think Dave Burbidge picked up their garbage this morning. But I'll tell you, when I put the name on the truck, it was earth shattering. I got a call from my aunt, and she said, "I can't believe it! I saw a garbage truck with my name on the side going down the street and found out you are the one that owns the truck. You've got to get our name off that truck." Well, the name stayed on and she got over it, but she was very upset.

Being out of school, I was able to really concentrate on my business. I worked the route every morning, came home and showered, then hit the streets selling dumpsters all afternoon. Everybody I saw I'd say, "Where do you work?" They would say, "At a furniture store," and I would say, "Who hauls your garbage away?" Next thing you know I'd be in that store asking their boss if I could haul their garbage.

Another thing we did was put a big, quarter-page ad in the Yellow Pages. It was more than we could afford at the time, $500 per month, but it brought in a lot of business. Since we had a new baby, my wife stayed home to answer the calls and give the sales pitch. She would say, "We would love to do your garbage, sir. I'll have our salesman drop by and give you an estimate." Well, I was the salesman. Since we didn't have a radio in the truck, she didn't know where I was from hour to hour, so I'd take a bunch of dimes with me and call in each day to see who wanted bids. I'd pull the truck behind the business, strip right down to my underwear, switch into my clothes, put on my salesman's hat, and go in and say, "Hi, I'm with Burbidge Disposal." If they liked my price, we'd fill out a contract right there. Then I'd say, "OK, I'll have the driver come by with a container tomorrow." That was me too! I was everything! Then I'd go back to the truck, take off my clothes, put my overalls back on, and go back to slinging garbage. It was crazy! My biggest worry was my one truck, and it was an old truck. My sales pitch was great service, dependability, and "Johnny-on-the-spot" problem-solving. I had nightmares about this truck breaking down and not being able to service those customers. Our first month of business we billed $105. After two years we were billing out $8,000 a month, so the truck was pretty busy. So I checked on the price of a new garbage truck—it was $45,000 complete with a packer. I went to several banks, and they all said "No," "No," "No." So I went back to my original banker and said, "I need a one-year promissory note for $40,000." He said, "Gee, are you buying a lot of dumpsters?" I said, "No, it's for a new truck." He wouldn't do anything long-term, but he gave me the note. I paid it all off but $5,000 in one year.

This first truck was very important to our growth because it was brand new and very reliable. The next year, the bank decided we were a legitimate business, and we bought a second new truck on a five-year amortization, just like a normal company. So now we had three trucks. I drove one and hired a friend of mine to drive the second—I trained him and turned him loose. I kept the old '65 Ford in the yard as a spare and ran the two new trucks full bore everyday, all day long.

After this second new truck, we really started to grow. The key to it early on was that we did things the other companies wouldn't do. For example, most companies are unionized, so their drivers won't ever get out of their trucks. The problem is that containers overflow, and people can't or won't lift their sacks up to the dumpster. Drivers from the other companies pull up, empty the container, then drive away leaving a huge mess around the enclosure. The maintenance people from the building then have to come every morning and clean up the trash. Right from the beginning, we got out of our trucks and cleaned up the entire area—it only takes a few extra seconds at each stop. It wasn't long before the maintenance people realized they no longer had to clean up the garbage—which they had done for years with the other companies—and the word got out. Most management companies manage several complexes. We picked up one building from a company one year, and the next year we got twelve more from the same company. So that's been a big one for us, and it's still our policy today.

At Christmas, we really go the extra mile to give excellent service. Every year we add three extra trucks, ten additional people, and get out at two in the morning the day after Christmas. Some places have so much stuff—trees, boxes, wrappers—you can't even see the dumpster. It's unbelievable! We dump the container, then start shoveling garbage. We reload then dump, reload then dump, reload then dump. We've done some dumpsters as many as twelve times—it's just a big mountain! It's unbelievable work—a real backbreaker! But when the maintenance people show up in the morning, they don't even know it was Christmas. (Chuckles.) Occasionally we lose a customer on a bid basis, but they always call back and say, "We didn't realize what you were doing for us." They always come back, low bid or not, because they want the service back.

In addition to the service, we've tried to create a whole new image for our business. When I started the company, it seemed to me that garbage companies were very sloppy. They had sloppy old trucks and beat-up old containers. I decided that if I was going to be in the business, I was going to change that. I had bright red, white, and blue trucks that were always clean. My dumpsters were bright white with red and blue stripes and a sticker on them—they always looked sharp. I figured if I was going to be in the business, I wasn't going to be a garbage man—at least the stigma that everybody always sees of the guy. I would go downtown, see people I know, honk my horn, and wave to them. I'm sure they were walking away saying, "Geez, I hope Dave gets a decent job someday." But I was proud of what I was doing. My equipment was on the road, and it looked good.

Anyway, over the years, we've just kept adding trucks and employees. I had no idea! If you had told me we would be one of the biggest independent garbage companies in the state, I would have said, "No way, there's too many." But we just kept working hard, giving fabulous service, and taking care of the customers. The first five or six years, our business doubled every year. Now it grows by about 10 percent each year. We pay for all or our growth with cash flow and don't borrow money anymore.

I said, "I'll have the part here in your shop Friday morning." He said, "Yeah, sure, I've heard that before." I flew the part in on an airplane, had to buy a seat for it. Friday morning I had the part to him, we fixed the truck, and it was on the road in an hour.

It's been slow, controlled growth. To this day, I still train all the new drivers. A driver that works with me has driven with me. He may say, "I've worked for other companies and know all about it." I say, "Well, we do things a little bit different around here."

Over the years we've also grown in areas other than garbage. A logical branch off the garbage business was the equipment business. You buy a truck—that's called a chassis—then you put a packer on the back which you dump the garbage into. I was buying a packer from a very good company in California. They have great, durable equipment that really works well. They also provide great support—if you ever need a cylinder or anything, they ship it right up. After a few years, when we had confidence in each other, they gave me the dealership for Arizona, Idaho, Wyoming, and Utah. Right off, I bid on six trucks for the county and was the low bid. At first, they were hesitant to even let me bid because they hadn't used me before. But I took a demo out to them, showed them how it worked, and took them to the factory, and they bought them.

I've kept an eye on the account and serviced them well. The one time we had a failure, their mechanic said, "I'm sure it's going to be five weeks till we get this part." This was on a Wednesday, and Thursday was Thanksgiving. I said, "I'll have the part here in your shop Friday morning." He said, "Yeah, sure, I've heard that before." I flew the part in on an airplane, had to buy a seat for it. Friday morning I had the part to him, we fixed the truck, and it was on the road in an hour. So the general manager called and said, "Hey, we've never seen service like that before. We'll be buying your equipment from now on." Apparently they'd been buying equipment from another company for twenty years. The only time they ever saw the salesman was at bid openings and when he came to pick up a check. The manager said to me, "You're in here all the time checking on these trucks. Don't you have anything better to do?" I said, "I'm just trying to make sure you're happy. I don't want any problems with this equipment." Because of that, we got the next bid for six more trucks. This year I'll probably sell thirty trucks. Next year I'll sell forty-five. Great service—a lot better than other companies provide—has been a key factor to our growth.

> ### TIPS FOR GIVING MIND-BOGGLING SERVICE

1. **OVERSHOOT CUSTOMERS' EXPECTATIONS.**

   Brainstorm ways to give your customers much more than they expect with every product and on every visit. This is critical to gaining the handful of patrons necessary to get a new venture off the ground. Over time, create mechanisms to include customers in the process to make sure your thinking is on track.

2. **GIVE CUSTOMERS MORE THAN YOUR COMPETITORS OFFER.**

   It's not only important to overshoot customers' expectations; you need to do it better than anyone else in your industry. If you exceed expectations but your competitors do as well, you won't enjoy long-term loyalty and commitment from your customers. Keep abreast of what other companies are doing and "one-up-them" each year.

3. **STAGE REGULAR EVENTS TO BLOW CUSTOMERS' MINDS.**

   As often as possible, create wild, wacky, mind-boggling events for your customers to enjoy. This is an excellent utilization of marketing dollars. It creates excitement in the community and further endears customers to your business.

4. **CREATE SYSTEMS TO PERPETUATE SUPERB SERVICE.**

   Make sure all your human-resource systems, policies, and procedures operate in harmony to produce extraordinary service with every customer on an ongoing basis.

Chapter · 7

BUILDING
THE TEAM

---

*R*afael Rubio and his family brought the fish taco to America in
*1983. It's a white fish rolled in a soft corn tortilla and seasoned with
salsa, a special white sauce, cabbage, and a squeeze of lime. They got the
recipe from a beach vendor named Carlos in the Baja town of San
Felipe. Their first location was a defunct hamburger stand near Mission
Bay in San Diego—just a few blocks from the place Rafael began sweep-
ing floors when he immigrated to America. At first, the business was a
bona fide family affair: Dad and sons Ralph and Robert cooked, Richard
rang up customers, and Mom bagged the orders. The family knew they
had a real opportunity, but they lacked experience in the restaurant
business. To add muscle to their zeal, they brought in a first-class team of
veterans from the fast-food industry: John Gorman from Jack-in-the-
Box, Taco Bell, and Good Earth; James Stryker from El Torito
Restaurants and Spectrum Foods; and Stephen Sather from Rally's
Hamburgers, La Salsa, and Taco Bell. They also created teamwork at the
store level by promoting managers from within, offering attractive
salaries, and creating a supportive work environment. Rubio's Fish Tacos
was named California's 1993 Entrepreneurial Success by the Small
Business Association. Today, Rubio's has more than fifty locations and*

800 employees, and it serves 15,000 fish tacos a day. The company is approaching $30 million in annual sales.

A common misconception about entrepreneurs is that they are mavericks who like to tinker and muddle alone until they figure things out. To the contrary, the entrepreneurs I interviewed thrive on the experience of others. Like Rafael Rubio, they quickly recognize their limitations, identify people to fill in the holes, and persuade them to join the team. They also build a network of stalwart relationships with advisors, manufacturers, suppliers, distributors, designers, printers, and contractors. In essence, they are master puzzle makers, astute at finding and "locking in" all the pieces. In today's oscillating business world, there isn't a lot of time to tinker and muddle alone.

THE POWER OF TEAMS

The team is everything in entrepreneuring! The whole is indeed greater than the sum of its parts. You get a lot more from a zealous group slugging it out together than you do from individuals working alone. *Synergy* is the term used to describe this phenomenon. The experience base is greater, perspectives are broader, ideas are better, skills are enhanced, and self-confidence is built when motivated individuals hum as a team. That is why young entrepreneurial companies are able to outsmart large, humdrum bureaucracies where the gusto left long ago.

Successful entrepreneurs build teamwork at various levels. Many of the business founders I interviewed started with a team of advisors. This group can range from a loose-knit collection of individuals to a formal board of directors. These people are generally outsiders with a wealth of experience to offer the growing organization; they provide knowledge of the industry, information about related industries, and help with business strategy. They also help the entrepreneur make important contacts to move the business forward. Usually, these advisors are "locked in" with some form of ownership—they either invest in the company or receive stock to participate.

In the stories that follow, you'll see how Mary Naylor's business, Capitol Concierge, was floundering until she brought in two investors who serve as her advisors. She meets with them every month and finds their insights invaluable. Because they are removed from the day-to-day details, they are able to evaluate the business in a more objective way than she can. Though Mary had to give up ownership to attract their money and expertise, as she puts it, "For me, 50 percent of something is better than 100 percent of nothing." Her business really took off after Mark and Cal got involved! We had a similar experience at Golden Swirl. Since our business was very capital intensive, we found two investment groups to join our team. While I had the zeal, tenacity, and academic expertise, they had the practical horsepower. When we sat down together, we had well over a hundred years of business experience in the room. From them I learned how to structure the organization, work with attorneys, document critical events, negotiate real-estate leases, and build stores. They were the best group of partners you could ever hope for! Without a doubt, we could not have achieved what we did early on without them.

The second type of team found in our stories is the management group—the folks who run the company from day to day. This group functions much like a sports team, requiring skilled players in specific positions. It would be unlikely, if not impossible, that an aspiring entrepreneur would have the complete package of skills needed to launch and build a successful new venture. The savvy entrepreneurs I interviewed clearly understood their strengths and weaknesses, and they sought out strong people to pick up the slack and round out the team. To attract these people, our entrepreneurs offered enticing incentives, and in many cases, ownership in the company. Hyrum Smith, whose story you'll read below, is an exceptional role model! Even though he didn't need the capital, he took his company public for the very reason of "sharing the rock" with his key people. He was genuinely enthusiastic about rewarding the people who helped build what eventually became FranklinCovey. He also felt that "owners" would act differently than "employees." In other words, if you hire strong team members but don't give them a chance to participate in the upside of the venture—stock options, performance bonuses, profit sharing—your company will never run as well as it might otherwise. Not only will your people lack motivation, but you won't be able to attract and keep top talent.

Building a strong team at Golden Swirl was both exciting and challenging. In the early days, Mary and I did all the work ourselves, which is the most efficient way to get started. As we grew larger, it became clear that we needed a general manager—we were running ragged! We kept saying, "We need someone like Gregg Morrow," a friend of ours who had the perfect temperament for the job—he worked hard, liked teenagers, was great with customers, had real integrity, and was very practical—a "Mr. Fix It" by nature. We finally decided to talk with Gregg. He turned us down the first time but joined our team a year later. He was marvelous in the field, which gave Mary and me time to work on product development, marketing, and business strategy. Each time we needed a key player, we had a similar experience. When we decided to manufacture our own products, we teamed up with Marlin Harmon, a Ph.D. in microbiology I met in graduate school at Purdue University. Marlin created a superb line of products on a shoestring budget. Later, we rounded out the team with Gordon Carmen and Lane Vance, two talented guys who added invaluable expertise in accounting, finance, sales, and distribution. Clearly, there was no way Mary and I could have covered all these bases.

In addition to the management team, the entrepreneurs I interviewed developed strong partnerships with critical players outside the company. Once mutually beneficial relationships were formed, they stayed with that supplier, distributor, manufacturer, or contractor while they rolled out their business. This process of partnering keeps distractions to a minimum, allows for rapid growth, and helps the company focus on what it does best. Here's how this process works: You approach your potential partners and tell them you want to give all your business to one company, but you want the best possible price for a long-term commitment and increasing volume. As my business-man father used to say, "You make money on the purchase, not on the sale." It works best if you reach a cost-plus agreement with your part-ners; then you don't have to worry about arbitrary price hikes or shop-ping your account around every year. While they may not make a killing off your account, you will help provide their bread and butter as you grow and give them ongoing business. Obviously, your ability to negotiate great prices increases as your volume grows. The impor-tant thing is to find people you like working with, then let them do their job so you can do yours. Along the way, it's also very important to communicate what excellent performance means to you, so they understand your standards and know how to keep you happy.

Just as some executives don't have a team mentality, some com-panies don't have a knack for partnering. This is very shortsighted in today's jarring business climate. One company we serviced through our wholesale business, Northern Lights, was notorious for beating suppliers down to nothing; they also changed suppliers frequently. If you won their account, it was good news and bad news; you increased your distribution but didn't make any money. Suppliers soon realized the account wasn't worth having. Today, this company is out of busi-ness. So you need to let your partners make money—remember, the relationship has to be mutually rewarding to work long-term. During our growth phase, we limited our relationships to one great architect, one product manufacturer, one cabinetry company, one equipment supplier, and one major distributor in each region. And it worked great! Certainly, some of our success must be attributed to these out-standing partners.

Finally, the entrepreneurs I interviewed work hard to develop teamwork throughout the organization. I included Pam Walsh's story in this chapter because her company does this exceptionally well. The company's structure is flat, and employees are organized into teams. The team coaches report directly to the head coach. Employees are team players, and customers are fans. The entire company meets briefly each morning for a pep rally. Team coaches take turns leading the hoorays. They report on past goals, set new goals, and establish incentives for accomplishment. A host of rewards are then offered when teams achieve their objectives: movie tickets, barbecues, awards, bonuses, profit sharing, and so on. The company recently created an "action board" where any team player can recognize any other team player for work well done. Together, these programs bring a spirit of fun and enthusiasm to the workplace.

Although this type of teamwork is difficult to maintain, the entrepreneurs I interviewed work at it constantly. They offer attractive salaries, bonuses, profit sharing, stock options, and a host of non-monetary rewards. They get to know their employees, give them credit for work well done, provide recognition, and promote from within. In sum, they try to build great organizations to work for—from the employees' point of view!

FINDING THE RIGHT MIX

Teamwork is hard work! Success at the highest level has to be won—it doesn't happen overnight. It takes patience, perseverance, and the right personalities. And just as a healthy team is greater than the sum of its parts, an unhealthy team is worse than the sum of its parts. In other words, a dysfunctional team of five is much worse than five individuals working alone. You not only have a loss in individual performance stemming from the conflict, but you also have to run damage control to stop the ripple it produces throughout the organization.

So how do you build a high-performance team? First, you need the right mix of skills. Every team member must contribute unique expertise required by the organization—and all the bases must be covered. This is the easy part! Next, you need the right personalities. Here's where things get messy. Fortunately, we have decades of research and practical experience to guide us. Ideal team members enjoy working in groups, believe everyone has something to contribute, understand their strengths and weaknesses, respect other people's position, feel optimism for the task, and don't crave personal credit. Most important, they check their egos at the door and work toward a team consciousness. Their objective is to produce a team success, not an individual success.

An organization that produces some of the most elite teams in America is the U.S. Navy's SEAL division. Only three out of ten people recruited for this job actually become Navy SEALs. The fastest, strongest, and best athletes are often the first to wash out. The ones who survive drop their individual egos, make a total commitment to the unit, and do all they can to help other team members excel. Team builders in companies can learn from this example. People who have uncontrollable egos, who think they are smarter than everyone else, who need to be in charge and hog all the credit just don't make good team players. It's better to choose someone with adequate talent and a passion for teamwork than a superstar with an anti-team personality.

Many of the entrepreneurs I interviewed have a special sense for selecting team members. Luckily, the early stages of entrepreneuring are highly conducive to teamwork. You're forging new ground and taking on corporate giants, and everyone is scared to death. Going up against big odds naturally produces humility and a team consciousness. It's when the company becomes successful that the terrified posture is replaced with pride and conflict. Bickering, backbiting, negative attitudes, staking out territory, and claiming credit often result. Here's how a team leader quoted in *Fortune Magazine* (February 19, 1996) puts it: "A team is like having a baby tiger given to you at Christmas. It does a wonderful job of keeping the mice away for about 12 months, and then it starts to eat your kids." Well said! So just as the right team members are important to initial success, keeping the mix right over time is important as well. Its hard to replace people when things aren't working out, but it may be necessary to preserve the team. Many of our entrepreneurs talked about facing this painstaking challenge. Not only did team members occasionally snap, but their industries changed too, making new talent necessary. Remember how Tony Conza of Blimpie replaced people from the old regime with negative attitudes and outdated skills just prior to his finest surge? This is a hard lesson for most entrepreneurs to learn, but it's critical for continued success. When someone isn't working out and you finally take action, you always wonder why you didn't do it sooner.

One final comment: People often ask me if friends and family members make good team players. It's a compelling question since aspiring entrepreneurs often have limited talent to draw from early on. Sometimes those closest to you are the only ones you can coopt to help. Some of the entrepreneurs I interviewed have built their entire company with friends or family members, so it can work. Frieda Caplan, Sean Nguyen, Mary Ellen Sheets, Jason Olim, Pam Walsh, and others have had positive experiences. However, it can change your association. Often you have to decide whether to put the business first or the relationship first. If you put the business first, the relationship may suffer; if you put the relationship first, the business may suffer. Teams can be tough enough without this added pressure. But if the parties are mature and understand the inherent conflict in their roles, things can work out fine. So my answer to the question is this: Don't hire people *just* because they are friends or family members. On the other hand, don't *not* hire people because they are friends or family members. Use the same objective selection criteria for everyone you consider. When a friend or family member has both the required skills and personality, you can have a very rich experience.

Anyway, it would take an entire book to outline the ins and outs of teamwork. But successful entrepreneurs work hard to create motivated teams at all levels of the organization. They link up with key advisors, create a powerful management team, partner with outside companies, and foster teamwork throughout the organization. And this effort has tremendous payoffs for the growing venture. You'll love the three stories that follow. Pam Walsh, Mary Naylor, and Hyrum Smith are great team builders!

OUR ROLE MODELS

Pam Walsh

Pam is the cofounder of Our Secret, a company in Albuquerque, New Mexico, that produces handcrafted gifts and decorative accessories for the home. Scented candles are the company's major product line. Pam is the "coach" of the product design team. A strong initial partnership and teamwork throughout the organization—particularly during disasters— have helped Our Secret reach $15 million in annual sales. Here's how Pam describes her experience:

When my husband and I got married in 1987, we decided we wanted to start our own business. I had been working for my parents for several years down in old-town Albuquerque; they have a store that sells pottery, furniture, and handcrafts. At the time, I was also making my own wreaths from dried flowers, evergreens, different kinds of bows, and selling them at the store.

In November of that year, we did a show called Holiday Olé, which was sponsored by the Junior League. A woman from the power company, P & M, came by and said she was looking for artists to be in a show in Dallas called "Point of View Southwest." The show was for buyers of gift stores, card shops, department stores, and home-accessory chains. My ears perked up, and I went, "Wow! That sounds kind of neat! I know how to make wreaths, so we can start there." (Laughs.) Well, the booths for that show were about a thousand dollars, which was a lot of money for us, so we told her we would have to think about it. But she called back a week later and said, "Great news! P & M has decided to pay half the cost of booths for artists who want to show their products." Now it was $500 for us, and we thought, "We can come up with 500 bucks." So we decided to go for it.

This was November of '87, and the show was in January. So we had to come up with a name for our business. We really wanted something nonspecific so we wouldn't have to change it if the business evolved over time. We didn't want Pam & Matt's, because we didn't know how things were going to turn out. (Laughs.) At the time, we were watching a miniseries called "My Secret Garden," and we liked the name secret. So we thought, "My Secret" . . . "Your Secret" . . . "Our Secret"—and that hit us just right. It was kind of intriguing yet didn't say what the business was, so it could be almost anything. About this time, we also asked my brother if he wanted to get involved, and he said, "Yeah, that kind of sounds good." (Laughs.) I was twenty-four and he was barely twenty. So we all three decided to go into business together. We got our license, registered our name, and formed a simple partnership. We just divvied it up equally with each person owning a third.

We started working in the two-bedroom house my husband and I rented, which was very small. (Laughs.) The first thing we did was build the booth. We really didn't know much about setting up a show, but we tried to be as creative as we could. We got all this canvas and stretched it out on PVC pipe, then splatched it up with paint. Then we decided to distribute other people's products in our booth along with my wreaths. We approached two or three artists I knew from my parents' store and worked out an arrangement to show their work. We ended up with my wreaths and two or three kinds of candles and pottery.

This first show was a total bomb! (Laughs.) We really had no clue about how to dress or how to do much of anything. The first two days we wrote no business. None! Matt and Greg were standing in front of the booth wearing suits and ties, like Mafia men. (Laughs.) I think it was very intimidating to people; they would stop and look but not come into the booth. So we decided, "Okay, that's enough of that." They dressed more casually the next two days, and we wrote about $15,000 worth of business. We were excited about that and thought, "Well, we learned a lot; we know what we did wrong, and we can sure improve on it next time." So we went home, shipped our orders, got a couple reorders, and eventually moved into a bigger house with a two-car garage.

We went to our next big show in July of 1988, which was also in Dallas. We changed our concept a bit and got two booths instead of one. We added a few rugs and some pillows, and I made my wreaths a lot more southwestern. I used feathers, little ceramic calf skulls, things like that, so our products were very different from anybody else's. We also built a fireplace and made things look real homey. This is kind of funny because we didn't think we would be very busy the first couple days since we weren't at the last show. So the night before the show, we went out partying, stayed out real late, and had a great time. (Laughs.) The next morning, the show opened at 9:00 A.M., and from 9:30 until 6:00, we were writing orders nonstop. Nonstop! So that show was extremely successful for us. Our sales were between $70,000 and $80,000. It was very, very exciting!

In September of '88, we got our first building, which was 4,000 square feet. The day we got the keys, it was totally empty. We brought some Stouffer's lasagna and a bottle of champagne, sat on the floor, and thought, "What in the world are we going to do with all this space?" Today, we have 42,000 square feet, but back then this was a big commitment. We started making our wreaths there but continued pouring candles in our two-car garage at home. We also hired our first employee about that time—today we have over 100.

We were still selling through shows until July of '89, when we took on a rep for the eastern part of the country. That was a big step for us. Then in December of '89, we took on another building—6,000 square feet—because the one we had was already too small. We continued making wreaths out of the first building and moved our candle production into the second building. Our original product was a little brown ceramic container that we poured different kinds of fragrances in. Then a month later, our first building burned to the ground, and we lost everything! We still had candles, but we didn't have any wreaths. This was three days before our January show in Dallas. At the time, we had taken on a second rep in Colorado, and we begged and pleaded with him for the wreaths in his showroom. He sent them to us overnight, and we reconstructed our booth in two days. I mean, we worked around the clock and got it done. It was pretty elaborate. It had a brick floor, a fountain, and tile everywhere. It ended up looking just like what we planned, so we were able to salvage a huge disaster.

After the show, we had to produce like mad 'cause we were out of inventory. During this time, we decided to narrow our focus because the wreaths were expensive and time consuming, and the profit margin wasn't there. So much to my chagrin—I didn't like the idea at all (laughs)—we decided to tighten up what we were doing. In July of 1990, we moved into our current building—which is ten times bigger than our first location—and moved full bore into candles. We continued to produce our brown container but also added a white stoneware container. We sold nothing but these products for a long time, and they were very, very successful. Later we added "Candlecakes," which are perfect refills for our containers. Then we introduced a product line called Ironworks. These are attractive iron stands that hold glass containers—our Candlecakes fit in them. This line has also been extremely successful for us.

In 1995 we had another big disaster. It was February 3 at about 3:30 in the morning when the alarm company called and said our building was on fire. Matt was so petrified he couldn't do anything. All he could think about was what happened before, only this time we had everything in one building. So I drove down, and it was pitch dark because all the power was out. The fire department was just hangin' around outside. They were thinkin' one of our kilns was smoking, which had happened a couple months before. It took them about half an hour to figure out there really was a fire. Well, it was pitch black inside, and there was so much smoke you couldn't see three inches in front of your face. So I went home, and Matt came down at about 6:30. On his way he stopped and picked up some notepads and pens so he could give our people instructions when they showed up to work at 7:00.

For several hours they wouldn't let anyone in the building because it was totally filled with smoke. Finally, at 10:00, they let a couple people in to take a look around. Apparently, one of the roll-around wax tanks we use to pour our Candlecakes had overheated and the bottom fell out. The wax got so hot it caught fire and slowly spread across the floor. It torched different areas of the factory and produced an incredible amount of thick, waxy smoke that blackened everything. I mean everything! All the computers were black, the ceiling was black, and all of our products were black. Everyone who saw the place said, "You're not going to be in business for two or three months!" And we said, "We can't afford not to be in business!"

We had all our employees helping, plus another 100 temporaries. We also had lots of volunteers from the community. We took everything out of the building and steamed the ceilings, steamed the floors, steamed everything. We had assembly lines of people wiping down our products. A lot of our inventory was completely ruined and had to be thrown out. There was over a million dollars of damages. But we all rallied together, worked around the clock, and were back in business in ten days.

It was during the cleanup that we started our pep rally. It seemed like a great idea, so we just kept doing it. Our company is organized according to teams, so we have coaches rather than managers. Matt is the head coach, and we have coaches under him that head up the different departments. I'm a design coach. Our employees are team players, and our customers are our fans. We really don't have a deep structure. Anyway, we meet every morning for about ten minutes or so. Each coach gets an opportunity to lead the pep rally for a couple days or however long they want. Then they pass a shirt to another coach—it's like passing the gavel. What they do is go over their goals—they talk about what they accomplished yesterday and what they want to accomplish today. It's real simple, nothing fancy. We just all get together and root 'n' rah and do cheers. It's everyone who works here, every morning.

> We meet every morning for about ten minutes or so. Each coach gets an opportunity to lead the pep rally for a couple days or however long they want. Then they pass a shirt to another coach—it's like passing the gavel.

To summarize our growth, we now do all the major gift shows: Dallas, Atlanta, L.A., New York, Miami, Boston, Seattle, Minneapolis, Detroit, Phoenix, Denver. We also have fourteen organizations that represent our products. A rep may have twenty different lines—it could be stationery, it could be balls, it could be almost anything. We try to find reps who sell mostly home accessory and gift-store items. We also try to find people who only represent one candle line. Customers only have so many dollars to spend on a particular type of product, so we don't want to give them a lot of choice. Basically, the orders come in from our customers and reps, and we make and ship the products. Our first year of business, which was 1988, we did around $110,000 in sales. It's doubled or tripled every year since then. We now do around $15 million a year. Basically, our growth has come from desire. So it's been really neat.

I think one of the reasons we've been so successful is that we didn't have anything to lose. We started out young and didn't take big risks. My brother invested $2,000 when he came in, and a year later Matt's folks loaned us $10,000. That was all. We grew as our cash allowed. What we would do is ask our customers to either prepay or pay COD. Then we went to our suppliers and said, "Can we please have sixty days instead of thirty for this particular bill?" They were always more than willing to help us. So we never risked large sums of money to start and grow the company. Never!

Another reason for our success is probably our customer service. Our philosophy is, "Our customers are always right." We believe that 100 percent. We never deviate from that. We always say, "What can we do to make you happy?" There are very few times someone is so unreasonable you just want to slug 'em. (Laughs.) When you put it in their lap and say, "What can we do to make you happy?" they are usually very fair and easier on us than we would be on ourselves.

Anyway, I'm very happy with what we've done. It's really neat creating something from the beginning and then marketing it to our fans. I love it! And I think anybody who has the desire to do it, can. It takes a lot of effort, though. You have to work hard to get where you want to go. You also have to have vision. You need to think about what you want to do and where you want to be in five years. If you don't, you're just going to spin your wheels. So hard work and vision are important. And let's see, what else . . . I don't know . . . maybe inspiration? (Laughs.)

Mary Naylor

Mary is the founder of Capitol Concierge, a company that provides lobby services to building owners and office tenants in Washington, D.C. The company struggled financially until Mary brought in two partners who provided both capital and management expertise. Mary credits these partners with the tremendous growth and success the company has enjoyed in recent years. Today, Capitol Concierge is the largest company of its kind in the country. Mary explains:

This idea came one day when I was traveling on an airplane. I read an article about a woman doing it in California and thought it was a great idea. I gave her a call and went out to visit her in Irvine. She wanted $10,000 to train me for three days and 6 percent of my gross revenue indefinitely. I was interested but didn't have the money. At the time, I was involved in another company I'd started with an old family friend. He was funding it, and I was doing the work. We were offering a training program on career planning for liberal-arts college students. That business was winding down because the funding was drying up, so I was looking for something new when this idea hit.

What I ended up doing was moving back home with my mother and working out of the basement. I borrowed $2,000 from her and rented an address from a mailbox company. Then I left the other entity and started researching the real-estate industry. I put together a program proposal, made a list of companies, and started making calls. This was in October of 1987. The challenge was that this was a totally new industry in D.C. and there were no models of the service here. I was calling building owners and property management companies, and they were saying , "Great idea, but we don't want to be your guinea pig. Come back when you've done it."

Finally, the John Akridge Company, a very prominent local developer said, "We'll do it." That was in March of '88, so I'd been at it for five or six months. During this time, I was locating vendors for the services and developing the systems, so I was ready to go. We signed the contract in March and started in our first building in June. As it turned out, they were a great referral that helped us get more business. So the tip here is to start at the top and get the cream of the crop as your first client. If they have a great reputation in your market, it will open up a lot of doors.

So I hired my first employee to be the concierge in the lobby of this building. Here's how the business works: The property management company pays me a monthly fee that covers the direct expenses of operating the desk; it also contributes a small amount to our company overhead. We then charge our customers for the services they buy. We get a discount from the florist, the dry cleaner, the sedan service, the travel agent, etc., which is our profit center. So we just started marketing in the building via literature and lobby events. You know, "Come down for free pastries and meet the new concierge." During this time, I got some free furniture from my mother's law firm and moved into a 200-square-foot sub-let. I also continued to go out and meet with property managers. We picked up two more contracts in '88 and six more in '89.

As it turned out, the projections I had made were completely off—I mean completely off! I had gathered information on how many flowers people buy each year, how many rolls of film they develop, and so on, to determine how much business we might get from a building based on its population. What I extrapolated from that information was just wrong— totally wrong! My numbers were way high! I didn't plan on all the work that was required to get people in the building to use the concierge. In addition, I had undercharged our first client to get the contract—that was just a strategic decision on my part.

So we were growing, but we weren't making any money. And I was doing all the work myself. I had one employee in each building, but they couldn't leave the desk. For them it's pretty much an eight-to-five job. So I was securing tickets, delivering videos, you name it. I was running around doing everything. I was also trying to manage the finances, but I had no training in profit-and-loss statements, payroll taxes, any of that. It was "lifestyles of the poor and pitiful." It was insane!

Then in 1990 we saw a downturn in the real-estate market, which turned out to be a big boom for us. Buildings owners were looking for competitive advantages to attract tenants. However, they weren't paying their fees on time either, and I didn't have the personal cash to make this happen. What I did was leverage a life-insurance policy through my mother and took an additional $15,000 from her. So my total capital contribution was the initial $2,000 plus this $15,000. That was it!

In April that year I started seeking bank financing. I put together a business plan, but no bank would touch it. I hadn't been in business long enough, and I wasn't profitable. I've since learned that banks only lend you money if you don't need it. I now have more money available to me than I can use. Anyway, I gave my business plan to a CPA in an accounting firm—a lot of his clients were private investors. I made a presentation to five gentlemen, and two of them picked me up—their names are Mark and Cal. That was one of my toughest decisions because I was giving up 50 percent of the company. They each have 25 percent, and nothing can be done without a 75 percent vote. So I have to persuade them to support my ideas, and they can't move without me. But they made a partial loan, partial investment, which helped me expand even further. The next year we went from twelve to fifty-five locations. It was just incredible! It was me out marketing, showing what we had. All the systems were being developed as we went along.

> I wouldn't go into business now if I was the sole owner. Filling in the pieces where you are deficient is an important part of success.

We now have nearly 100 buildings. We do around $7 million in sales with over a hundred employees. Our core services include flowers, gifts, catering, sedan service, dry cleaning, theater and event tickets. We also do unique things people ask, as long as they are legal: track down a rare book, pick up a prescription, purchase an engagement ring, make arrangements at a restaurant, you name it. We've even found pet food for someone's tarantula. So we're basically a broker of services. We've heard it all and we try to deliver on every request—we really do. It's amazing. We develop great relationships with all kinds of people. And I think we're just scratching the surface. We're currently designing the systems and activities to position ourselves for the next wave of growth. It's one set of strategies to go from $1 to $5 million; it's a whole 'nother set to go from $5 to $10 million. It's putting people and systems in place to launch that kind of growth.

I think a critical program any business owner needs is a board of advisors. Many entrepreneurs run aground because they get so involved in the day-to-day details they never pull back and analyze the business in a more objective way. I have a monthly meeting with Mark and Cal, and it's invaluable to me. They are invested in probably forty other businesses here locally, and watching them work has made all the difference in the world. Fortunately, I have a great relationship with them. But some entrepreneurs miss this advantage because they don't want to give up control or equity. Personally, I wouldn't go into business now if I was the sole owner. Filling in the pieces where you are deficient is an important part of success. For me, 50 percent of something is better than 100 percent of nothing. So I think it's shortsighted to not take on partners.

> I'm a big believer that you create your own opportunities. You can't succeed in business if you don't feel that way!

I think it's also important to include employees in the business. All of our people understand how this company works. I spend a half day with them as part of their training. We talk about our sources of revenue, our profit-and-loss statement, how the company makes money, and how they fit into the big picture. This is very important! Otherwise, team members become shortsighted. I also encourage their input through a variety of committees. We have a bonus committee, an employee appreciation committee, and a vendor review board, so everyone can learn various aspects of the business. When a position opens up, lots of people have exposure to that area.

Another important key is planning. We write a business plan every year. It's not a big plan you would submit for financing but a simple, one-page strategy. It outlines our expected growth, desired profit margin, six or seven key objectives we want to accomplish, and the target dates. We use it as a tool to measure ourselves against every month. Then we stay flexible and open to new opportunities, which are thrown at us everyday. When an opportunity arises, I prepare a concept paper stating why we should do it and why we shouldn't do it. Then we sit around and talk about it. If we decide to proceed, we plan how it is going to be realized. What are the steps? I'd say this is my greatest strength. I can sit down and write up a plan and the steps that are needed to accomplish it. To me, this is critical. Execution is everything! So we use this idea of planned opportunism every year. I think we are the largest in this industry because we take the time to step back and plan strategy and direction. Then we take responsibility to make things happen. I'm a big believer that you create your own opportunities. You can't succeed in business if you don't feel that way!

Hyrum Smith

Hyrum is the cofounder and former chairman of Franklin Quest, a company that conducts personal productivity seminars across America. The company also produces and sells the Franklin Day Planner, both at seminars and in its 120-plus retail stores. In 1997, Franklin Quest merged with the Covey Leadership Center. At the time, Franklin had 3,000 employees and Covey had 700, making FranklinCovey one of the largest training and development companies in the world. The business now exceeds $400 million in annual revenue. Here's Hyrum's story:

In my senior year of college I discovered I could sell things. I made $22,000 that year selling stuff. I sold cars, I sold anything that wasn't nailed down. All the offers I was getting from companies at the time were for considerably less money than that, and I thought, "Geez, this doesn't compute." So I decided to take a position selling insurance with Connecticut Mutual Life in Hawaii. Moved my family there and did very well for a year. My problem was that I was selling life insurance to people who couldn't afford it but were buying it anyway.

So I left the life-insurance business and joined a computer firm in

Portland. It was later acquired by ADP, and we became their largest division. We grew the business from $6 million to about $40 million while I was the senior vice president of sales. During this time, I grew the sales force from twenty people to 300. I was training all these people and discovered I really enjoyed teaching. So I looked at the academic world as a possibility, but I had two problems: one, I didn't have the credentials, and two, I couldn't make a living there. So I decided I'd teach in the corporate world—they'll take anybody. (Laughs.)

What I did was create a company called Golden Eagle Motivation. I have this thing about eagles. It's been funny; people send me eagles from all over the world. Anyway, I created a sales seminar because that was my background. From July of '81 to July of '82, I knocked on lots of doors and taught lots of seminars for four or five people. (Laughs.) It was a grim year, but I learned a lot about the seminar business.

During that period, I discovered that corporate America was really hungry for productivity management. So I joined forces with a guy in Salt Lake named Charles Hobbs who had a time-management seminar. I moved here in July of '82 and worked with Charles for a little over a year. Then in 1983, I left Hobbs and started H. W. Smith and Associates, which was the forerunner to Franklin. Dick Winwood, a friend of mine from ADP, joined me. We decided we could really teach people how to get control of their lives, so we created a seminar and started selling it. (Laughs.) We told people, "If you go to our seminar, you'll realize a measurable increase in your personal productivity." At the time, we were giving out a Day Timer because people needed a tool to implement what we were teaching.

We did a lot of free seminars to get started, but the thing that launched us was a relationship with Merrill Lynch. Merrill Lynch had seen me do a seminar for Charles Hobbs and liked it very much. When we went out on our own, they came to me and said, "We want you to teach." And I said, "I'm not teaching Hobbs's stuff anymore, I'm teaching my own stuff." And they said, "Well, let's look at it." So we did the seminar and they liked it a lot. That's how I met Arlen Crouch, their regional director of Southern California. I trained all of his people, then ended up back in New

York. We now train every broker that Merrill Lynch hires. So it really took off! We were stunned by it!

A lot of our early success resulted from the people we brought in to help: Dennis Webb, Lynn Robbins, and Bob Bennett. Bob is now a U.S. senator from Utah. As the seminars started taking off, I called him on the phone and said, "Bob, I think we've got something here that's going to work, but I can't run it from an airplane. I need someone on the ground running things." He came up from California and got real excited. He commuted for a year, then moved here and became our president.

So in 1984 Dick and I were teaching seminars twenty days a month, and Bob was here running things. That's when we decided to create our own device. Actually, we were so convinced we were a training company it didn't occur to us to create a planner. But Day Timer was not willing to make their product more closely fit what we were teaching in our seminar. So we decided almost by accident to create our own. I wish I could say it was revealed to me in the night ten years ago, but really, it was a glorious accident.

Anyway, we mocked up a sample planner, then started looking for financing. See, the seminar business is easy to get into because there are no big capital expenses. But now we needed to raise money to build this new concept. Well, a guy came forward who had been to one of our seminars and said, "I'll give you $200,000 for 20 percent of the company. So we signed a deal with him. Of course, at that time we would have given him 50 percent. Fifty percent of nothing is nothing—that's what the company was worth in 1984. But the week the planner was coming off the press, this guy got cold feet. His partner came up from California and said, "There are hundreds of day organizers out there; we're crazy to do this." So our guy comes back and says, "Hyrum, you've got to let me out of this deal. I really don't think you guys have a future. Blah, blah, blah . . ." And I said, "Well, I've got to pay an $80,000 bill on Friday to release 5,000 of our first day planners." He said, "Well, what can I do? I really want out of this deal." I said, "I'll tell you what: if you'll loan me 80,000 bucks for ninety days interest free, I'll let you out." He said, "Great!" (Laughs.) So we got our first day planners funded and paid him back in ninety days. That was a bullet that missed us, because 20 percent of our market cap right now is not a bad number.

So we got our day planners produced and started giving them away at the seminars. We had 5,000 of these dated items aging every day, and I thought, "Oh, man!" I looked at the mountain of day planners in the warehouse and thought we had made a big mistake. Well, we had to print 3,000 more before the end of the year, which was pretty neat. Then the big question was, will anyone renew their day planner? We had sold 8,000, and here we were at the end of '84. Well, to our amazement and delight, 90 percent of our customers renewed them. And that 90 percent has continued every year since. But back then, people would call in and order the stuff and we'd go down and ship it out. Our first order-entry clerk was Karma with a yellow pad, bless her heart. I mean, the whole manufacturing and distribution system we have created from a yellow pad is really incredible. We now have over 400 people answering phones twenty-four hours a day, six days a week, and taking more than 6,000 orders a day. Karma is now our senior vice president over that division; she has around 500 people reporting to her. She's a high-school graduate and a millionaire 'cause we gave her stock.

Anyway, our first year, which was 1984, our revenue was $300,000. It was all seminar revenue because the planner was given out as part of the price. We doubled that figure every year until 1989, when we did $30 million in seminars and planners combined. By this time, a lot of people were buying planners that had not been to the seminar. We discovered by accident that retail stores work for us. We were on the third floor of a bank building downtown, and people kept coming in to buy stuff. So we rented 600 square feet on the first floor from November to January, thinking we'd shut it down at the first of the year. Well, the next year, that 600 square feet did a million dollars in sales of day planners. It just blew us away! So now we have over a hundred retail stores all over the country. And every store we've opened has done a million dollars in the first year. It's just been incredible! Of course, we don't open a store until we have 10,000 day planner users within a thirty-minute drive of a location. This produces what we call a breeder effect. We've discovered that the 25,000 people we teach every month will bring in another 10,000 to 15,000 users because they get excited about it. "Man, you've got to get a Franklin Day Planner!" Then people show up in our stores saying, "Hey, my friend says I've got to have one. What do I need?" We can then sell them the day planner and our retail kit, which is our seminar on audio. We find when they get the training, they are more committed to use the planner. The kit also includes a book I've written called *The 10 Natural Laws of Successful Time and Life Management*. I've got one around here somewhere I'll give you. Here's one in Chinese. (Laughs.)

So back to 1989. We had just finished a $30-million year, and Arlen Crouch from Merrill Lynch joined our team. He and I had become great friends, and I have to give him the credit for our current financial condition. When he came on board we were pretaxing about 6 percent—and I didn't know that! But I recognized early on there were a lot of things I didn't know how to do. And frankly, one of them is reading and understanding a financial statement. (Laughs.) I am really good at growing a top line, but I don't like to worry about the bottom line. So our sales were growing like crazy, but we didn't know how to manage a big company. When I signed every check we had pretty good control, but all of a sudden we had fifty people spending money.

Anyway, Arlen was a twenty-six-year veteran at Merrill Lynch and really had the skills. He took a major pay cut to come, but I gave him a bunch of my stock. He joined us on the "come" because he believed in what we were doing. It turned out to be a very good decision for both of us. In ninety days he cut our expenses by $300,000. In two years he took us from 6 percent to 22 percent pretax. At the end of his first year we did $52 million in sales. During the next three years he put us in great financial shape. He also got Price Waterhouse in here to do three years of audited statements in case we decided to go public. Financially, we didn't need to do it, but I really wanted our people to "own the rock." So in 1992 Merrill Lynch took us public on the New York Stock Exchange. I think we did $116 million that year and $160 million the next year. A few years later we hit $300 million.

Over the years, time management has continued to be the flagship of what we do. All of the stuff we sell revolves around that concept of personal productivity. We made a conscious decision to stay with what we are good at. Our clients come to us and say, "Gee, we love your time-management piece, but what else do you do?" We've added two or three other curriculums, but they are minor for us. I watched what happened to Larry Wilson at Larry Wilson Learning. He had four seminars that corporate America loved, and he was growing like crazy. His customers came to him and said, "Can you teach this, can you teach that?" His answer was always, "Sure." He ended up with ninety-four curriculums, and it put him under. Funny thing was, 90 percent of his revenue was still coming from the four core concepts he was really good at. So we've just stuck with what we do best.

Our basic approach to selling our seminars has been classic network marketing. We got into Dow Chemical and Merrill Lynch because a couple guys saw me speak. Then we got into General Motors because of Dow Chemical. We got into Chrysler because of General Motors. We got into Ford because of General Motors and Chrysler. It's fascinating how it happens. You know, a kid goes to Dow Chemical as an intern from Michigan State University. He gets his planner and goes to the seminar. Then he gets his first job at Proctor & Gamble. We've now trained 30,000 people at Proctor & Gamble. (Laughs.) I mean, we just haven't advertised. We grew that way in the beginning because we didn't have any money. Now it's our strategy! We grow that way by design because it's a healthy way to grow.

Our first few years we only did corporate seminars. We'd sell the program and the company would fill the seats. A few years later, we started doing public seminars. We contacted our day planner users in a given area and asked them to send their friends. We now do public seminars in over 200 cities every month. We bring in about a million dollars a month from these seminars. It turns out they are a great way to market the seminar to prospective corporations. Our marketing people follow up on leads, call the corporations, and schedule the seminars. We've got fifty sales people earning an average of $120,000 a year selling seminars—they get paid by the number of people they put in the seats. Our best salespeople make $300,000 a year. (Laughs.) It's a great job!

So our seminars combined with our planner and retail products have made us a very healthy company. A lot of seminar companies are struggling because they don't have any follow-on revenue after the seminar. So they are always looking for new bodies. Well, we're after new bodies too, but our company breeds itself—it finds new bodies on its own!

Anyway, a lot of people ask, "What do you attribute the success of the firm to?" There are several things. First, we have products that really work, and we guarantee those products. If you don't like the seminar, you get your money back. If you don't like the planner, you get your money back. And we've never had to pay on those guarantees. Fortunately, we have an ageless concept; personal productivity is going to be around as long as people are out of control, and people will always be out of control. (Laughs.)

A second thing is that we've surrounded ourselves with incredible people. I mean, there are now 3,000 stories like Bob Bennett and Arlen Crouch. When we needed a specific talent, the talent was always there. And the way we made the firm attractive to people is by spreading the ownership around. I believe this has been a significant factor in our success. When we were a sub-S corporation we could only have thirty-five owners. For me, the major motivation for going public was to put ownership in the hands of everybody else. We've created over thirty millionaires because of this crazy thing. That's exciting to me, because owners act differently than employees.

> The major motivation for going public was to put ownership in the hands of everybody else. We've created over thirty millionaires because of this crazy thing.

Actually, I can't believe it happened. A lot of people have asked, "Is this something you envisioned?" The fact is, this is a glorious accident. The analogy that paints the best picture is this: You're fighting in a trench with your samurai sword, and you're killing everything you come across. Then every once in a while you get up out of the trench to see where things are going. And we didn't do that very often. I mean, we couldn't even spell strategic planning in the beginning. (Laughs.) We didn't even have financial records the first few years. Talk about gunslingers! Wow! It was scary!

But we've had a real passion for what we are doing. When we get up in front of fifty people and turn them on to this concept, it has a major impact on their lives. There's tremendous passion in that. And somehow we've been able to pass that on to our people. Talk to any of them, and you'll see there's real passion about what they do. People are walking out of our seminar today just as excited as they were ten years ago. Frankly, the principles of human productivity haven't changed for thousands of years. We have fancier devices, we move faster, and we live in fancier caves, but the things that make us productive haven't changed. And we teach people those things.

> My advice to anyone who wants to start a business is to find something you really believe in. In my opinion, financial rewards are always a byproduct of some other success.

My advice to anyone who wants to start a business is to find something you really believe in. In my opinion, financial rewards are always a byproduct of some other success. If you're just in it for the money, it won't last. So find something you feel strongly about, something that makes a difference in people's lives; then make it happen. If you want to do it, you can, no question. The opportunities in this country are better than ever before. And if the passion is there, the money will be there. I guess my passion for personal productivity started when I was young. My mother asked me constantly what I was doing to justify my existence. (Laughs.) She really did! If I wasn't moving, she said, "What are you doing?" "I'm just sitting here." "Well do something to justify your existence!" Man, I heard that a million times.

TIPS FOR BUILDING THE TEAM

1. **ASSESS YOUR OWN STRENGTHS AND WEAKNESSES.**

   Start off by making a list of the things you do well. Then make a list of the business skills you don't have or don't understand. These are the holes you'll eventually need to fill as your company grows.

2. **FIND PEOPLE WITH THE MISSING SKILLS.**

   Take your list of weaknesses and organize them into company roles. Identify people who can fill those roles, even if you don't need or can't afford them right now. Be prepared when you are ready.

3. **FIND PEOPLE WITH A TEAM PERSONALITY.**

   Make sure you hire people with personalities conducive to teamwork. Find players who will harness their egos, help other members excel, and work toward a team success.

4. **CREATE INCENTIVES TO KEEP STRONG PLAYERS.**

   Offer key people attractive monetary incentives: performance bonuses, profit sharing, stock options. Also, provide a host of non-monetary rewards: praise, recognition, tickets, parties, trips, days off, and so on.

5. **FIX CHEMISTRY PROBLEMS AS THEY ARISE.**

   When someone isn't working out, take care of the problem. This will earn you respect from team members and restore balance to the group. Remember, part of being the leader is making the tough decisions.

Chapter • 8

GETTING MORE
FROM LESS

---

*D*ebra Fugal bought a lollipop-making kit in a hobby store for $19.95. *She thought it would be fun to make lollipops in the kitchen with her kids during summer vacation. Her husband, Lowell, told her she would never use the machine more than once or twice. Before long, the kids were selling the colorful lollipops throughout the neighborhood—they were mobbed every time they showed up at the pool with a batch. Then when Lowell's business suffered a setback, he started selling them to candy stores in the area to supplement his income. The family stayed up late at night making batch after batch to meet their orders. That's when the health inspector found them and made them move to a commercial setting. Today, Custom Confections, Inc., located in Boise, Idaho, is a multimillion dollar business, producing nearly 20 million lollipops a year. The company sells the fun-filled treats in the shape of teddy bears, roses, hearts, bunnies, and ice-cream cones to toy stores and other companies nationwide. One of their latest creations, the Worm—a portrayal of the tattoo-covered, cross-dressing Dennis Rodman—has sold to a million fans. And it all started in the family kitchen with a $19.95 lollipop-making kit!*

The Fugals are frugal! Creating a multimillion dollar business from a

$19.95 lollipop-making kit is unbelievable! Funny thing is, their experience is not an exception to the many stories I collected—it's the rule! Most of the entrepreneurs I interviewed started with very little money, grew their business with cash flow, and remained frugal along the way. Simply put, these successful entrepreneurs are not lavish risk-takers.

GOING IN LEAN

In their book *The Millionaire Next Door,* Thomas Stanley and William Danko review twenty years of research on America's wealthiest individuals. The first time they interviewed people worth at least $10 million, they rented a posh suite on Manhattan's east side. They served four patés, three kinds of caviar, and several vintage wines. To their surprise, these decamillionaires drove up in ordinary cars wearing ordinary clothes—and not one touched the food. Hundreds of interviews later, Stanley and Danko report their surprising findings: most millionaires live in modest homes, drive average cars, wear common clothes, and own ordinary businesses. They've made their money from hard work, perseverance, and self-discipline. The word that describes them best is *frugal!* They've learned one of life's most important lessons: wealth is a function of living below your means, not total income. As the authors point out, people with incredible salaries who live extravagant lifestyles are some of the poorest people in America.

These findings describe our entrepreneurs to a tee! Rather than risk large amounts of money, they figure out how to do things with limited resources. I was shocked at how many of these multimillion dollar businesses were started with little or no capital. Here are a few examples: Rick McCloskey, founder of Systems Connection, started his business in a one-bedroom basement apartment. He bought computer cables for $6 wholesale and sold them for around $15—most retail stores were selling them for $30 plus. He worked on a desk made of particle board and cardboard boxes and stored his inventory under the kitchen table, in the living room, and in the closets. At the end of the day, Rick would load his orders on the back of his wife's moped—their only vehicle—and head down to the post office. A few years later, Systems Connection had more than 100 employees and $20 million in sales. Likewise, Teresa McBride, whom you met briefly in chapter 2, started her $100-million-plus consulting business on a bootlace budget. She turned her home into an office for half a dozen people; the hallway was the receiving area, her garage the shipping dock. Being short on space, she met clients in a local restaurant—the waitress would cue them up for her throughout the day. Even Jon Huntsman, in the capital-intensive petrochemical business, bought his first polystyrene plant with a down payment of $500,000—the plant cost $42 million. The executives at Shell Oil Company nearly tossed him out of the office when he first proposed the deal. But as Jon explains, "I was able to string together the most unique financing arrangement ever concocted. It was literally hooked together with chewing gum and bailing wire."

Going in lean has real advantages. First, you find out if your venture works before making major financial commitments. Take the Fugals' lollipop business: They spent little on equipment, worked out of their home, built a decent clientele, and proved the business worked before going to the next level. Only then did Lowell rent commercial space and leave his former business. If they had borrowed money, purchased equipment, leased a plant, and hired employees right from the first, they would have experienced enormous pressure to perform. If they didn't move truckloads of lollipops, they would have had a financial nightmare. As it turned out, they risked only their time. A second advantage of starting lean is that you have a lower cost structure than your competitors in the industry—fewer expenses and no debt. This allows you to sell at lower prices and quickly pick up market share. Rick McCloskey sold a zillion computer cables because they were half the market price. If you gradually bring your prices closer to market, your profits increase considerably, which provides other luxuries: You can offer attractive salaries, spend more on product development, and build cash to fund growth.

While we can praise our entrepreneurs for these insights, most of them developed their frugality out of necessity—they didn't have any money! Many of these folks contacted banks initially but were turned down. A common line I heard was, "Banks only loan you money when you don't need it." Blessed with bank rejection, these entrepreneurs had to finagle to get open and consequently learned an important lesson: You can make things happen even if you don't have a lot of money! This awareness fosters creativity in problem-solving, which serves the business well down the road. This is a talent business executives, community leaders, and politicians would do well to cultivate!

Of course, some will quarrel that you can't take advantage of windows of opportunity if you are undercapitalized, which may be true with some businesses. But why would you want to rush into an industry with a short life cycle? The truth is, just as many "adequately" capitalized companies fail as those that are cash strapped. Many would-be entrepreneurs write marvelous business plans and raise a bunch of money only to rent office suites, lease phone systems, buy mahogany desks, pay themselves salaries, and hire helpers—all before they have final products, customers, sales, cash flow, and profits—have money, spend money! In other words, they create a splendid illusion of a company, then have to "jack it up" and put a business underneath it. And here's the challenge: New ventures often take longer, cost more, and earn less than anyone imagined. So if you have to achieve your best-case scenario to succeed, you've got trouble! While you may produce a "business" success eventually, you won't enjoy a "financial" success if the capital meter ticks indefinitely without revenue. Yet it happens all the time! A company I met with recently spent millions of dollars over a decade trying to create a state-of-the-art technology. While reviewing their history, I discovered they had a marketable version of the product during their second year of funding. Had they introduced this product, it could have produced the revenue needed to support their ongoing development. But they had money . . .

In contrast, the entrepreneurs I interviewed created a product or service they could take to market immediately—even if it wasn't what they wanted to sell long-term—then used their cash flow to figure out where to go next. Remember how Joe Montgomery of Cannondale wanted to produce bicycles all along but lacked the capital for equipment. His solution? He started selling bike accessories, some of which were stitched in a basement. But it produced revenue and got him into the industry. Also, Jon Huntsman had real success running his first few plants by taking them out of the R & D mode they had been in for years and putting tangible products into the marketplace. This strategy has helped him to pay off debt quickly with every new plant he has purchased.

So, many of our entrepreneurs created something from practically nothing. This gave them competitive advantages and fostered an efficient mindset. Hence, the age-old adage "Don't go in undercapitalized" may not always hold true. Going in overcapitalized may be just as big a problem—you spend money you don't need to, which puts you in a hole early. Being short on dough, our entrepreneurs quickly and creatively developed products or services, then focused on generating revenue. They found a handful of customers, received market feedback, and tweaked their products as they went along—all while keeping their overhead low. The lessons for wanna-be entrepreneurs are many: Don't fall into the capital trap! Money is not the solution to every problem! Think how you might do things differently! Focus on making sales! Produce a small success early and use it as a springboard to other things! In sum, the entrepreneurs I interviewed who started out on metal desks in basements are like the millionaires in Stanley and Danko's book. They may not look like they have much, but they really do. On the other hand, high rollers who start on mahogany desks in fancy offices may look like they have a lot, but they often don't.

STAYING LEAN
AS STANDARD PROCEDURE

Not only did our entrepreneurs start off lean, but they also continued to practice frugality during their growth stages. They fine-tuned their products, built a loyal clientele, and produced profit in their core business before moving to the next level. For example, they didn't open ten stores until the first one was working well; they didn't schedule twenty seminars until the first one was a hit; they didn't lease five helicopters until the first one was fully booked; and they didn't sell dozens of franchises until the first few paid off. Put simply, they didn't make commitments to become big until they were successful being small. So they proved each step before taking the next step. And since most of them funded their growth with cash flow, there was never much risk of losing big. Granted, some will argue that you can't grow as fast that way. True, but the growth is sound! Over time, many of our entrepreneurs caught up with and even surpassed competitors that grew more rapidly, because they were built upon a stronger foundation. In the next chapter you'll see how these folks continue to notch things upward and onward as they enjoy success and gain more confidence at each plateau.

In addition to controlled, conservative growth, our entrepreneurs exercise frugality in their basic operations. Again, some of this stems from a lack of resources. Nonetheless, many of these entrepreneurs are masters of efficiency, getting the most out of every dollar they spend. Here's an analogy I like to use: Suppose your goal is to eliminate a killer bee that's buzzing around your kitchen. One strategy is to get your sledgehammer and whack away; another is to use a flyswatter; a third is to simply open the door. While all three strategies accomplish the goal, they range from costly to efficient: the sledgehammer damages walls and tables, the flyswatter is standard practice, and opening the door is the most efficient. As simple as this analogy is, our entrepreneurs learn to open doors. They figure out the most efficient way to achieve objectives and solve problems.

We learned this strategy at Golden Swirl out of necessity. We needed to bring people into our stores quickly but had little cash the first few years. We looked at the traditional media—radio, TV, print— and realized the costs were high and the response rates low. For example, the typical weekend radio campaign might run $10,000, reach

100,000 people, and produce a 1-percent response rate. This would put 1,000 people in our stores for $10,000—a cost of $10 per person. If you're having a weekend automobile sale this would be a great return since your average profit per car might be several hundred dollars. But we were selling $2.00 cups of frozen dessert! A thousand buying customers would never come close to paying the cost of the promotion. So we racked our brains to figure out other ways to bring people to our stores. We soon learned we could produce a 20-percent response rate by distributing coupons at schools, health clubs, races, and other businesses. We could thus attract 1,000 people to our stores with 5,000 coupons, and the only cost was the printing. Now our cost per buying customer was a few cents rather than ten bucks. It didn't take rocket scientists . . . So with every challenge, we learned to ask, "How can we do this with fewer resources?" There are always ways!

Unfortunately, many companies, particularly large corporations, use sledgehammers to achieve objectives and solve problems. Throwing lots of money at things seems to be standard procedure, even though there are other ways to get things done. I recently met with an advertising executive who told me that some clients spend millions of dollars with prestigious firms only to have the project done by a couple of guys on a computer. These firms then have to wait to submit the work so it doesn't look too easy and inexpensive. Interestingly, several of the entrepreneurs I interviewed admitted falling off the frugality bandwagon after enjoying success. When they finally had cash they got "fat in their thinking" and starting spending like everyone else. Seeing the folly of their ways, they went back to getting more for less—the strategy that produced their success in the first place. It's funny how our greatest errors are often committed during our periods of triumph. How important it is to maintain humility and frugality during all phases of business growth and development.

Here are three masters at getting more for less. Robin Petgrave launched his flight school with $300. He convinced another company to waive its $6,000 deposit, rented one of their helicopters for $67 an hour, then charged his students $105. Debra Charatan started her commercial real-estate company in New York with $2,000 she borrowed from a friend in the industry. She managed to finagle a free office in a prestigious location as part of the deal. And Jonathan Altman capitalized his pasta-making company well below industry levels by buying used equipment and delivering products in his Volkswagen Rabbit. For nearly ten years before moving into a 42,000-square-foot production facility, he made pasta in his barn in Vermont.

OUR ROLE MODELS

Robin Petgrave

Robin is the founder of Bravo Helicopters of Torrance, California. He started the company in 1991 with virtually no money, then used creative, low-cost marketing strategies to find customers. Today, with fifteen helicopters, fourteen airplanes, and nearly sixty employees, he operates one of the top flight schools and charter-tour companies in the country. He says:

I came to America from Jamaica when I was ten years old. Right off I got into learnin' how this country works. I'm basically a people watcher. I always want to know "why." I quickly learned that America was a different way of life. In Jamaica, I was a very bad kid. I used to lie, steal, and beat up kids. My family wasn't all that great—my father ran off and left my mom and all that stuff. We had no money, and when you're poor you just don't have the luxuries you do otherwise. I mean, when your biggest concern is how you're going to eat, you don't have time to think about, "Oh, did I hurt this guy's feelings?"

So when I came here, everybody seemed so soft. I was like—whoa! I felt like I was takin' advantage of everybody. I mean, the kids couldn't fight. The first time I got into a fight and beat this kid up, everybody yelled at me because I didn't fight fair. I was like, "You have rules for fighting? Man!" So I had to take a step back and see how this place worked. It made me crazy when I didn't understand something.

This big curiosity is something I've always had, even as a little kid in

Jamaica. You know when you see a bus go one way, then you see a bus go the other way? Well, I always wondered, is it the same bus? How did it turn around? Did somethin' pick it up, turn it around, and put it back down on the ground so it could go the other way? Did they switch drivers? Did the people get off? I always wanted to follow it to the end of the line just to see what happened. I spent a whole summer one time in Jamaica scroungin' up enough money to take this bus the whole way 'cause I wanted to see where it went.

So when I came to this country, that's one of the things I did in elementary school and junior high. I used to take my lunch money and get on the bus to see where it went. I'd have a certain amount of money, go a certain distance, then turn around and come back. Then I'd find out that that bus connected to another bus or a train that went someplace else. I was like, "Whoa, where did that go?" So I used to do that all the time, and I went further and further and further.

One day I wound up at Logan Airport in Boston. I saw these jets taking off and thought, "Cool!" Big thing sittin' there, all these people coming and going, everybody's hugging. I thought it was the coolest thing ever! Then I saw a helicopter come in, and everything stopped—the whole world stopped! I was watching this thing come down and thinking, "How's it going to move around?" It hovered for a minute, landed, all these people got out, then it took off. I was like, "Now that's cool. The airplane guys think they're cool, but this is totally cool!" That was my first experience with a helicopter.

Anyway, I really got into sports while I was in high school. I played softball, baseball, hockey. I was an East Coast champion in karate and a national-class runner. I also got into acting and started doing commercials, TV shows, and modeling. So I did a lot of stuff. All along, my career counselor kept asking me, "What do you want to be when you grow up?" I'm like, "I don't know. I'd like to be a cop, but they get shot, so that's no fun." Then one day I asked him, "What about flying helicopters? Can I do that?" And he goes, "Well, let's see." So he did some research and found a company with a helicopter and arranged for me to go with 'em for a whole day.

So I showed up there and flew on their helicopter, I mean, everything just stopped! I was totally blown away! I was like, "This is it, man! Now I know what I want to do!" So at the end of the day I asked the guy flying, "How do I do this?" And the guy's like, "Well, you have to go through the military. I did two tours in Vietnam." I was like, "I don't want to do that. Police get shot, but army guys get shot even more." Plus, I didn't think I could take being bossed around in the army. I'm very strong willed. If somebody tells me to do something, I automatically don't want to do it, even if it's for my own good and even if I was going to do it anyway. That's just my nature. So when this guy was telling me all this stuff, I was like, "Okay, forget that." I pictured some little army weenie in my face telling me all this stuff, and the only brains he had on me was he joined the army sooner. That wouldn't cut it with me. I'd wind up beating him up and goin' to jail.

So anyways, I went to college in Connecticut on a track scholarship. I studied acting and minored in communication. I never went near a business course. I thought you had to be really smart to do that kind of stuff. I also thought you had to sit down behind a desk all day. That's what my impression of business was, and it wasn't for me. I figured since I was already acting anyway, I might as well major in it.

During this time I was training for the '84 Olympics. I went home for spring break because I had a part in a film there, and the camera truck ran over me and punched a hole in my leg. It put me in the hospital for ten days. I was supposed to be there a month, but after ten days, I'm like, "I've got to leave. I'm not going to miss a semester of school 'cause I'm in the hospital. This is stupid!" So as soon as I got on crutches, I left the hospital against their request. I went back to college and started running again. I still did pretty well, but it wasn't the same. I went to the Olympic trials anyway but didn't do well. There was really nothing I could do about that. Looking at my times before the accident, I would have placed third in the '84 games.

When I got out of college I went to New York to act. Most of the stuff I did came from California. So my logic was, if I want to get one of these huge, huge parts, I'm in the wrong place. I eventually moved to L.A. and started doin' pretty well. After I'd been there a while, I went back to New York on a trip with some friends of mine. While we were there, we went on a helicopter ride. The guy that was flying was about my age, and I was like, "Cool man. You must have joined the army when you were young." He says, "No. I just paid for lessons." And I was like, "You can do that?" He says, "Yeah." I was like, "How come no one ever told me that?" I figured if this guy could do it, I could definitely do it!

So I came back to California, looked in the phone book for flight schools, and started taking lessons. Within a year, I got my license. From that time on, everything stopped: the acting, the sports, all that stuff. I thought those things were nice, but flying was much better. You know what it was? I used to dream I was some kind of superhero who figured out something nobody else in the world had figured out. If I dove at the ground with my arms back and had total faith and didn't flinch, I would defy gravity and start to fly. The reason nobody else had figured it out was because they all flinched. When they flinched, it showed a lack of faith, and they were subject to the laws of gravity. Sometimes, I'd get so close to the ground my skin was almost touching, but if I had total faith and didn't flinch, I would start to fly. Of course, I never really tried it; these were just dreams! But almost every night, I'd be flying around saving people and doing all this Superman stuff. In the morning I was like, "Man! That was cool!" But once I had my first lesson in the helicopter, the dreams stopped. I haven't dreamt them since because I started doing it every day. I mean, what I'm doing now beats working for a living.

Anyway, when I got out of flight school, it took two weeks to find a job teaching. I did that for about a year and a half until my boss and I got into a disagreement. He thought maintenance was an option and wanted me to fly a helicopter that was having some problems. I wouldn't do it! So to show me who was boss, he grounded the helicopter for four days to do an inspection that normally takes half a day. It was basically to punish me so I couldn't work. At the time, I was having serious financial trouble and only had three hundred bucks. I was like, "Okay, let's see what we can do."

So I went and talked to a company that leased helicopters that had been after me. You know, "Why don't you think about starting a school or somethin'? We have these helicopters, and we could lease you one." I'm like, "Well, I don't have any money, and you've got to have money to do these things." So when my boss grounded me, I went to see 'em. Normally, you had to pay a $6,000 deposit and guarantee 'em eighty hours a month. If you didn't fly eighty hours, you had to pay for it anyway. I was like, "There's no way I can do that." And the guy goes, "I'll tell you what; we'll be nice to you because we've seen how much you fly. You don't have to give us the $6,000 deposit, and you only have to pay when you fly." I'm like, "Okay, that's painless. What do I have to lose?" And within four days, I opened up a flight school right next door.

So I started leasing the helicopter and just paid for the time I used it. The leasing company was charging me $67 an hour, and I was charging people $105. That was just for the flight time, not the instruction. With the difference, I had to pay for fuel, the advertisements, the computer, the building. After all the expenses were taken out, I was making about five dollars an hour off the helicopter. This is pretty much the way all businesses work. When you buy something in the store, you're not gettin' it for what it costs; you're paying five different parties along the way: the guy who owns the land, the guy who picks the thing, the guy who washes it, the guy who does the packaging, the guy who sells it, the guy who tells you it's in the store, and the guy who owns the store. That's why some things are so expensive.

Anyway, my first customers came with me from the other flight school.

I called the newspapers and said, "We're thinking about putting an ad in the paper, but you guys have to do a story on us first." And they were like, "Okay, tell us about your company." So we did a lot of stuff like that—it was all very cost-effective advertising.

I didn't badmouth the guy, but the students knew what was going on. I have certain standards, and I didn't want to jeopardize people's safety, especially when I was in the helicopter with them. They respected the fact that I stood up for that. I think I also train people really well. I'm not the smartest guy in the world; I'm not the best pilot in the world; I'm not the best instructor in the world. But I do know how to get people to do things well. I can't make someone the best pilot in the world, but I can make them the best pilot they can possibly be. And so I had a pretty big following, and when people found out I was doing this, they came with me.

I also started advertising right off. I had a different theory on this whole flight school. The other schools were doing very little advertising. They put a few signs outside their buildings and waited for people to find them. I kept thinking, "This is absolutely amazing! If I wanted to learn to fly a helicopter and kept driving by this street but never looked over, I wouldn't know this place was here." So the first thing I did was make some flyers. You know, "Bravo Helicopters, blah, blah, blah." At the time, there was an air show at Hawthorne Airport, and I was trying to figure out how to get the helicopter over there because I didn't have the money. So I had a student fly over for a lesson, then brought him back in my car. Now the helicopter was there all day. So I'm standing there passing out stuff: "Hi, I'm Robin. I teach people to fly." Well, the newspaper came by and took a picture of me, and all of a sudden everybody started calling. So I'm going, "Ummm, this is interesting. If we're good guys, the newspapers will write about us and more people will call."

So we started doing things to get the public's attention: we went to air shows, we did a lot of community things, and I always sent out press releases. I also called the newspapers and said, "We're thinking about putting an ad in the paper, but you guys have to do a story on us first." And they were like, "Okay, tell us about your company." So we did a lot of stuff like that—it was all very-cost effective advertising. And we grew from one helicopter and me to five helicopters and other pilots.

During this whole time, I never raised any money or went into debt. I started off with $300, spent $70 on a business license and the rest on business cards and flyers. What I did was set it up so people paid for things before they got them. And while they were paying for things, we used the money. So I just kept jugglin'. As it turned out, we took in $18,000 our first month, so things started off really well. Then about a year after leasing the five helicopters, we bought our first helicopter. It cost $117,000.

So we've just kept advertising, and we've kept growing. Right now we're getting pretty big. We're one of the best flight schools in the world. We're considered a vocational school, so we can do V.A. funding and non-immigrant visas. We have fifteen helicopters on our fleet and nearly sixty employees. We've also done a lot of aerial photography, and we're just gettin' into movies. It's funny how flying has gotten me back into acting. All of a sudden I'm a rare commodity: a fairly good-looking black guy who can act and fly a helicopter pretty good. I just did the movie *Broken Arrow* with John Travolta, Christian Slater, and Howie Long. So people are starting to jump on that.

We've also grown into a tour and charter business. We pick people up in one of our limousines, bring 'em down to the airport, fly 'em around Los Angeles, land 'em at a restaurant, then drive 'em back home in the limousine. We also do things with the studios. We fly people where they want to go and charge 'em by the hour. In addition, we help scope out locations. Basically, we do anything anybody wants. You tell us what you need, and we'll do it. As I said, we did $18,000 our first month; now we do that much in a couple of days. We'll do over three million this year.

I don't know what the American dream is (laughs), but I'm livin' mine. And other people can live theirs, too. Starting a company just isn't that hard. I mean, if you had asked me about this when I was in high school or college, I would have thought "impossible." But now I look at the whole formula, and it isn't that difficult. If somebody wants to start a business, I can tell them how to do it. (Laughs.) And you don't have to have a lot of money. I mean, people call me up, "Hey man, I like what you're doing. I want to start a helicopter company too. Do I have to buy a helicopter?" I'm like, "No! There's a lot of people with more money than you'll ever have who own a lot of stuff they're not usin'. So just tell 'em, 'Hey dude, let me use this for ya. I'll pay you somethin' when I use it. It's no money out of your pocket.' So if you want to try somethin', just go ahead and do it."

Then when you're getting started, I think it's real important to listen to other people. Tell 'em about your idea and hear what they have to say. When they tell you why you can or can't do something, listen to the reasons. You're always going to get both sides of the coin. They'll give you two good reasons why something will work and about ten reasons why it won't: "You're going to hate this." "You're not going to have any days off." "You're going to be a slave." I think you need to know the downside factors and prepare for 'em, but don't take 'em to heart. If you believe all the negative things people say, you'll never start anything. Just because this guy had a terrible time or that guy went bankrupt doesn't mean that you're going to. Learn why it happened, then make sure it doesn't happen to you.

I really think you make life what you choose to make it. You have to decide what you want, then do the things to achieve it. That doesn't mean you have complete control over everything. I got run over by a truck, and it wasn't my fault. It was just one of those things that happen. So you can't control everything, but when you face a tough situation, don't sit there and say, "Life sucks because I'm not gettin' what I want." You take the best of what you've got and make something happen!

Debrah Charatan

Debrah is the founder and president of Debrah Lee Charatan Realty, a brokerage firm that sells commercial real estate throughout Manhattan. Debrah started her first company in 1980 when she was twenty-three years old. At the time, it was the first and only woman-owned commercial real-estate company in New York. Debrah has sold more than 1,200 notable properties during her career. Here's her story:

I grew up in Howard Beach, a middle-class area of Queens. My parents were survivors of the holocaust, and we didn't have a lot of money. My first entrepreneurial experience occurred when I was seven. I used to go to the candy store, but instead of being fascinated with the candy, I was fascinated with the store. I wanted to know where they got their inventory and how they made money.

By the time I was ten, I was babysitting every day after school, often till 11:00 P.M. I also tutored two kids in math, which paid $5 an hour. Relatively speaking, I was making a lot of money. I really liked it. I needed to be independent, and money gave me freedom. I could go into a store and buy whatever I wanted. This was the beginning of my entrepreneurial spirit.

When I was fourteen I got a job in a bakery. This had a major effect on my life. I learned how to work, how to run a business, and how to make money. I worked there forty-plus hours a week while I was simultaneously going to high school. I worked every day after school, then ten to twelve hours every Saturday and Sunday. I started off making $1.85 an hour and left there making $3.50 an hour. I worked for a tyrant, but he taught me many important lessons. If a bottle of milk would fit in a #3 shopping bag and I put it in a #5 bag—which cost perhaps a tenth of a cent more—he would go crazy. He taught me how to be a good worker, and eventually I was opening up the store in the morning and closing it at night. As a result, I developed a lot of confidence there as a young kid.

When I graduated from high school I wanted to work in the big city. Unfortunately, the first question everybody asked a girl lookin' for a job in 1974 was, "Can you type?" Guess what? I couldn't! I was very proud of my experience, but no one was really interested in my job at the bakery. Eventually I was offered a three-day job at a real-estate company writing invitations to a party. I said to myself, "I've got three days to show them how good I am, and hopefully then they'll hire me." That's exactly what happened. They paid me $115 a week, which was not much back then; my take-home was $82.47. Nevertheless, I had a job, and I wanted to learn. My employer was Martin J. Raynes. He was twenty-nine, gorgeous, and rich. He had a chauffeur and lived a New York jet-set lifestyle, which I had never seen before. I liked it! This was my first year of college. I was going to school in the morning and staying at the office until nine at night. I did whatever it took. During the next six months, I realized I loved the opportunity and decided to work days and go to school at night.

Soon thereafter, the woman who managed our properties decided to leave the company. She was responsible for a thousand apartments in New York; I was doing the secretarial work. They didn't consider me for the position because I was only eighteen, but I decided to ask anyway. I told my boss I believed I was well qualified because I had been de facto doing the job. I asked him to give me a chance and told him he could fire me if I failed. He gave me a shot. I got a raise to $200 a week; now my take-home was $143.05; I remember it vividly because it was nothing. Nevertheless, I managed these thousand apartments and learned so much. I was still going to college at night because I wanted to finish my degree.

I worked there for five years before I got bored with my responsibilities—it just wasn't challenging anymore. During this time, I had picked up my broker's license. I decided to try commercial real estate. I was offered a job for $25,000, which seemed like a lot of money at the time—especially for a woman. I took the job and learned the side of real estate that I still do today. Even though I was paid a salary, I did a lot of the same things commissioned brokers do: I found tenants, negotiated deals, and managed projects. I was very much a self-starter; I felt very capable and did a good job.

> I needed a lot of things that I couldn't afford, but that didn't stop me.

During that year I came in touch with some unimpressive brokers who were nevertheless walking out with $50,000 commission checks. I was making $500 a week. I said to myself, "If they can do this, I can do it!" Until this point in my life, I was a very salary-focused person. The idea of commission was frightening to me. Nevertheless, when my employer offered to switch me to commission, I said to myself, "Why do I need you if I work for nothing? I can work for myself." I simultaneously went into the marketplace and investigated other brokerage firms. I felt I could do better on my own.

I decided to open my own business and determined I would sell buildings. It was 1980 and I was twenty-three years old. I didn't understand that nobody in New York operated a business that just sold buildings, because they didn't believe you could make a living doing it. Most management companies managed buildings for owners. This was their bread and butter. If they ever sold a building, it was their gravy. But I felt I could do it. I didn't have any money, so I asked someone in the business to loan me $2,000, which he did. The same friend gave me a room in the basement of his building at 48th and Madison. I was at 18th East 48th Street, which was a substantial address—and I got the room for free! I needed a lot of other things that I couldn't afford, but that didn't stop me. I borrowed a desk, I borrowed a typewriter. There was a book I needed called the *Owners' Book,* which listed all the people who owned buildings. I had to have it, but it cost a thousand dollars a year to rent. I copied it by hand. I got a telephone, stationery, and a typing service, and I was in business. I hoped I could sell something quick before the money ran out. Unfortunately, I didn't have anyone to support me.

I opened up in May of 1980. I started calling people from the *Owner's Book* and asking them if they wanted to sell their building. These were all cold calls. "Hi, I'm Debrah Charatan, I'm calling . . ." Women didn't do that at the time, so people would always ask, "Are you working for your husband or your father?"

After about 200 calls someone said yes. I place a $21 ad in the *New York Times.* People started calling, and I'm in business. Instead of trying to sell them that building, I asked them what they were looking for. I made my first deal in four months and made $4,375. I paid back the $2,000, and I was in the black. So I made my first deal in September, two deals in October, and another deal in December—$20,000 commissions, $40,000 commissions.

In October of that year, I moved upstairs to the tenth floor. Now I had 300 square feet. I hired a part-time high-school kid to come in half a day to be my secretary. I started hiring people. I asked myself, "How can I be different from everyone else?" When you don't have any money you have to be different; otherwise, you don't get anybody's attention. I decided to hire all women so I would stick out.

The timing was perfect! The real-estate market was booming, and I just walked into it. I earned my first $100,000 when I was twenty-four. Then it just took off! Someone wrote an article about me, and before I knew it, I was on every television station. I became well known and well respected in the industry. Everybody knew my name, and everybody wanted me to sell their buildings. Things mushroomed. I made my first million dollars when I was twenty-six. It was unbelievable!

In 1983 I expanded further. I took the whole second floor in the building. At my apex, I had thirty-five people working for me. I had $200 million in sales. What we were doing was unheard of, but it was wonderful and exciting. I won a number of awards: Woman of the Year, Working Woman of the Year, Business Owner of the Year. I even met President Reagan.

Inevitably, then it crashed! The Tax Reform Act of '86 started the decline. The stock market crash in '87 accelerated it. We also had a lot more competition. By the late eighties, everybody was going out of business, including us. It was a very rough time.

I've now started over, and it's very good again. I have a dozen associates, and we still sell commercial real estate. Many companies that left with us are slowly coming back into the market. As a result, the competition's heating up again. It's an easy business to open because it's not capital intensive. We face a lot of challenges every day, but we work hard to resolve them. My function in the office is to close all the deals. My associates do the legwork, and I finish things up. I do over two deals a week right now. So I've had some real ups and downs during my career, but I take full responsibility for both. I never blame my problems on someone else. I think that's a real key to being happy, well adjusted, and in control of your life.

> Early on I realized that selling is simply meeting people's needs. If I help people get what they want, I'll get what I want.

One philosophy has helped me succeed over the years. Early on I realized that selling is simply meeting people's needs. If I help people get what they want, I'll get what I want. If I make my clients happy, they'll make me happy. Today, I'm very happy.

Jonathan Altman

Jonathan and his wife, Carol Berry, are the founders of Putney Pasta Company. They started the business in a renovated horse barn on their dream property in Vermont. This allowed them to live in the country and *stay home with their two-year-old son. Initially, Jonathan delivered his wares to their first customers in his Volkswagen Rabbit. Today, Putney Pasta employees around forty people and exceeds $5 million in annual sales.*

I grew up in the food-manufacturing business. When my grandfather came to this country, he started a plant that manufactured deli products. Nathan Handwerker's business ultimately became Nathan's Famous of Coney Island. So the original Coney Island Hotdog was made by my family.

In the mid '70s I moved from New York to Vermont because I wanted to live in the country. I was committed to making the experience work, but the employment possibilities were not very strong. I had a host of jobs. I sold automobiles, I sold beautiful timber frame houses, I even fed people at rock-and-roll concerts. That was a business I did with Carol's brother. Historically, the feeders at these shows were large canteen operations, and we were just a couple of kids. But we had this notion that concert promoters would charge us less money up front if we gave them a bigger percent of our profits. So we did that for a brief while.

We finally realized we had to take some proactive steps in order to maintain our country lifestyle—which we absolutely loved! I ended up commuting to New York to attend the New York Restaurant School. I didn't want to start a restaurant because they depend on the traffic that goes by your front door. And the traffic here is not that great—that's why I moved here in the first place! But I figured I could use the location as a springboard to sell a product. As it turned out, an instructor at the school really influenced my thinking. He owned a wholesale bakery in New York City and took me under his wing. He showed me his business from the inside, and it was absolutely fascinating! So as time went on, Carol and I knew we wanted to manufacture some food stuff. We could stay in Vermont and sell the product down-country. That way we wouldn't be subject to the vagaries and vicissitudes of the tourist trade.

Concurrent with this, Carol and I finally found the piece of property we'd been searching for for five years. It was a beautiful, forty-acre parcel on a private road. The woman who owned it used to raise racehorses, so it had a new horse barn on it. We bought the property with the intent of razing the barn to build our house. We were three weeks away from digging a hole and starting construction when the woman next door decided to sell her home. She was a recent divorcee who felt the social opportunities in Vermont were lacking. Knowing we had purchased the land next door, she asked if we knew anybody who might want to buy her house. Her house turned out to be everything we wanted, so we bought it and moved in. Now, in order to keep the first piece of property, we had to figure out a way to generate some income. I realized we were sitting on a potential opportunity. I had a septic system, a well producing tremendous amounts of glorious water, and a 1,600-foot horse barn. And it's a magnificent spot! It sits on a hillside overlooking a private valley. From the ridge, we have the most beautiful color show you can imagine. We decided right then and there we would put my New York schooling to work—we would turn that building into a small food-processing plant!

So Carol and I sat down and made a very objective list of what we wanted this food stuff to be. We only had to examine our own lives to see what our needs were. We were two young people starting a family, faced with the possibility of having to both work long hours. Yet we wanted to be responsible to our two-year-old son; we wanted to feed him wholesome, nutritious foods that were easy and convenient to prepare. So as we went down our list, we realized that pasta suited our purposes very well. We knew we could make a clean product, one without additives or preservatives, which was of paramount importance to us. So we were going into the pasta business.

I wish I could tell you that all the recipes for our products were handed down from generation to generation, but growing up in the delicatessen business, I didn't have a long list of Italian pasta recipes. We realized, however, that the rest of the industry was making very traditional products: a meat product, a cheese product, a tomato sauce, an Alfredo sauce—just very basic fare. So we saw what appeared to be a niche or void in the market, which was unique, specialty fillings—something nobody else was doing. A friend of ours with a cooking background came to work for us part-time. The three of us knocked our heads together and came up with certain flavor combinations: three-cheese tortellini, spinach-

and-walnut-filled tortellini, mushroom-and-Gruyere-cheese-filled tortellini, garlic-and-herb-filled raviolini. And given the fact that we were manufacturing in Vermont, we took an aged, extra-sharp Vermont cheddar cheese and mixed it with walnuts to make a cheddar-and-walnut-filled raviolini. It was great! So that was basically our line.

We also decided we were going to sell our products frozen rather than refrigerated—the reason being, refrigerated products had to be pasteurized or heat-treated in order to have an extended shelf life. Once we began tasting the products in the marketplace, we realized that a pasteurized product was inferior to a truly fresh product or one that had been flash-frozen. So early on we dug in our heels and decided to make a flash-frozen product.

I should backtrack a little bit. When we realized this was what we wanted to do, we raised a very modest amount of money. It was a family loan for around $30,000. What we did was hire a couple of local nail-bangers and doubled the size of our barn—from 1,600 to 3,200 square

> We just picked up anything we could find; it was amazing how much equipment we got for so little money.

feet. And in the New England tradition, we just kept adding onto it over time. We ultimately ended up with about 4,000 square feet. At the same time, I started shopping around for used equipment. A friend of mine was moving his office-feeding company from New York to New Jersey. They were upgrading a lot of their equipment and allowed me to take anything I wanted for a nominal amount of money. So overnight I had stainless-steel tables, an old Garland stove, and a whole host of support equipment. I also went to a lot of used restaurant equipment places around the Bowery in Manhattan. I would buy a Hobart mixer in one place, a commercial sink in another, load them in my pickup truck, and drive up to Vermont. Then I'd head back down and buy some more.

Shortly thereafter, I contacted a manufacturer of pasta equipment. They sold us a modest machine that made noodles. I think the whole thing cost $10,000 brand spanking new. Although it was a lot of money, I soon learned it was not a lot for pasta-making equipment. Anyway, the manu-facturer's rep told us about a small facility in Jersey that was upgrading its equipment, and overnight we had two little tortellini machines and a machine that made raviolini—which is a little tiny ravioli. So we just picked up anything we could find; it was amazing how much equipment we got for so little money. And I have to say, we didn't pay ourselves much money during this time—we still don't today. Our main priority has always been to keep this company healthy and sound because it's our long-range nest egg. So the money went a long way!

Before long, we were making pasta. In the early days, we put it in a bag and heat-sealed it with one of those "seal-a-meal" things. We put a pressure-sensitive label on it, and out the door it went. Back then, we had to sell 200 pounds of pasta every week to pay the overhead. We kept thinking, "Where are we going to go to find someone to buy 200 pounds of pasta?" Well, I went out looking. At the time, I was driving a Volkswagen Rabbit, and on a real good day I had to take the back seat out to fit a second cooler in there—that was our delivery truck for the first year or two. So we'd produce the product and freeze it, and I'd drive around looking for sales. Our first two customers were the Putney General Store and the Putney Co-op. We used to sell them noodles and frozen filled pastas.

Soon thereafter, we moved upward and onward and bought a van that had been converted into a camper. I bought a commercial chest freezer and removed the lid because there wasn't enough height to open it in the camper. I took a piece of styrene insulation board and laid it across the top of the freezer to keep it cold. Every night I would back the van up, plug the freezer into a 110 outlet, chill it down, and stuff it with pasta. The next day I would take off and deliver my wares. That worked for a while; then we bought an eight-foot delivery truck that had just come off lease—we bought it for a song. I still own it today because I've had a hard time parting with it. So basically I'd sell three days a week and deliver two.

It didn't take long to pass the 200-pounds-a-week mark. There was a whole host of small general stores, natural food stores, and independently owned markets that were willing to carry our pastas. Then we picked up two natural-foods distributors that started selling our products throughout northern New England. Essentially, I was broadening my sales staff by working with their sales forces. This became my major focus during this period of growth. I would find a distributor, train their people at new-product meetings, preach the gospel according to Putney Pasta, then spend weeks at a time calling on their customers. I'd get up at five in the morning, cook all these different pastas, put them into beautiful salads, take them from account to account, and put them in people's mouths. Once they tasted our products, the sales were not that difficult.

A big break came for us about ten years ago. We went to a natural-foods trade show and came home with national distribution. Prior to this, the natural-foods industry was still in its infancy. Even though health-food stores had been around forever, the infrastructure for distribution was not in place. As the industry came of age, the stronger players started buying out the weaker players. Suddenly there were fewer but much larger companies in the industry. Eventually we gained a presence with all of them.

To summarize our growth, we did about $10,000 our first year, which was 1983. This year we'll exceed $5 million. We're now selling products from Bermuda to Hawaii. We sell through two primary channels: retail, which is general stores, natural-food stores, and supermarket chains; and food service, which is restaurants, hotels, and other types of feeding establishments. We have a whole host of both types of accounts, so we're doing very well. For the most part, we've financed our growth with the success we've had. Everything we've made has gone right back into the business, either to buy more equipment or to hire new employees. Carol and I have continued to draw relatively small salaries.

A few years ago we moved our manufacturing facility off our land. We now have about 42,000 square feet. We'd been searching for a new home, and we came across an old kiln-drying operation for fine furniture. It not only gave us more space, it solved the problems of manufacturing down a long dirt road. I could tell some wonderful stories. One day a vendor come up to see us in his Eldorado Cadillac. It was during mud season, and he was lucky enough to make it up the steep hill to our facility. But when he stepped out of his car, the mud sucked the Italian loafer right off of his foot. (Laughs.) He had to dig with great humility through the mud to find his shoe.

Anyway, over the years we've seen a lot of competition rise out of nowhere. You know, some well-heeled person buys all the equipment, builds a state-of-the-art plant, and tries to buy his way into the business. Well, it's not as simple as good financing. You need a passion for what you are doing. When I travel around the country, I generate a lot of excitement about our products—not because I'm a terrific salesman, but because I firmly believe in what we are doing. These poor distributors are subjected to endless presentations from a variety of manufacturers on why their sliced turkey breast is better than the next guy's. They have to listen to these things for hours on end. Then I get up and tell our story, and they all sign on. So my passion is contagious, and that helps more than anything else. You can have a well-financed company and even a good product, but if you can't get people to buy it, you've got a problem. Without the passion, many newcomers have a hard time moving through the entrepreneurial maze.

> Opportunities are wonderful, but they're only opportunities. Success comes from passionately exploiting those opportunities.

The other thing we've done is to stay very flexible with our customers. I'll give you an example: We had a stately old hotel up in the lakes region of New Hampshire that had used our products for years. The chef wanted to know if we could make him a special pasta for the summer. So I made a key-lime noodle which he used very successfully in a seafood dish. Another example involved Bill and Hillary Clinton. One of my distributors had a contract with Air Force One, so I visited the flight crew, and we really hit it off. I decided I would always go out of my way to give them a hand. Well, Bill and Hillary had our lemon-pepper fettuccine on a flight and really liked it. One night, Hillary called the steward and asked for that same dish on a flight the next day—they had a 5:30 A.M. departure time. So I woke up my food broker who woke up the distributor, and we got the lemon-pepper fettuccine on the flight. What I'm saying is that selling the customer is not just selling the product. It's being there for them! We do everything humanly possible to meet our customers' needs. And it comes back to us in spades!

Anyway, if you had told me fifteen years ago I would be making pasta for a living, I would have questioned you considerably. So I guess some of our success has been circumstantial: being in the right place at the right time. Nonetheless, I could give you a list of companies that were in the right place at the right time but didn't know how to makes things happen. So opportunities are wonderful, but they're only opportunities. Success comes from passionately exploiting those opportunities. I also think you can create opportunities by staying in motion. In other words, to be in the right place at the right time you have to "go there." You always need to be thinking about plan B if plan A doesn't work. I think successful entrepreneurs take a strong, proactive position as opposed to just responding to what comes their way.

I'll end with a little anecdote: When we first got started, someone from the pasta-equipment company said to me, "I love to sell to people like you." I said, "Why's that?" He said, "Because I get to resell this equipment in another year or two." I said, "I beg your pardon." And he says, "If you're going to the market with all these fancy vegetarian pastas, you'll be out of business in two years." Needless to say, a few years ago they invited Carol and me down to look at the latest pasta-manufacturing equipment—all at their expense. And I said to one of the reps, "A couple years back you guys said we would be out of business in two years. What seems to have changed?" He says, "Well, I didn't think you were going to change the industry." (Laughs.)

TIPS FOR GETTING MORE FOR LESS

1. **LOCK IN BEFORE LAUNCHING.**
   Do as much background work as you can before spending any money. Develop your products and services, identify your suppliers, and if possible, line up buying customers before opening your doors.

2. **LAUNCH AS LEAN AS YOU CAN.**

   Keep your initial expenses as low as possible. It's what you do that matters, not what you look like. A metal desk and low rent will pay off much more in the long run than a fancy office will in the short run.

3. **FOCUS ON EARLY SALES.**

   Winning over customers as quickly as possible should be the all-consuming focus at launch time. You can't survive many months with less cash coming in than you have going out.

4. **OUTLAW SLEDGEHAMMERS.**

   Constantly seek the most efficient way to achieve every objective. Never heft a sledgehammer when you can open a door. Don't commit to long-term practices that put a drain on your cash.

Chapter • 9

NOTCHING IT
UPWARD AND
ONWARD

Terry Neese worked for a personnel company in Norman, Oklahoma. When her boss failed to renew his business license, she moved across the hall and started her own personnel-services company—she was twenty-two years old, divorced with a child, and had $600. Within a few years, she had placed more than a thousand people in new jobs. Terry later started a second personnel business in Oklahoma City. As that business grew and stabilized, she started Terry Neese Temporaries as an extension of her permanent placement service. Along the way she bought her own building and started a real-estate company. Terry's entrepreneurial successes produced other opportunities as well. In the early '90s, she served as president of the National Association of Women Business Owners. As a Cherokee Indian, she worked on the National Advisory Council on Indian Education. She also served President George Bush as one of six senior advisors on small-business issues. Today, Terry's companies comprise one of the largest privately owned placement services in the country.

Terry's story is similar to most of the entrepreneurs I interviewed: they continue to grow, expand their services, diversify into new areas, and change the nature of their business. None of these entrepreneurs created a company that remained the same for any significant length of time. A thorough analysis of the stories helps us understand how entrepreneurs grow their businesses, and why continued growth is so important to long-term success.

GROWING FROM PROPELLING EVENTS

A clear pattern for business growth emerges from our stories. First, our entrepreneurs set a rather small objective, one they are sure they can attain (find a customer, buy a truck, open an office, get certified, write a story, design a product, rent a helicopter, build a prototype). Then they devise a method for accomplishing this objective; it's generally not a serious plan like we teach in business schools but rather a calculated scheme for realizing the goal. Next they plunge in with passion and tenacity. Eventually they hit the target and enjoy the rewards of conquest, which motivates them to keep going. Now the cycle begins again: (1) achievable objective, (2) roughed-out plan, (3) hard work, and (4) eventual success. Only this time our entrepreneurs have a bit more experience, a few more contacts, and most important, increased confidence to try something a little more challenging. In other words, they notch it up the next time around (find a few more customers, buy a second truck, open a satellite office, design another product, buy a bigger boat, open a second restaurant, try another acquisition).

I call these cycles "propelling events" because they continue to thrust the entrepreneur to higher levels following each success and as new opportunities arise. Not being huge risk-takers, they generally don't take the next step until they have succeeded and stabilized at the previous level. Interestingly enough, triumph at each plateau seems to be a function of the principles we've highlighted up to this point: knowing the terrain, radiating zeal, working with tenacity, giving mind-boggling service, building the team, getting more from less, and so on.

Most people who succeed in a career or business can trace their history through a series of "propelling events." In my life, a half-dozen stand out. As an undergraduate, I needed one last class in my major to graduate. The only course that fit my schedule that semester was a doctoral-level seminar. Reluctantly, the professor allowed me to sign up, but he warned, "You're going to have a tough time!" Inspired by an inferno of fear, I studied more that semester than ever before. When the course ended, I was stunned to learn that I had received the second-highest grade in the class. As you might guess, this event propelled me into graduate school, where I had a similar experience. My degree required a year of statistics with the notorious B.J. Winer, one of the top statisticians in the country at the time. The dreaded mountain of statistical formulas he wrote on the board each day convinced me I would fail his class. But thanks to an unstinting effort invoked by terror—manifested by memorizing flash cards during my daily runs—I not only passed both of his courses, but I also earned one of the few perfect scores he ever gave on a final exam. It was obvious to me I had more brawn than brains—and a bit of luck. Nonetheless, this experience, plus B.J.'s letter of recommendation, propelled me into my first academic position, which led to a full-time consulting practice, which thrust me into my own business.

In like manner, the entrepreneurs I interviewed experienced numerous propelling events that moved them into new business frontiers. We saw Joe Montgomery go from building the world's first bicycle-towed trailer to making bike accessories to manufacturing state-of-the-art aluminum bicycles. Jon Kittelsen went from playing hockey in high school to creating a new mouth guard to winning a national award for his invention to starting EZ-Gard Industries. Gail Frankel went from the Stroll'r Hold'r to several nifty gadgets to more than a dozen. Lori Line went from playing the piano in a department store to recording her own album to creating her own production company. Rob Olson went from working in an auction gallery to conducting auctions to becoming a full-time auctioneer. Perhaps most inspiring is Sally Gutierrez, who collected welfare, worked in a card shop, began cleaning the owner's home, started a residential cleaning service, then built a successful commercial cleaning business.

This pattern of growth is particularly dramatic in the three stories in this chapter. June Morris starts out as a travel agent, launches her own travel agency, jumps into the leisure travel business, begins chartering airplanes, then creates Morris Air—a major jet airline service. Zia Wesley-Hosford goes from solving her skin problems to becoming a cosmetologist to writing books about skin care to introducing a line of natural cosmetics. Scott Watterson begins importing home accessories from the Orient, adds wood-burning stoves to his product line, starts selling mini-trampolines, begins importing other types of home exercise equipment, and ends up manufacturing trampolines, treadmills, exercise bikes, and rowing machines. Today, Icon Health & Fitness is the largest manufacturer of home exercise equipment in the world.

So in a nutshell, entrepreneurs tend to build on their successes. They set attainable objectives, work hard to achieve them, stabilize at that level, set their sites on a slightly higher level, then keep on going. At each phase they implement principles that promote success, gain more industry knowledge, make more contacts, gain more confidence, and are well poised to take advantage of the next opportunity when it presents itself during their day-to-day business routine. Over time, this upward spiral of success, fueled by propelling events, leads them to places they never envisioned in the beginning. In many cases the end result is far beyond their dreams. That is why most of the entrepreneurs I interviewed described their business successes as accidents. That is, they couldn't see the end when they started because the path was not clear. Rather, it evolved along the way as a series of opportunities were made available from being in the thick of things. Obviously, their business planning was rather flexible. The long-term strategic plans often seen in more bureaucratic companies were seldom seen in these stories. Instead, successful entrepreneurs seem to zigzag around pursuing opportunities that happen to work best. Over time, they become experts at quickly shifting resources to more fruitful domains. Of course, this strategy will lead to some element of surprise down the road. The lesson for aspiring entrepreneurs: have small successes early, then build on each experience.

CHANGE AS STANDARD OPERATING PROCEDURE

Nothing stays the same very long in today's business environment. The shift from a national to a global economy has brought many more players to the field, and more and more companies are introducing marvelous innovations at an accelerated pace. Each year, changes in information technology, entertainment, automobiles, clothing, food choices, and so on, are more dramatic than the previous two or three years combined. Consequently, customers now have many more options and are starting to expect and seek out the "latest and greatest" products and services. Forecasts on all fronts say this pattern will continue, but the changes will be even bigger, faster, and more dramatic. In this highly competitive climate, companies need to constantly seek out new opportunities, new products, new services, and new ways to get things done. Those that are unwilling or unable to change will never survive the storm.

To help us cope with this breakneck speed of change, a host of management authorities have advised us to rethink, redesign, reengineer, redefine, and transform our corporations. In the clever book *Sacred Cows Make the Best Burgers,* Robert Kriegel and David Brandt argue that philosophies, strategies, and policies that help companies succeed initially may actually lead to their demise in the long run. They recommend that organizations put out to pasture all practices that don't improve productivity, increase quality, add value, or build morale. I have likewise seen countless companies religiously cling to the strategy that got them going, only to end up further and further behind their newer competitors as the industry changes. To endure over time, organizations must constantly scrutinize what works and what doesn't work, then channel resources accordingly.

Unfortunately, as many transition experts admit, redesign programs actually produce very little change in organizations. A recent study by the McKinsey group reveals that most companies experience less than a 5-percent change in the way they operate after reengineering. The problem? People don't like change and thus resist or even sabotage attempts to do things differently. Here's where our entrepreneurs have a real advantage: they thrive on change! And since they *are* the organization, particularly in the early days, they can make required changes quickly. Notice how the three entrepreneurs in the stories that follow are masters of change; they alter the nature of their business frequently and rapidly. June Morris, for example, transitioned her company from a charter plane service to a full-fledged airline nearly overnight. Obviously, a propensity for change and briskness of implementation are ideal management qualities for rapidly changing times. Entrepreneurship may be the perfect leadership model of the future, not only for business but for the public sector as well.

NOTCHING IT UPWARD

The entrepreneurs I interviewed change their businesses in two ways. First, they continue to *expand* what they are already doing—I call this "notching it upward." In other words, they go from one office to three, five ponies to twenty-two, one truck to ten, three plants to eight, two boats to four, and so on. There is little change in the core business, but they continue to expand it each year. This type of growth is critical to gaining market share and meeting consumer demand in a given region. Dave Burbidge, for example, could not sell garbage contracts to large real-estate companies or businesses with multiple sites without more trucks and additional dumpsters. Marti McMahon could not meet the growing demand for her yacht service in San Francisco without extra boats. And Mary Naylor could not offer her concierge service throughout Washington, D.C., until she was prepared to contract with additional buildings.

In our business, we tried to enter markets and quickly build as many stores as we could to cover the territory. It was hard to do in Los Angeles but easier in cities like Las Vegas and Salt Lake City. Greater market coverage yielded real competitive advantages. First, since everyone in the area could access our business, we were able to launch effective market-wide campaigns. Second, we could attract and hire stronger management in the region. And third, we could significantly lower our distribution costs because we were able to ship full trucks of product. These benefits enabled us to effectively compete with companies that were laden with high product costs, excessive marketing expenses, distribution burdens, and sparse coverage. That is why Jack Welch sold off all of GE's businesses that were not number one or number two in a given market: It's very difficult for a small guppy to remain alive in a large pool of piranhas!

Notching it upward also provides other advantages: You pick up tremendous economies in purchasing, you create more opportunities for your people, and you have more dollars for ongoing business development. But perhaps most important, continued growth has a real energizing effect on an organization. Having studied and taught all the theories of motivation, I believe there is nothing more exciting to team members than a company that is going places. On the other hand, there is nothing more discouraging than a business that is falling apart or losing market share each year. I've experienced both, and believe me, people prefer to play on a winning team!

NOTCHING IT ONWARD

A second way our entrepreneurs change is to *extend* their company into products and services outside the core business—I call this "notching it onward." Terry Neese, for example, started a personnel placement service for full-time positions, then added her temporary employment agency. Sally Gutierrez started a residential cleaning company, then launched her commercial cleaning business. John Solomon Sandridge opened his own art studio, then created LuvLife Collectibles to market his work. And you'll see how June Morris started a travel agency, then extended her business into charter air service.

Typically, notching it onward involves the same processes outlined in chapter 1, "Knowing the Terrain," and chapter 2, "Seizing the Opportunity." That is, our entrepreneurs discover a need while working in an industry, then realize they are uniquely qualified to meet the need—they have the contacts, credibility, resources, expertise, and even a few built-in customers. Only this time they seize the opportunity while working in their own business rather than someone else's. Other than that, the steps are the same. And having succeeded in their initial business, they are energized and full of confidence to launch the next venture.

But sometimes entrepreneurs notch it onward because the core business is no longer working. In that case, moving on is imperative to survival. Scott Watterson, for instance, had a wood-burning stove business that did great in the winter but died the rest of the year. To stay afloat in the spring and summer, he and his partners started selling trampolines to the same distributors. Later they abandoned both of these products and started importing mini-trampolines and other exercise products from Asia. When currency exchange rates started causing them grief, they began manufacturing these products themselves in the United States. Without these changes the company might not have survived. Likewise, Dave Burbidge's construction cleanup business hit the wall when new home starts died; Burbidge Disposal grew out of a last-ditch effort to utilize his equipment.

Notching it onward was critical to our experience at Golden Swirl. We kicked things off retailing frozen yogurt. After a few years, we hired a microbiologist and started creating and manufacturing our own products. As our reputation grew, more and more companies called and asked if they could buy our products. Our answer was always no because we didn't want the name we used on our retail stores— Golden Swirl—appearing in gas stations, hamburger joints, and convenience stores. But when a regional franchisee of Hardee's asked if he could sell our products in his stores, we knew we had an opportunity. We quickly launched a wholesale business under a new label—Northern Lights—and started selling to the food-service industry. Our products soon appeared in restaurants, convenience stores, hospitals, hotels, casinos, employee cafeterias, and even other frozen-dessert chains. Over the years, the combination of retail and wholesale was a marvelous marriage. The retail company provided the cash flow to create the products and launch the wholesale division, and the wholesale company increased our production volumes, lowered our costs, and contributed significantly to the bottom line. It wasn't long before we were selling more products to wholesale customers than we were to our own stores. In fact, wholesale profits pulled us through a major company redefinition when our stores became dated, labor skyrocketed, competition increased, and sales grew sluggish. Without the wholesale venture, we might not have survived long enough to reinvent our retail concept.

By far our biggest leap onward was selling the company to Yogen Fruz—the world's largest franchiser of frozen desserts. Though Golden Swirl was not for sale when they called, it was clear the acquisition would make both companies stronger. Yogen Fruz would gain a superb product line, an upscaled retail concept, and excellent sites throughout the western United States. Golden Swirl would obtain access to broader resources, multiple product lines, and greater economies of scale. Perhaps most significant, our basic business strategy would change. While our company-owned stores had done well for years, it was becoming harder to find and afford high-quality managers and employees. Yogen Fruz would sell all the units to individual franchisees—which would greatly alleviate our labor challenge. Rather than operate multiple sites, they would put people in business, then provide products, services, and support to help them succeed. In addition, the acquisition would significantly benefit our wholesale business; it would give us a larger sales force and many more channels of distribution. Clearly, selling the company was the right thing to do. It would transition Golden Swirl into a new entity—one that would be well poised for continued success in our new economy. So notching it onward may become the norm of the future as more and more companies find that their core business needs rethinking. My prediction is that numerous products, services, and entire industries will become obsolete as change continues at a supersonic pace.

It's important to note that many of the entrepreneurs I interviewed are masters at notching it both upward *and* onward. Charles Knauss of Palm Mortuaries is a great role model. When he started his business, he had one facility in downtown Las Vegas. When he realized that his ability to service the city was limited, he began acquiring both mortuaries and cemeteries. With multiple sites, Palm now handles more than half of the business in Las Vegas. Along the way, the company also became a partner in an insurance company to fund its "pre-need" program. In addition, Palm launched a flower business to meet its customers' floral needs. With multiple locations, "Flower Fare" is one of the more successful chains in Las Vegas. It now services more non-funeral customers than it does funeral patrons. So notching it upward and onward are both important to long-term success. In the future, companies will either grow or go away. Nothing stays the same anymore!

OUR ROLE MODELS

June Morris

June is the founder and former CEO of Morris Travel, the largest travel agency in Salt Lake City. She is also the founder and former CEO of Morris Air, a company she sold to Southwest Airlines in 1994. June is the only woman in America to own and operate a major jet airline service. Before being sold to Southwest, Morris Air had several thousand employees and hundreds of daily flights throughout the United States. June's story is the ultimate prototype for success! Every pattern highlighted in this book was proficiently implemented during the course of her business, as you'll see:

I had been a travel agent—I worked for the Automobile Association and American Express. When I remarried to my husband, Mitch, I wanted more freedom to go with him, so I decided to stay home for a while. I didn't like that very much, so Mitch suggested I start my own agency. I said, "Oh, no. I couldn't do that." Starting a business wasn't something I had thought about very much. But he really encouraged me, so I started a one-person travel agency, Morris Travel. I filed for the license and ordered all the brochures, and that's how it all began.

During the early years, Mitch was still very much involved in his business, but he was a great breakfast-table consultant—he was absolutely supportive. If he had said, "June, you're too dumb to do a travel agency," I probably wouldn't have done it. (Laughs.) But he was just very encouraging; there was so much I learned from him that helped. One of the things Mitch always stressed was to hire good people, then let them use their creativity to do their jobs rather than make them do things your way. So I followed that advice as I hired people: I gave them assignments and ownership of those assignments, then let them solve problems their way. I think that helped people take a real personal interest in what they did, and they put their hearts and souls into their work.

I've always been a little bit competitive, and I set my sights on being maybe number three in Salt Lake. In order for that to happen, I figured we had to have something special to offer to get the business. So we racked our brains over what we could do that would be different from the other companies. What we came up with was a computer program that gave companies management reports on their accounts—we gave them a computer printout every month. This was something no one else was doing, so it was really ahead of its time. That's really how we got the business—we met a need that no one else was meeting. We also created brochures that looked very slick and made nice presentations, which no one else was doing. We were just innovative. It wasn't always easy; I don't think there are any easy sales. But we ended up getting all the big corporate accounts. We also got the university, the government—and that's how we did it. As it turned out, it didn't take too long, just a few years, until we were number one!

Anyway, around 1978 the airlines were deregulated, and since our agency was 85 percent corporate travel, I was a little nervous. I thought the airlines would start going after corporate accounts directly and cause a shakeup in the industry. By then, Morris Travel was a big agency! We had lots of employees and all the major corporate accounts, so I was really afraid we were going to lose it all because of deregulation. This is when I first started thinking about leisure travel. Here again, how do you get into the leisure business big-time? You've got to offer something special, something different from what other companies offer. So I hired two or three more people, and we tried different things, but none of them worked very well.

Then I heard about David Neeleman. He was an agent with his own business. He was just a kid at the time; I think he was only twenty-four. Anyway, David had a successful Hawaii program. He bought a bunch of tickets from a charter operator on the west coast and had people driving down there to catch the plane. He was swiping some of my customers, and I thought, "Oh boy, that little brat. He's getting what little bit of Hawaii I've had." Anyway, his uncle, Stan Neeleman, happened to be our legal counsel—he's a great person, too, by the way. One day we were having a board meeting with Stan, and he told us the charter company Dave was using was going bankrupt, and consequently Dave was having some problems. Everyone said, "Oh good, we're glad to get rid of him." But I found out where he was and told him we wanted to work with him. So my son Rick and I—he was the president of our company at that time—took off for Minneapolis and got some really good fares on Northwest Airlines. We combined those with the land packages David had worked out in Hawaii and continued on with everything he was doing. But now with the support of a big travel agency, we launched into leisure seriously and were selling tons of tickets.

This was when the idea came to charter our own flights rather than fly our passengers on the scheduled airlines. We chartered our first flight to Hawaii and then expanded into Florida and other locations. The charter business was totally different from the travel agency, but the nice thing was that our name recognition in travel really helped launch the charter business. At first we didn't lease any planes, we just chartered them. When you charter an airplane, the airline provides the crew and everything; all you do is buy the seats. So basically we were a marketing company, marketing the same way we'd been marketing travel, only now we were selling our own product. We were using newspaper, radio, TV, you name it. If we didn't fill the seats, we ate 'em. (Laughs.) When we first started, it was just a kick, because we even traded things for seats. We didn't want any vacant. We had motorcycles, drapes, everything you can imagine; it was just a riot, all the things we did to fill those seats.

But you know, we were profitable right from the first. It was a real plus for people to fly to Hawaii for $399 when they'd been paying about $800. So it really opened up a huge market for us. I don't want to imply that this was easy. The charter operators weren't always reliable, and it got frustrating after a while. Finally, we decided to do our own thing. We leased a big plane and were going to fly to London. We had our own pilots, we were training flight attendants and doing everything. It was amazing. (Laughs.) About the time we got that going, Reagan bombed Khadafi, and all of our passengers canceled their reservations. We had leased the jet for ten years, so we were really in trouble. It's very expensive to lease an airplane!

Then we had an engine go out on the plane, not anything major, but they found something in testing that didn't look good, and it grounded our plane. David Neeleman located this operator in Denver that had a bunch of jets, Sky World, and they came in and picked up the passengers we would have left stranded when this happened. So that was a very, very hectic time. But we got through it all right because of my husband's connections with Transamerica. They were the company we leased the plane from. Mitch had a photo-finishing company which he sold to Transamerica and then ran that subsidiary for them for ten years. He became very good friends with the president and chairman, so that helped out. The lease contract was renegotiated; otherwise it would have cost us millions of dollars. We were very lucky! So our first attempt at the airlines business was very scary—we about lost it all. (Laughs.)

At the time, the agency was really cookin' and providing the cash flow. We didn't do any borrowing for either the agency or the charter company, so we were in really good shape. In fact, we had a zero start-up cost at first because I had experience in the industry and my husband had an office. I just rented a corner of his building, so we got off very cheaply. I think it is very important to start small and not get yourself into too much debt. If we had borrowed a bunch of money to go into business, we would have been in real trouble during this time. Anyway, things worked out fine, and we were able to unload that plane.

After that, we continued to charter planes from Sky World for quite a while. While we were with them, we kept expanding and adding cities. We were still just a charter company doing leisure, but we added Los Angeles. There was a huge pent-up demand for Los Angeles from people traveling back and forth from Salt Lake. The other airlines were charging a minimum of $400 round trip, and of course, we were selling seats for $59 each way. (Laughs.) As time went on, we started getting more and more like a regular airline and had different companies chartering for us. At one time we had thousands of people flying on hundreds of flights on Braniff's planes. One morning at eleven o'clock we got a call from a friend who said, "Braniff is going down!" All of a sudden we had thousands of passengers booked all around the place, and we didn't have any airplanes.

We all started running around the office like crazy, each person took a flight, and we went to work figuring out how we were going to take care of all our passengers. David and a couple of the other guys got on the phones and soon had a couple of charter planes coming in. Then we called United and Delta and negotiated special prices for tickets on their flights. As it turned out, we were able to get everyone on a flight. The press was standing by hoping for a stranded passenger story, but we fooled them. (Laughs.) All we had were two- or three-hour delays on some of the flights. So that was very exciting! (Laughs.)

We were starting to feel that we couldn't count on other people's planes—it was so frustrating. They'd be late, and other things would happen over which we had no control. We couldn't control the flight attendants, their customer service, things like that. At that point we had so many scheduled flights going: Idaho, Washington, Oregon, Alaska, Hawaii, Los Angeles. About that time, Alaska Airlines made a complaint against us. They said we were really a scheduled airline pretending to be a charter company. That turned out to be really good for us because we said, "OK, if that's the way it's going to be, then we're going to be an airline." So we started taking steps to become an official, scheduled airline, Morris Air.

We hired a fellow who had been with the FAA named Usto Shulz, and boy did he go to work! He got our license, met all the other requirements, and got us ready to fly. This was not that long ago—it was in November of 1992. We immediately started leasing planes on long-term leases and replacing all the chartered flights. We hired all of our own crews—hundreds of pilots and hundreds of flight attendants—and got them all trained and certified. So now we were in the airlines business in a big way, and it was very exciting. Of course, we had to have our own reservation center, our own telephone operators, and all of those things. Fortunately, during the time we were chartering, we hired a lot of real sharp people to work on things like that. We had developed our own reservation system and our own computer system, so when we became an airline, we already had a lot of those things in place for all of our markets. I guess we had a couple thousand employees by then.

A few years before all this when we were doing the chartering, our travel agency and our air charter company started having a bunch of conflict. You see, the charter company was punishing the travel agency by directly booking passengers. And the other travel agencies didn't want to buy from Morris Air because it was stealing their business—they didn't like the idea of Morris Air in the first place. So the travel agency was actually becoming a liability to the charter operation. After a while, we decided to sell Morris Travel, which we did—we sold it to some of our employees in the late '80s. Things were much better after that because all the travel agencies now felt free to buy from Morris Air.

So at this point, we were just running an airline. We flew to about thirty cities, mostly in the western U.S., but we did go to Orlando and several places in Mexico. We only had 737s, so we couldn't fly to Hawaii anymore because it requires longer-range planes, but we were becoming very successful and very profitable. Of course, Delta was getting more and more nervous. At first they thought we would self-destruct, but they started becoming concerned about the increased traffic we were causing at the airport. In fact, I think a lot of what has happened to the airport, including the new parking structure, was largely because of us. We really changed the face of travel out of here; things were working very well.

One of the things I think entrepreneurs need to know is that you can never really stay the same. You have to constantly keep growing; otherwise you're going to shrink—you just have to keep changing. To grow in this business you need more and more aircraft, which means you really need huge dollars. Up until now, we were still funding our growth with cash flow—it was just like a little goose laying a golden egg! We had twenty-four planes at the time and hundreds of daily flights all over the place. We were still expanding and moving like crazy, so we decided it was time to do a public offering. We had a number of investment banking firms interested in taking us public. When they came in and saw what we were doing and looked at our books, they were really excited about it. They were all licking their chops over this— they thought they had a real good one.

> One of the things I think entrepreneurs need to know is that you can never really stay the same. You have to constantly keep growing; otherwise you're going to shrink.

Because of our size, we had just hired a really good CFO, Glenn Schaab, to help with all of this. He was kind of an entrepreneur himself and had become available, so we got him on board. He knew the accounting firm that handled Southwest Airlines—a few of the guys there. He said to us, "What do you think about selling to Southwest?" We had patterned ourselves after them in many ways and were doing a lot of the low-cost operations they were doing. So our CFO contacted their people and said, "Do you think Herb might be interested in talking with the Morris folks?" Of course, he said yes, so we met with Herb Kelleher and decided it was a perfect fit. At that time we were in a very good position to negotiate: we had real strengths, we were profitable, and we were ready to do a public offering. We wanted them to continue servicing Salt Lake—that was real important to us; we wanted our employees to be taken care of, which was also very important; and of course, we wanted a darn good price. And we got all of it! It was a stock transaction, so we got Southwest Airlines stock. At the time, our company was valued at $139 million.

I'm now sitting on the board of directors for Southwest, and it's a very nice board. They get right down to business and are very serious about what they're doing. They're also a casual group and very fun to be around. Last summer they gave me a party—it was a hangar party—and I guess a couple thousand people came. They rolled out this brand new 737 they had just picked up at Boeing, and it had my name on it—the "June M. Morris." It literally had my signature on the plane! Then they showed a video that was just great! It talked about me as a little girl in a little country town, and how I used to look up into the sky and watch the airplanes and wonder where they were going and what it would be like to be on one. It ended by saying, "Now little girls looking up at airplanes will see June M. Morris's airplane." I must say it was very exciting!

Zia Wesley-Hosford

Zia is the cofounder and former president of Zia Cosmetics, a San Francisco–based company that sells a line of natural cosmetics to the health-food industry. The company has twenty reps that sell to 2,000 health-food stores nationwide. Before starting the business, Zia was a cosmetologist, author, and consumer advocate in the cosmetic industry. She knew if she could create products that would really work—clear up problem skin, even out skin tones, take away signs of aging—women would buy them and tell their friends. With sales of $7 million, it's working quite well. In 1996, Zia sold her interest in the company to her partner, Fran Strachan. Here's her story:

It really began in my late twenties when I started having skin problems. I always had good skin when I was younger; then all of a sudden I had this horrendous acne. I always thought teenagers were the ones that had skin problems, but I've learned that adult acne is not that uncommon. At the time, I was living on the beach in Malibu—I lived there for a total of about ten years. So combined with the acne, I was beginning to see the effects of all my years of tanning, which is when you usually see it—late twenties, early thirties.

So faced with acne as well as sun damage, I began making the rounds to dermatologists. I did all of the things dermatologists do, which are mostly drug-related—topical antibiotics and taking antibiotics internally. I also had this treatment twice a week called a flush treatment, which I hope they don't do anymore. They took dry ice, put it in a cheesecloth, rubbed it directly on my skin, then put me under a sun lamp for ten minutes. Ohhh! Horrible damage! My skin always looked horrible! So things went from bad to worse. Of course, being female, I also tried every cosmetic on the market. I would go into department stores, and they'd look at my face and say, "Oh, use this, this, and this," then sell me two hundred dollars worth of products, which invariably made things worse—irritated my skin, clogged the pores. I don't think there were any good cosmetics on the market at the time—they were more a cover-up than a treatment. It was all perfume, artificial fragrance, and artificial coloring.

Because I wasn't getting any results, I started looking at some alternative treatments. That's when things started getting interesting. I found that diet made a big difference in my skin. In all my previous treatment, no one had ever mentioned food to me. If there was a list of foods to stay away from at the time, it probably consisted of fried foods and chocolate. That doesn't even scratch the surface of what foods are terrible for your skin. So I put together a diet that gave me all the vitamins, minerals, and protein I needed. I got rid of meat and actually became a vegetarian. I cut out sugar, caffeine, dairy, and processed foods. Later I found that iodine is terrible for acne as well. Fortunately, I am a good cook, so I made everything taste great. Changing my diet was a big help!

At the time, people also believed that once sun damage occurred it was irreversible. If your skin looked like leather, it was there for good. In my quest for good skin, I came across several practitioners who thought skin could be healed by using topical ointments and taking antioxidants—just like you heal a cut or scrape. So the first thing I put on my skin was aloe vera, which made an enormous difference. I had spent thousands of dollars on expensive cosmetics and prescription drugs, and within three days my skin had totally changed with pure aloe vera! I also started drinking aloe vera juice—it cleanses the body and is a wonderful oxygenator for the blood—and that made a difference. So my personal problems were the beginning of where I am now. I discovered that all the typical places I thought I could get help were no help. I found there was an alternative way to help the skin, but the information was generally not available. And because the results I had experienced were so extraordinary, I passed the information on to whomever wanted it. And I found that other people were really interested.

A couple years later I decided to leave southern California and move to the Bay Area. I also made a career change. I had been a singer and a dancer, but I wanted to do something different. My family and all my good friends said, "You've been helping everybody with their skin and their makeup for years. Why don't you get a cosmetologist's license and have people pay you?" It made a lot of sense. So I took something that I loved and was already doing and went to San Francisco. I attended the Vadelsa Student Academy for a year and received my license as a cosmetologist. Then I apprenticed for another year and a half with a former instructor at the academy.

In 1980 I rented half a salon in Sausalito. I decided to offer facials along with haircuts, perms, and everything else I was doing. To do facials you have to use products that cleanse, heal, and moisturize the skin, so I started looking for products. The first place I went was where everybody else went: to the labs that offer private-label cosmetics. I probably talked to six or seven of them in the Bay Area, and their products were all the same junk. I mean, it was the stuff that was sold in the five-and-dimes. And this is what everybody was putting their own label on and selling at whatever price they wanted to! The average cost for a two-ounce jar was probably seventy-five cents. People would then sell it for $20 and $30. So when you went into a Beverly Hills salon and bought a moisturizer with their label on it, this is what it was! I was appalled! I couldn't believe this was going on and nobody knew about it. So I started writing up pages of information and telling all my clients what was in these products and why they were so bad.

Remember, I had been on this quest of finding out what was good for the skin for several years. Now I was learning what was bad for the skin, and I had a lot of information no one else had. One day a client of mine, Shakti Gawain—author of *Creative Visualization, Living in the Light,* and all those bestselling books—looked at the things I was handing out and said, "You have enough information for a book! Let me publish it for you." So her company published my first book, *Being Beautiful.* It was an all-purpose, holistic beauty book. It contained the first ingredient dictionary plus everything on skin care, good hair, and wardrobe. When it came out, we went to the American Booksellers' Convention, and they had a tiny little booth. To attract people we offered ten-minute consultations. A sign said, "Ask Zia, Ten-Minute Consultation." I was busy all day, every day!

On the second day of the convention, this woman came in who had just about everything wrong with her skin you could possibly imagine: dark circles under her eyes, acne, blackheads, excess oil, uneven color, and premature aging. She said she was thirty-two years old and sick of the bad skin. I guessed she was ten years older than that. I told her in order for her to have really good skin she had to change her diet and lifestyle; she also had to start exercising and give up smoking. She said, "You just tell me what to do, and I'm going do it." She was ready. So I gave her this whole long list of recommendations.

Three weeks later I got a phone call from her. She said, "I don't know if you remember me. My name is Tobi Sanders. You did a consultation." I remembered her immediately. "I just have to tell you I followed what you said to the letter, and although it's only been three weeks, I already have better skin than I've ever had in my life. If you can do this for me, you can probably do it for thousands of other people. I'm a senior editor at Bantam Books, and I'd like you to write a book for me." So I ended up writing three books for Bantam, two of which were bestsellers. The first one was called *Putting On Your Face: The Ultimate Guide to Cosmetics.* The next one was called *Face Value: Skin Care for Women over 35.* The third one was the *Beautiful Body Book.*

In *Putting on Your Face,* I recommended products for women to use. In the chapter on moisturization, I discussed why moisturizers are good or bad. At the end of the chapter, I listed five or six products I had tested which were well made and did what they claimed. But I couldn't recommend any products for the eye area. The skin around the eyes is the thinnest on the entire body, so it's very sensitive. And because there are no oil glands there, it doesn't get natural lubrication like the rest of the face. You have to use something very pure and clean, because if it gets in the eyes, you're in trouble; if it's greasy, it causes makeup to run; anything oil-based used at night will make the eyes puffy.

Several years before this, I had tested all the eye products available, and they were the worst on the market. So I worked with a female chemist in the Bay Area to develop a product I could use myself, recommend to my clients and friends, and sell in my salon. I was mixing the ingredients in bottles on my own. It was a water-soluble oil, yet it penetrated the skin. So when it came to recommending eye moisturizers, I said to my editor, "What do I do in this category? There aren't any products I can recommend other than my own, and that sounds a little self-serving." She said, "No, I think you're absolutely right. I've been using your product for a year, and it's the best thing I've ever used. All my friends use it, everybody loves it, it works! I think that you should explain why it's the only product you will recommend."

So on her advice I wrote a paragraph in the book explaining why mine was the only product I could recommend and why everything else on the market didn't meet my standards. I said to my boyfriend, "You know, I'm goin' to talk about my product in the book, and I've got to be able to sell it mail order. Would you be willing to set up a little business with me to do this?" He said, "People aren't going to read your book and send away for a product without trying it." And I said, "I'll bet they do." So he said, "I'll tell ya' what—if they do, I'll manage it for you." So I got a post office box and put the number in the book.

When the book came out the following year, I was already working on my next book and had forgotten all about the post office box. About three months later, I remembered the box and said to my boyfriend, "Oh no! I completely forgot about the post office box. I've got to go see if anybody sent me any checks." So I went to the post office, and the box was stuffed! And there was a note in it saying there was another box in the back! Now that I had all these checks coming in, my boyfriend, Fran Strachan, had to honor his commitment to help me sell the product. So we set up a production line in our kitchen. We bottled, labeled, and wrapped the eye oil in a little paper with the instructions and ingredients on it. Then we packaged it in a padded mailing envelope and sent it out. And that was how Zia Cosmetics was born in 1983.

Simultaneously, I started getting letters from people asking about skin care. A big portion of my time was spent answering these letters. I began noticing a similarity in the questions asked and decided to do a newsletter as a way of updating information in my book. Fran thought it was a good idea too, so I started a quarterly newsletter called *The Great Face*. I sent it to those who wrote to me, and we sold subscriptions—something like $8.00 a year. These people would tell their friends about it, and pretty soon we had a list of several thousand subscribers. We published our phone number and address in the letter, and the phone started ringing off the hook. About this same time, I had another book coming out and was going on a major radio and television tour. We knew the number of calls would go up and decided to get an 800 number. And sure enough, during the entire time I was on tour we got 500 to 1,000 calls daily. We sent all these people newsletters—most of them became subscribers, and most of them bought the eye oil. Based on these results, we decided it was time to offer more products: a couple of cleansers, a toner, and a few moisturizers. This was really the beginning of our product line.

When the new products came out, Fran was the sales force. He made the calls, got the feedback, and tracked how things were going. Initially, we thought we would go into the salons first, but we soon discovered they were much more accustomed to the junky, high-markup products. You know, it didn't matter what was in them; what mattered was the

> I knew if I offered a product that really did what we said it would . . . women would tell each other.

profit margin. Within a year, it was very clear the full line of products belonged in the natural-foods industry. People who frequented health-food stores were very excited about Zia Cosmetics because they were all natural. And since they were already very conscious about what they were putting into their bodies, we didn't have to educate them.

Initially, we entered the market with one of the biggest health-food distributors on the West Coast—this was around 1988. We did a lot of training with them but soon discovered, through no fault of theirs, that distribution reps go into stores with 300 products, not just ours. They might say, "I have this new cosmetic line, and I think you'll really like it." And the store owner might say, "Well, I'm not really into cosmetics today. What have you got in soap?" Then the rep goes right on to soap or incense or fried rice or whatever else they're selling. (Laughs.) So things were very slow at first. It took a while to realize that if we trained reps to just sell Zia Cosmetics they would sell a lot more Zia Cosmetics. So after about six months, we left that distributor and went with direct reps who only sell our product and maybe one or two others that complement ours. We look for people with experience in the industry who are excited about our line and understand what it's all about. It has worked very well for us because our products take a lot of education.

To summarize our growth, we now have twenty reps who sell our products to 2,000 health-food stores across the United States, Canada, and overseas. Our reps are paid a combination wage and commission. We are the leader in facial skin care in Whole Foods and Wild Oats Market, the two largest chains in the country. We currently manufacture over fifty products and have thirty-five in-house employees.

I think the most important piece of information I can pass on has to do with our selling strategy. In the very beginning, when we only had the eye oil, Fran and I spent many, many days going back and forth about whether we should start this company. I had a vision of creating a whole line of products that were as beneficial as the little one we already had. Playing devil's advocate, Fran would say, "How are you going to compete with Revlon, Estée Lauder, and all these companies that spend millions of dollars just to launch one new product? And I said, "If it works, women will use it, and they'll tell all their friends." See, I know how women are—

they are very observant. Let's say a woman has skin problems, then all of a sudden the problems go away. She is very verbal with her friends about what she used. Or if she doesn't offer the information, her friends will be the first ones to say, "Your skin looks incredible. What did you do?" We women pass around a lot of information about stuff like that. I knew if I offered a product that really did what we said it would—clear up problem skin, even out skin tones, take away signs of aging—women would tell each other. So with a great product and word-of-mouth advertising, I knew we could keep our costs down and grow to be a pretty good-sized company. And you know, to this day we've never advertised. It must be working pretty well because we're selling around $7 million worth of all-natural cosmetics that really work!

Scott Watterson

Scott is the cofounder, chairman, and CEO of Icon Health & Fitness, the largest manufacturer of fitness equipment in the world. The company makes treadmills, exercise bikes, strength-training equipment, mini-trampolines, and other fitness products under brand names such as ProForm, Image, HealthRider, Reebok, Weider, Weslo, JumpKing, and Legend. Icon employs approximately 6,500 people in its production facilities in Utah, Colorado, Texas, Quebec, England, Italy, and China. Here is Scott's story:

Gary Stevenson and I started the business while we were in school. During the summer, we had a choice of either working for the city water department or doing something on our own. We had both lived in Asia—Gary in Japan and I in Taiwan—and we wanted to use some of our experience there. So we decided to start importing products out of Asia to offset some of our expenses as students. Gary, myself, and another guy, Brad Sorenson, got together to form a company. We went to the least-expensive attorney we could find, and his first question was, "What's the name of the company?" Of course, we hadn't thought of that yet, so we just combined some of our initials and came up with "Weslo."

We started importing things from Taiwan that could be used by interior designers: brass accessories, candlesticks, marble fireplace hearths, marble accessories. Before our first products arrived, we bought a sample in a store and started making sales calls. We took the sample upstairs to the buying office of a large department store, gave them a price, and they bought it—that's how we made our first sale. Then we started selling fireplace hearths to another company. I would make one sale, Gary would make another one, and Brad would make the next one. We took turns being the delivery boy because we wanted people to think we were a legitimate company. Of course, at that time we were students and a little naive, but we worked hard and had some success.

As school continued to demand more of our time, Brad got married and decided he wasn't interested in staying with the company. It wasn't particularly profitable at the time, although we did make some money. When Brad left, Gary and I picked up another partner, Blaine Hancey, who is a relative of mine. At the time we still had the marble business going and were importing some sporting-good products out of Taiwan. During this time, we got into wood-burning stoves because the energy crisis was growing, and Blaine had a neighbor named Ron Larson who couldn't build these stoves fast enough. He wasn't sales and marketing oriented, but Gary and I were, so we became partners to build and sell wood-burning stoves.

Ron built the first stoves in a little garage. He had built fifty or so before we got involved with him. Later, when the four of us were partners, we ended up getting outside manufacturers to build them for us up in Oregon. It was quite an experience! If our competition had a stove with quarter-inch plate, then we made ours with half-inch plate. Another advantage we had was that we imported the door fronts from Taiwan; they were nickel-plated and casted—an expensive part of the stove. Of course, by then we were able to utilize our contacts to get those at a competitive price.

So we started going to trade shows and marketing the product to fireplace shops and wood-burning–stove dealers. We'd sell a bunch of stoves and have a great year; then the snow would melt. (Laughs.) When the snow melted, so did our dealer base, and we'd lose most of our income during the summer. So we started looking for something that was counter-seasonal to wood-burning stoves. Of all things, we found a large, outdoor trampoline which was a summer specialty item. Blaine Hancey had one in his backyard. We looked up the manufacturer—a company called Round Trampoline in Florida—and contacted them.

We created an agreement with them that would give us an exclusive for the entire country if we could sell 500 of their stitchless trampolines. What we did was set up our stove dealers as trampoline dealers. They thought we were crazy, but we gave them the trampolines on consignment and told them we would pick them up in ten days if they didn't sell. We didn't have to pick up a single consignment. We ended up selling 500 trampolines in about three weeks, which was a total surprise to the trampoline company. They backed out of our agreement because they realized there was a much bigger market than they had expected. Instead of pursuing legal remedies, we realized we had a tiger by the tail and started making our own trampolines. We brought in the raw materials—the steel, the springs, the fabric—and had someone else manufacture them for us. We were responsible for the inventory, parts, marketing, and sales. So we ended up selling wood-burning stoves through the fall season, and trampolines in the spring and summer—that gave us a more level cash flow.

Anyway, we did all this while we were in school. We capitalized these early ventures with $2,000—Gary's father lent him $1,000, and my father lent me $1,000. After that, we didn't really capitalize any of our other deals—we basically leveraged ourselves or used cash flow. It's unusual that we've made money every year we've been in business. Even when we were doing brass accessories, wood-burning stoves, and these big trampolines, we always managed to make a little bit of profit. By the second year of trampolines, we were out of school, and Gary had a big decision to make because he was now married—I was only engaged. (Laughs.) We were both extended offers from different companies but decided to pursue some of our entrepreneurial instincts.

The stove business kept getting more difficult, but we found we could sell trampolines to people other than wood-burning–stove dealers. At some point, we saw there was also a market for mini-trampolines, a product fitness activists could use indoors. So we started importing a mini-trampoline from Taiwan to sell to the sporting-goods channels of distribution. We went to our first trade show in Chicago, and I'll never forget it! There were about forty of us selling mini-trampolines, and we were all on the same aisle. (Laughs.) The price started out at about $40 a trampoline, but by the end of the trade show it was down to about $20. It seemed like people changed their prices every day, but we managed to be competitive because we sourced our products out of Asia. With our contacts, I was able to go right to the factory; other people had to go through a trading company. During this time, we developed some good vendor relationships that we still use today. The mini-trampoline really got us into the sporting goods and fitness industry. Although it was very competitive, there were substantial volumes in the business. It opened up whole new channels of distribution for us. We quickly saw we could go from mini-trampolines to exercise bikes to rowing machines to other fitness products—and we started importing these from Taiwan.

After a while, we found that the currency was changing and the valuation of the dollar was causing us problems. The mini-trampolines were also freight intensive. At this time, we started a metamorphosis; we went from being an importer to a light assembler. For the trampolines, we had the fabric and the pad stitched in Taiwan, then all the parts shipped over in bulk. We welded the rings ourselves, assembled the springs to the trampoline, then shipped—so it became a domestic product. We'd make money, then use our cash flow or leverage from bank lines to grow the business. Occasionally we'd borrow from people, then pay them back with a handsome interest rate. But other than the initial $2,000, there was no new infusion of capital.

We soon grew to be a $30-million business. We made mini-trampolines in our own assembly plant, we had outdoor trampolines made for us, and we imported exercise bikes from Taiwan. By then, the stove business had all but gone away, and Ron Larson had left to pursue other things. Blaine also became interested in selling because he didn't like the risk of leverage. Gary and I didn't like it either, so we started looking for a new partner. We had several people interested in our business but elected to sell 55 percent of the company to Stan Tuttleman from Philadelphia. He had asked Mellon Bank to search for small companies that had good growth opportunities, and they found us. So in 1983 Stan became our money guy. Blaine eventually left the company; he was ten years our elder, and Gary and I were still young and hungry.

Stan was very helpful because he was on the board of directors of the Limited Corporation—the company that sells women's apparel. He had also started a company called Mast Industries which was the import arm of the Limited. Through his experiences, he brought a lot of professional leadership and formality to our business: new reports, how to hold board meetings, and so on. And because he still had an appetite for business, we quickly grew to around $60 million. Then Stan got cancer and found himself in a tough situation with one of his partners, so we decided to sell the business again. We ended up selling 100 percent of our stock to Weider Health and Fitness, and they gave Gary and me substantial stock options to stay and run the company. So Stan got his investment back, made some money, and left the business.

At the time, we were getting into other exercise products, such as motorized treadmills. Since the currency situation in Taiwan continued to be a problem, we realized it was going to be necessary to manufacture here in the United States. We ended up going through another metamorphosis, taking a lot of our offshore manufacturing and bringing it here. We started as an assembler of treadmills and really grew that market. At the time, treadmills were only sold to hospitals and health clubs, and since they're so big and bulky, it was cost effective to manufacture them here. We now have over a million square feet of manufacturing. We manufacture trampolines, exercise bikes, rowing machines, and treadmills. We still import both materials and finished goods out of Asia. So we've been able to integrate our manufacturing while still keeping our import advantage. We've really been able to just add on to what we've done as we've gone along. We've also been able to broaden our channels of distribution, selling not just to sporting goods but to large mass merchandisers: Sears, Montgomery Ward, JC Penney. There's not a large distributor or retail outlet of exercise equipment that doesn't carry something from us.

Along the way, Weslo wanted to develop other brand names. We were selling to one channel of distribution and wanted to sell to others. At the time, Nike had a company for sale, which was ProForm. It was a small company that only did $1 or $2 million in sales. We bought their finished goods, acquired the name ProForm in the transaction, then started growing the brand. Today we have seven significant brands, and we're still adding lines. ProForm is the high-end sporting-goods brand for fitness equipment—we introduce a lot of our technology innovations through this line. Weslo is a fitness-equipment brand for the mass marketer—it's the value or discount brand. Image is the high-end specialty fitness brand of institutional and traditional exercise equipment—it's sold by specialty dealers who cater to the more discriminating consumers. Then we have Weider, the brand for traditional anaerobic strength-training products—weights, benches, weight systems.

A couple of years ago, we were preparing to go public and had actually filed our S-1. Bain Capital, a leveraged buyout group in Boston, came to us and said, "Why don't you let us buy the company? That way your shareholders can monetize their investment and you can still go public later." We completed the sale with Bain in November of 1994. The total transaction was over $400 million, replacing the old credit lines and raising $250 million worth of bonds. Gary and I have sold the business three times. Each time we sell it, we put money in our pockets, then get stock back from the new group to stay and run the company. Of course, with the Bain transaction, we were able to significantly broaden the group of management that owns stock. We even extended stock options to a lot of middle managers in the company. We're now looking at a public offering sometime in the future.

To summarize our story, we've had phenomenal growth all along. We'll do approximately $890 million this year, and we're chasing a billion dollars real quick. We've integrated our manufacturing to include injection molding and metal fabrication. We have 6,500 employees and distribute our products throughout the world. With that ensues a whole lot of different challenges. But what's invigorating for me today is molding this company into a $2-billion business. I find that entrepreneurial skills are needed regardless of the size of your company—whether you're $10 million, $100 million, or a billion. I'm sure we'll meet our goals if we follow the same approach we've taken up to this point.

As a manufacturer, a real key to our success has been our flexibility. Some of our competitors have become inflexible through bricks and mortar. They've created facilities that are so large that in any economic downturn or change of products, they get hurt. I think it's very important to always look outside first. There should be a real economic purpose for producing something yourself. Then try to over-utilize your manufacturing space at all times. If we have a million square feet now, we could probably have two million. But we're a consumer company, and consumers' tastes and needs change. I mean, we've been from A to Z in terms of products. As products come and go, and as currencies change to favor offshore again, we must have a factory floor and a whole philosophy based on flexibility. That way, we can grow with consumer interests and shrink at the same time. I would say don't be an empire builder, a bricks-and-mortar guy. Retain enough flexibility to follow opportunities.

> Growth is just a matter of setting new goals for yourself, building on your successes, challenging your peaks, not limiting your vision, and surrounding yourself with capable people that can share that vision.

My advice to aspiring entrepreneurs is to have successes early! When you set your mind to something, make sure you finish it. I think it's a real challenge to stay in school once a business opportunity comes your way. But I think it's wrong to drop out. I think it's right to say, "No, I've got to discipline myself to finish my education." Then, as you start out in any business activity, whether you're your own boss or working for somebody else, set targets, have successes, and recognize those achievements—that will reinforce your ability to expand your opportunities. Growth is just a matter of setting new goals for yourself, building on your successes, challenging your peaks, not limiting your vision, and surrounding yourself with capable people that can share that vision. Period!

1. **WORK TO ACHIEVE SMALL SUCCESSES,
   THEN BUILD ON EACH EXPERIENCE.**
   Set reasonable objectives and work hard to attain them. Never bite off more than you can chew. When you reach one plateau, look for the next opportunity, then repeat the process. Let success bolster your confidence, skills, and contacts.

2. **EXPAND YOUR BUSINESS TO GAIN
   COMPETITIVE ADVANTAGES.**
   Steadily notch your business upward each year, but no faster than you can stabilize and effectively manage. Remember, it's better to have a strong presence in one market than a weak presence in several markets. Ongoing growth produces wonderful economies, opportunities for people, and enthusiasm in the organization.

3. **EXTEND YOUR BUSINESS INTO
   NEW PRODUCTS AND SERVICES.**
   Continually scan the horizon for opportunities to add fresh products and services and new divisions. Have the courage to seize opportunities for which you are uniquely qualified that will add value to the company. Notch it onward before it's too late!

4. **MAINTAIN SUFFICIENT FLEXIBILITY TO CHANGE QUICKLY.**
   Keep all your systems, procedures, and facilities pliable enough to change swiftly when necessary or to pursue bright opportunities. Don't lock into anything long term that will inhibit your ability to change on the short run. Being able to transform the company quickly will keep you alive!

5. **CREATE THE NEXT TREND RATHER THAN CHASE IT.**

   Constantly ask the question, "What might customers want in the future that they don't have today?" Hold regular "new trend" debates about which products and services might create the next market frenzy. Start working today on what you need to be tomorrow. Become a company that leads out rather than follows.

Chapter · 10

GIVING
SOMETHING BACK

---

*A*nnie Meadows's life was a disaster. She played in a rock-and-roll
band, used drugs and alcohol, read palms, gazed into crystal balls,
and practiced witchcraft. Though drawn to this lifestyle, she was very
unhappy. One day, while working on the island of Kauai in Hawaii, she
got down on her knees and prayed, "If there's a God up there, get me out
of this situation." The next day, the island was devastated by a hurricane.
When Annie went to her insurance company to file a claim, she was told,
"There is no insurance because it was an act of God." She terminated her
employment contract, went back to the mainland, and turned her life
around. From that point on, Annie had a genuine desire to help other
people find the truth, peace, and freedom she had discovered. Before long,
she and her husband, Peter, launched a company, Exodus Concert
Ministries, to spread basic Christian values. Later they formed a second
business, ECM Records. Today, these companies produce and distribute
CDs, help promote new Christian artists, counsel with people on the
phone, and respond to letters from those in need. In addition, Annie
speaks to youth groups and performs at more than 100 concerts a year,
both nationally and internationally. Her business objective is to earn
enough money to support her growing enterprise—not to become rich.

Annie's story is a great example of something I heard over and over in my interviews: Most successful entrepreneurs have a genuine desire to help other people—not just make piles of money. And this desire leads to action. I was impressed by how many of our entrepreneurs are passionately involved in giving something back to their communities. In some cases, like Annie's, this is the primary goal of the organization. In the end, both parties benefit—the company and the community.

THE PASSION FOR GIVING BACK

Having been around business startups much of my career, I had some idea of the patterns I might find before beginning my three-year adventure. Nonetheless, I remained true to my scientific upbringing and let the trends emerge from the interviews. I have to admit, a heartfelt passion for "giving something back" was not on my list of expected keys to success. Robin Petgrave, whom you met in chapter 8, summarizes the attitude of many of the entrepreneurs I interviewed:

> *One final thing I think is most important: When I started this company, I decided people would be more important than money. I knew I had to make money, but the money would go to creating jobs and doing stuff for the community. It's really twofold: one, the people you help really like it, and two, the news media loves it, which brings in more people to experience all the stuff you're doing. It's a cycle that feeds itself, and it's really cool! So I don't look at this place as a way to make millions for me. We might make millions, but we'll put it back into the community.*

One of the things Robin does is help kids stay off drugs. He takes a helicopter to schools and speaks to the children. He tells them about his past and about his present business success. He explains that if he can do it, they can certainly do it! "You guys think you have it hard; you haven't seen nothing," he says. "You've got shoes on your feet; I didn't have no shoes!" Then he helps create contests to keep them in school and off drugs. "And they go absolutely nuts!" he says. Another thing Robin does is take children with terminal illnesses for helicopter rides. One Christmas, he picked up two families in his limousine, drove them to his office, gave the kids presents, then flew them all over Los Angeles. Knowing it would probably be their last Christmas together, the families were notably touched. "The kids dug it, the moms cried, it was totally cool!"

Like Robin, Mary Ellen Sheets of Two Men And A Truck sees her company as a "way to provide funds and manpower to worthwhile community projects." She is constantly doing free or discounted moves for a number of organizations. The interesting thing is that the spirit of service seems to rub off on her employees. They say, "We take pride in a company that does right for the people of this town." Now she encourages all of her franchisees to get involved in worthy community projects.

Gail Frankel, whom you met in chapter 5, is another great role model. Her parents brought her up "to believe in giving something back." So as her company, Kel-Gar, began enjoying success, she looked for ways to contribute. Here's one of the things she is doing:

> We decided to link up with the Susan G. Komen Breast Cancer Foundation. Obviously, a lot of women buy our products. Some of them may think, "I'm immune from cancer because it doesn't run in my family." Or, "I'm not fifty years old yet." Well, one of my best friends at the age of thirty-one discovered a cancerous tumor, which gave me greater awareness of the problem. So I wanted to convey a message about breast health care and give women a number they can call if they have questions. We put an insert in every package even though it costs us more money. I figure if we help one person, it will be well worth the cost.

So a strong interest in serving the community is a common theme in our stories. It actually makes a lot of sense. Many of these people were the "less fortunate" themselves at one point in their lives. In addition, many have worked for large corporations where making money was the only thing that mattered. Now that these folks are running their own show, they want to do things differently. Not only do they want to help those in need, but they also want to pay back the community that helped them achieve their own American dream. In the stories that follow, you'll see how three everyday Americans—Marty Shih, Ruffin Slater, and Jon Huntsman—have created wildly successful companies for the benefit of the community.

THE POWER OF GIVING BACK

Dale Aramaki is a hero in our neighborhood. A few years ago, he opened a Phillip's 66 service station just up the street. He's very friendly, likes our kids, hires our teenagers, provides free popcorn, gives kids discounts on candy so they can sell it at school for a profit, answers our car questions, puts air in our tires, offers good prices, and can fix almost anything—quickly! One of the first summers Dale was open, he came to our block party, even though he lives outside the neighborhood. The fun thing was that he brought party poppers for all the kids, which kicked off the street dance with a bang! The following year he brought free Icees for everyone. All the women in the neighborhood love him because they can take their cars in for repairs, walk home, know they'll get a fair price, and most important, not have to rely on their husbands to solve the problem. Many people in the neighborhood won't take their cars anywhere else. My wife, Mary, even feels guilty if she ever goes to another gas station. So Dale serves the community, and the community is loyal to Dale. We all want him to survive so we don't lose his presence in our neighborhood. During the next few months the road in front of his station will be torn up, and Dale is worried about losing business. I know one family that will figure out a way to get around the construction to patronize his store.

Dale's story is similar to many of our entrepreneurs: The business supports the community, and the community supports the business. This was critical in the early days of our company. We had little money to advertise but needed to win customers over quickly. Our strategy was to support as many community groups as possible. Giving away free product was not very expensive and probably did more for our company than donating money might have. You've already read about our free nights in chapter 6. In addition, we gave away free product to schools, churches, birthday parties, cultural groups, handicapped events, and fund raisers. We let high-school teams and pep clubs sell our gift certificates and keep the money to buy their uniforms. We sponsored every major 5K, 10K, and marathon in the community. Our crews would get up early in the morning, make anywhere from several hundred to several thousand cups of yogurt, pack them in dry ice, take them to the event, and pass them out for free! We had wonderful team members who provided this service with real enthusiasm. We even sponsored our own race each year and donated the money to a local nonprofit organization that helped the mentally ill find jobs. Just about anytime anyone called and asked for free product, we would say yes.

Over the years we had debates about how valuable our giving program was—because it was a lot of work! There is no question in my mind that it helped jump-start our sales in the early days. We attracted more people to our business than we would have without our generosity in the community. It was also satisfying to be part of something larger than ourselves and to pay back the community that helped our fragile new company "take" and eventually expand way beyond our initial expectations.

It's my observation that giving back works best under certain conditions. First, you must have a heartfelt desire to participate. If you give a gift begrudgingly, it's generally not well received. When our managers were enthusiastic about donating free product, the enthusiasm came back to our stores. When they became burned out, lost interest, or had the customer pick up the product rather than distribute it themselves, our giving had little benefit. So you have to "be there" with a genuine fire burning. Second, you have to participate at the local level with community groups in a position to support your business. Our customer was the middle- to upper-class individual with disposable income and a health and fitness orientation. We served 2,000 cups of yogurt at NBA games but only forty-three at an Oingo Boingo concert. So we supported health and fitness organizations, the running and cycling communities, schools, hospitals, cancer research groups, and the cultural arts—and we always contributed at the local level. Stated differently, donating money to save the rain forests in Brazil is a worthy cause but may not bring customers into your business in Chicago. So you have to build relationships with compatible, local organizations.

Finally, charitable giving must be a part of a sound, overall business strategy. Remember, giving something back is one of ten important keys to success; it won't save a struggling company if the other nine factors are missing. So you have to create great products, work with tenacity, build a strong team, get more for less, and so on. Giving something back then brings a powerful spirit into the organization, blesses the community, and builds mutually rewarding relationships—providing it's done with a genuine desire to serve. In other words, when the other nine cylinders are humming, charitable giving is the capstone to long-term success. I love Jon Huntsman's philosophy; his profits first go to paying off debt, next to updating his facilities, then to charitable giving. So he maintains the integrity of his business, then gives away millions every year!

In sum, there is nothing wrong with wanting to make loads of money in life. I know a lot of people who do it, and do it very successfully. However, a tremendous amount of energy comes from working for the good of others. We draw personal power and support from a variety of sources when we serve. Doors open, paths are provided, things work out. Call it synergy, karma, the law of the harvest, whatever. The fact is, we reap what we sow in life; and the more positive energy we send out, the more comes our way. Businesses that emphasize giving back to the community have a much better chance of thriving in that community. This is especially critical during the start-up phase. In some cases, it may be what helps the vulnerable new venture survive.

Following are three incredible stories of giving back to the community. Notice how the growth of Marty Shih's new venture was aided by the free 411 service he offers Asian-Americans. Also observe how the overarching objective of Ruffin Slater's grocery store is to benefit his employees and the community at large. And Jon Huntsman is the utmost example. He sees himself as a steward of resources to enhance the quality of life of those around him. Jon has donated millions of dollars to help find a cure for cancer, alleviate human suffering throughout the world, and foster education and the cultural arts. Notice how he tries to support a humanitarian project in every new country in which he does business. Prepare to be touched by these marvelous American heroes.

OUR ROLE MODELS

Marty Shih

Marty is the founder and chairman of "800-777-CLUB," an elaborate network of support services and products for Asian-Americans. Originally, the company was a flower business, but Marty realized that Asian immigrants, unfamiliar with the language and culture, have a host of additional needs. The free information and services the company offers have aided its rapid growth and remarkable success. In less than ten years, the business has grown to 900 employees and $180 million in services provided, making it the largest organization of its kind in the country. Here's his story:

I came here from Taiwan in 1979 to go to school. My sister Helen had already been here for two years. When we got here, my mom had already brainwashed us. From the time we were kids she told us, "When you grow up, you go to the United States. The ocean is wider, the sky is higher, and the moon is bigger there!" She knew that wasn't true, but she said it to stimulate us. When she was seventeen, she got a chance to go to an American School in Beijing for a couple of months, and from that point on she wanted to live in the United States. That was her dream because America was the free world. But during World War II she lost all her money and ended up in Taiwan. She eventually got married, had kids, and never got to immigrate to the United States. So we came here to live out her dream.

When I got here I had $500 and was going to study mathematics. But since my mom told me this was the land of opportunity and I could do whatever I wanted, I decided to start my own business. With the language and cultural barriers, it would have been very difficult for me to work for someone else. I finally decided to sell flowers on the street. The first day Helen and I went to the flower market and bought about $100 worth of flowers. That whole day we only sold one bunch for $1.99. (Laughs.) I can still remember it like yesterday. I told myself, "Marty, you're going to be the McDonald's of the flower industry." I kept telling myself that because McDonald's was the entrepreneur's dream. I'm not a very smart guy, and I didn't finish my studies, but I had a real passion to achieve that dream.

So we just kept selling everyday on the street corner. At the time, I was twenty-five years old and didn't speak English well. Soon we got up to $30 to $50 a day. Then an old gentleman who passed by every day offered to let us sell flowers in his building for free. So we set up a stand in his lobby in downtown Los Angeles. We gradually started selling more and more flowers and opened up a second stand. Our vision to be the McDonald's of the flower industry really influenced our thinking. The Chinese always say, "If you have a one-degree different thought, you'll end up a hundred miles different over time." So not only did we open more stands, we used catchy names for bunches of flowers. Just like McDonald's has the Big Mac, Chicken McNuggets, and all those things, we had the "Love Bouquet," the "Tickler Bouquet," and other menu items. This made it simple for both the customers and the street boys we hired to sell for us. So we standardized everything.

Before long we had six or seven flower stands in downtown Los Angeles. Then we started opening retail flower shops. In the shops, people generally bought flowers for birthdays, anniversaries, and other special occasions. So we created a computerized database of our customers' needs. The next time a birthday came around, we would call or send a letter saying, "Your girlfriend's birthday is coming up, do you want to send her flowers again?" So we started marketing to our own customers. We got up to sixteen retail shops in nine years.

At the time, I had a joint project with Flora Fax and the Direct Marketing Center at American Airlines—they were answering our phones. You see, in the flower business you get really busy with walk-in customers during holidays and don't have enough manpower to take phone orders. So the Direct Marketing Center was answering our phones with "She's Flowers Shops," then punching orders into the computer, taking credit-card numbers, and forwarding the information to our stores. That project was very successful, and I realized the world was changing from an industrial society to an information society. I figured we could operate a flower business twenty-four hours a day, seven days a week on the phone without needing salespeople in our shops. At the same time, I realized that Asian immigrants were becoming a major buying power in the United States. I was thinking if I could break through the language and cultural barriers using new-wave technology, I could create a great business opportunity.

So one day on a flight from the call center in Dallas back to Los Angeles, I told my sister I was going to quit the flower industry and start this company, 800-777-CLUB. I figured we could link Asian-Americans to a variety of products and services through the computer—and we could talk to them in their own languages! I was thinking way beyond flowers. I told Helen, "If American Airlines can sell flowers so successfully, I'll bet I can sell airlines tickets." So I was thinking about airline tickets, hotel reservations, flowers, gifts, cakes, long-distance services. AT&T had already broken up, so we could shop long-distance rates for our customers. We would make our money by getting a commission on everything we sold. For example, if you want to send flowers to your girlfriend who lives in New York, you go to a flower shop and pay $100. Well, that shop only ships $75 to the flower shop in New York and keeps $25. Also, travel agencies pay a standard commission of around 10 percent. So we could make money without charging our customers any more. We would basically provide a free service but do it in the new immigrant's language— that would be our niche market. I also knew if I could get customers comfortable with the phone, the computer, and E-mail, I wouldn't have to pay up to $3 per square foot each month for retail space.

So we started the business in November of 1989 in the basement of my flower shop. We had ten services to offer. I had been to these companies and arranged to sell their services for a commission. I had to promise them we would bring thousands of people to their business to get the deal. This was very important because we had to tell our customers we had lots of services to offer. So I did a lot of juggling in the beginning. To kick things off, we did a big grand opening and invited our friends and flower-shop customers. I also put a little ad in the Chinese newspaper. It said, "One phone call and the world is in the palm of your hand." There were three of us in the basement to answer the phones. People nicknamed us the three stooges because we aren't very smart. I am a very short Chinese guy, Steve Wang had a bum leg, and David Lin was a dreamer—so the three stooges. (Laughs.)

> One of the things people can do is go into our Web site and send a greeting card for free—we call it CardMaster.Com. Everyday, about 30,000 people send free cards for different occasions.

After our grand opening, we were all very excited, but the phone didn't ring that much. Most of the calls were for flowers because people thought I was a flower boy; with sixteen shops in the area, I was known in the Chinese community. So we started asking ourselves, "How can we get the phone to ring." One day I got this idea: "What if we check information for everybody for free?" I was thinking of a 411 service in the Asian languages, but my colleagues said, "Oh no, we can't do that; once the phone starts ringing we are going to lose money." But I felt that sooner or later people would use one of our services. And that's exactly what happened. We now receive more than a thousand calls a day for this free service, and we provide it twenty-four hours a day, seven days a week. People just call 800-777-CLUB, then transfer to our Asian 411 information service. We not only function as a 411, we act as a 911. For example, we might get a call from someone who has lost a child, a wife who is being beaten by her husband, or someone who took the wrong Greyhound, got off, and doesn't know where he is because he doesn't speak English. So we try to help these people in their own languages. I think it's definitely a worthy cause. Our whole society is built up by people helping people.

Anyway, during 1990, the phone slowly started ringing, and we went from three people to seven people. One of the big things we sold back then was MCI long distance because new immigrants didn't know they could get phone service cheaper. Over the years we've continued to add services that people need, and our sales have doubled every year. We've come from two telephone lines to 600. We've come from three people to 900. We do about 10,000 phone calls an hour during our busy times. We're also on the Asian Internet and get about two million hits per day. And we get calls from all over the country because the Asian market is so big—about twelve million people in the United States. People not only call us, we call them, so we are doing a lot of telemarketing. This year we will provide around $180 million in services in six different languages: Mandarin, Cantonese, Korean, Vietnamese, Japanese, and Filipino.

We also have a service called our Professional Employee Organization (PEO). It provides services for new businesses started by Asian immigrants: insurance, payroll, labor law, 401Ks, workers compensation, things like that. Small business is hard enough for the general public because you have to deal with all the government regulations. Think about how it is for the new immigrant! So we have a professional team to help with those things, and we're doing very well because Asians have an entrepreneurial spirit.

So anyway, I really think our 411 service has helped our growth. We do other community services as well. One of the things people can do is go into our Web site and send a greeting card for free—we call it CardMaster.Com. Everyday, about 30,000 people send free cards for different occasions. They construct the cards from our database and ship them E-mail. As people use CardMaster, the people who get the cards start using it, so it produces more leads for our company. And everything is free!

We also have a big ballroom in our building that we let community organizations use for cost plus a cleaning fee—it's about 10,000 square feet. You know, new Asian immigrants are very thrifty and don't want to use the Marriott or the Hilton because they are too costly. So we make our ballroom available, and people really like coming here. It's in El Monte, right off the 10 Freeway, so it's very convenient. It's used almost everyday for seminars, training, and special events. It's even used on Sunday for a church service. So I think these things we do have attached the community to our company. In fact, many people think we are a nonprofit organization, but we're not.

> Let's say there's a flower boy on the other corner doing the same thing I did, but he always says, "I want to own a flower shop someday." Well, that's the most he can do, because people usually don't go beyond their goal. But if you set a big goal, even if you only finish 70 percent of it, you are far better off than the street boy who only wants a flower shop, because you are thinking differently.

My advice to entrepreneurs is to have a clear vision. I wanted to be the McDonald's of the flower industry, and that really guided us. But if you ask me today, "Marty, did you become the McDonald's of the flower industry?" Well, I didn't. We eventually sold our stores to the managers because we wanted to build our new business. But I feel that is secondary. The important thing is that I had the dream. Let's say there's a flower boy on the other corner doing the same thing I did, but he always says, "I want to own a flower shop someday." Well, that's the most he can do, because people usually don't go beyond their goal. But if you set a big goal, even if you only finish 70 percent of it, you are far better off than the street boy who only wants a flower shop, because you are thinking differently.

We now have a new vision for our company. When you walk into our building, you'll see a big plaque on the side of our elevator. It has our four objectives listed. The first one is "To Honor the American Dream." Ninety-nine percent of us new immigrants come here to find this dream. The second is "To Be the Bridge to Asia." That's our strong point! The third one is "To Develop People's Potential." I'm a good example; I'm just a normal guy with a dream. The fourth one is "To Be the Best We Can Be." We always ask ourselves, "What is next?" Like my wife always says, "This is just a big dream for us. What if we wake up?" (Laughs.) Or what if this dream continues to grow? What if we grow to 5,000 people or branch out to Asia? Is our American dream fulfilled already, or do we still have a long way to go? America is still the best country on earth to do this!

Ruffin Slater

Ruffin is the founder and general manager of Weaver Street Market, a full-service grocery store located in Carrboro, North Carolina. According to Ruffin, the business "is a small-scale experiment in democracy." From the beginning, the goal was to make ownership available to the employees who work there and the customers who shop there. With more than seventy employees and $6 million in sales, the experiment seems to be working pretty well. Here's Ruffin's story:

I majored in history at Duke University. After graduating, I worked for a nonprofit, public-interest company for a couple years. When we lost our funding, I starting working at a little grocery store in Durham. It was a natural-foods cooperative—sort of a leftover from the hippie days. After a couple of years I became the manager. I really liked working there, but it was kind of dying down.

One day I started thinking it would be fun to open my own store. I got in the car with someone who worked with me and started looking for locations. We wanted a place where people could do all their shopping— you know, a produce department, a meat and fish department, a bakery, a deli—sort of the natural foods equivalent of a full-service grocery store. We really had two objectives in mind. First, we wanted to entice people to change their diets and experiment with healthier, natural foods. Second, we wanted to try an alternative system of ownership. We wanted both the people who worked there and the people who shopped there to own the business, which really hadn't been done before. There were other cooperative businesses out there, but none where the workers and customers owned the store together. We really wanted people to have a stake in how things went, so we sort of coined the idea of a community-owned grocery store.

The first real challenge was getting the money. We needed about $500,000 to lease the building, do the improvements, and get the inventory. Well, the money came from different sources. There's an alternative lending institution in Durham called the Center for Community Self Help. Its purpose is to lend money to small businesses, minority-owned companies, cooperatives. We got $100,000 from them, but it required a personal cosignature and a first lien on all our fixtures and inventory. It also required that we get the rest of the money. Then the town of Carrboro just happened to have a new loan fund for businesses willing to locate downtown—they were trying to revitalize the area. We explained the project to them, got letters of support from local business people, and talked to their board members. They finally approved a loan for $90,000. Next, we went to individuals we knew in the community and borrowed amounts up to $10,000. These loans totaled about $120,000. The rest of the money came in the form of inventory from suppliers who were willing to finance us on thirty- to sixty-day terms.

So we raised the $500,000 and outfitted the building, which is about 10,000 square feet. We wanted a clean and simple look with an open-grid ceiling. We wanted the food to be what the customer would see, so we didn't try anything fancy. The amazing thing is that we were able to do all this with debt, so we didn't have to dilute the ownership to people who provided the capital. This kept the shares available to our employees and customers, which was our major objective. So everything just worked out!

We opened in June of 1988 and did well right from the first. Our location is extremely unique and unconventional for a grocery store because we're right in the middle of town. There's like a town green in front of the building, and we get a lot of foot traffic. We also have a real nice outdoor eating area where people can get together. So it's sort of the crossroads of town with a town-hall atmosphere. I mean, from the second we opened, people felt really comfortable here. It was almost like the store had been open forever. People just showed up to shop, meet their friends, have a cup of coffee, try some pasta salad, have a business meeting, or buy a deli sandwich. We did a few things to alert people that we were comin', but it sort of just took without a lot of advertising or attention.

Right off we started selling shares to our customers and employees. This is how it works: Customers can buy a share of ownership for about $100. This entitles them to a discount when they shop, so they see an immediate benefit from their investment. We actually sold about 200 shares before we opened, and we've continued to sell them since. The employee shares are a little different. They can buy a share for $400, and they get dividends based on store performance. So we've made it easy for people to become part owners, and it's a good investment. We've now sold nearly 4,000 shares, so we've been able to pay back the money we borrowed.

> We really wanted people to have a stake in how things went, so we sort of coined the idea of a community-owned grocery store.

Anyway, that's the model. It was ambitious at first, but it's worked out really well. Most of our managers are owners or becoming owners, which has been critical to our success. In the beginning it was a struggle, because there were parts of the business I didn't know anything about. You know a grocery store is logically divided into departments like the produce department, the grocery department, the cashier department, the meat and fish department, the deli and food-service department. It's just been critical to find people with expertise in those areas to come in and round out our team. At first I was inexperienced in identifying who the right person might be. Some people worked out great and others didn't. Now we have ten managers who have been here for a while, and they are all strong in their areas. We have a management meeting every week, and everybody participates. We take turns running the meeting, so each week we have a new leader. We share information, identify issues, look at financial statements, and review customers' suggestions.

Having all our higher-ups right here in the store has been really important. We're not like a typical chain where all the executives work in a main office somewhere. I mean, it really feels like a small business. Most of the people who work here know the customers, and the customers know us. People who shop here know if they ask for something they're going to get it. In the very beginning we decided we were not going to be bureaucratic or complicated in how we treated our customers—because they're owners, too. You know, if they say a product they took home was bad, we don't care if they bring it back or have a receipt or anything. We just figure they are tellin' the truth. Or if I see a customer at the back of the store and a price on something is missing or ambiguous, I just say, "Tell the cashier this is $1.49." I don't have to write it down or tell the cashier—I know he'll ring it up for $1.49. We tell everyone who works here this is the way we want to run our business.

I think a lot of people support this store because it puts into practice a dream they have. It's not a dream of getting rich but the dream of a town working together in a democratic way for the good of us all.

How has our philosophy worked? I think it's worked great! Occasionally someone might grab a bottle of vitamins off the shelf, take it to the checkout stand, and ask for a refund, but basically it's worked wonderfully. I think it really contributes to the atmosphere of our store. Most people have had the experience of waiting in a checkout line while the cashier asks for a price check, then waits for the price to come back. Meanwhile, the line gets longer and longer, and everybody starts rolling their eyes. I think it's refreshing to come to a store where you just tell the cashier, "This is $2.99," and he rings it up. We don't hold up our lines forever waiting for someone to confirm something. So our customers feel like it really is their place.

Anyway, I feel like I'm living a version of the American dream—although the American dream typically involves people working hard to get what they want as individuals. What I've tried to do is help the community create a store for itself, so there is a greater communal or social aspect to our business. It sort of goes back to an earlier day of small towns where the shopkeeper provided credit to farmers in the spring so they could plant their crops, then waited to get paid in the fall. I think this is that angle on the American dream—the community working together to help each other out. There aren't a lot of opportunities for people to really participate in the businesses they patronize. Sure you can buy stock in companies from a broker, but they are generally somewhere "over there." I think a lot of people support this store because it puts into practice a dream they have. It's not a dream of getting rich but the dream of a town working together in a democratic way for the good of us all. I think that's our biggest contribution, and it's the most exciting part of the business. I can get a good salary and meet my needs while helping other people meet their needs.

Actually, I'm surprised about what I'm doin'. I had no intention of making this a career—it sort of just happened. The thing I like about it is the combination of the theoretical and the very concrete, hands-on work. On the one hand, I think about social responsibility, how to structure our company, and how to run a $6-million business for the benefit of everybody in the community. Generally I think democracy is a hard thing; it's often frustrating and doesn't always work. But when it does work, I think people see possibilities in other aspects of their life, and that's very rewarding to me. Then on the other hand, I order groceries, put them out, and people come in and buy them—it's very simple and clear. So when I get frustrated about something, I can go out and stock shelves for an hour, you know? Or I can go out and help customers, which is what we're here to do. So this is a nice combination of both of those things.

Jon Huntsman

Jon is the founder, chairman, and CEO of Huntsman Chemical Corporation, the largest privately held petrochemical company in the world. Jon's first company, Huntsman Container Corporation, pioneered *the polystyrene "clamshell" for the McDonald's Big Mac. Today, Huntsman Chemical owns more than eighty manufacturing facilities in more than twenty nations. Each year, the company donates a significant portion of its profits to humanitarian projects. Jon and his family recently donated $100 million to help find a cure for cancer. Jon says, "It's our way of saying to the world, 'Thank you for permitting a very ordinary family, and a very common individual from a common background . . . the opportunity to build a global empire.'" Here's how it happened:*

The early days were difficult. My father was a music teacher, both in junior high and high school. The only job he could find happened to be in Blackfoot, Idaho, so I was born in Blackfoot. I came two-and-a-half-months premature. My father was on a fishing trip and had no idea my mother would be delivering over two months early. There was no doctor present, so a midwife, a Mrs. Olson, came and helped my mother. I was what they call a blue baby—the circulation was very poor. When the doctor finally came, he looked at me and said, "This child is dead; let's work to save the mother." In the meantime, my father showed up, and he and Mrs. Olson put me in hot and cold water to get the circulation going, then wrapped me in a blanket. Little by little they got a few peeps out of me— to Doctor Miller's amazement. My wife and I visited him on our honeymoon some twenty-two years later, and he told us I was one of three babies, of the thousands he delivered in rural Idaho, who had absolutely no chance of surviving and yet lived.

In any event, we lived in little Idaho towns from Blackfoot to Thomas to Pocatello, where my father taught school. In 1950 at age forty, he decided to go back to college. He went to Stanford University, and we lived in married-student housing for three years. My brother Blaine and I were the oldest kids living in Stanford Village. Everyone else was newly married with little babies, and here my father was going back to college. During those years, he only made $120 a month, so it was a difficult time for our family. My responsibility was to pay for family medical expenses and the family automobile—that meant I had to have two or three jobs. After school I worked in a grocery store cleaning out the meat market; at night and on Saturdays I worked for JC Penney; when I got home I would often babysit late at night. Incredibly enough, I was able to play sports and still get rather good grades during that time.

So my upbringing was very meager. We would have been clearly considered on the poverty level. I remember as a freshman I had one shirt! I would wear it to school every day and wash it on weekends. Also, my mother would go to the meat market after it closed to get parts of meat that hadn't been sold so our family could get by on $120 a month. But you know, at the time, I didn't know we were poor. I was both junior class president, then student-body president of Palo Alto High School, one of the most affluent high schools in America. I was without question the poorest kid in the class, but it didn't ever occur to me I was different from anybody else. I just couldn't invite people to a home while we were at Stanford Village because we didn't have a home.

During my senior year, our teachers had a two-day conference, and classes were adjourned on Thursday and Friday. Our principal called me at home and told me that Dr. Raymond Saalbach, the director of admissions from the University of Pennsylvania, and Mr. Harold Zellerbach, chairman of the board of Crown-Zellerbach Paper Company and president of the Northern California Alumni, were coming to Palo Alto High to see any students interested in attending the Wharton School of Finance. He had failed to tell them it was a teachers' conference and there were no students for them to interview. He asked if I would come in and pretend I was interested in the University of Pennsylvania. I was planning to go to Stanford, but I knew I had to go where I could get the best scholarship. So I went in and met with them, and they were absolutely phenomenal! They came to our basketball game that evening and watched me play, then followed up with letters. They eventually offered me two scholarships—the Northern California Alumni Scholarship and the Harold L. and William Zellerbach Scholarship.

So I went back there to a school I'd never heard of and found out that 70 percent of my classmates had been to prep schools attuned to Ivy League academics—something which was very foreign to me. When I got there, they listed the SAT scores of the incoming freshmen. I scored very high in math because it was easy for me. In English, however, the scores ranged from 511 to 800, and 511 was the score I had received. It occurred to me that perhaps I was their token Californian, and to some extent their token Christian. It's a school where the top business leaders in America send their children, and many of them come from wealthy Jewish families. These students had prepared for years to go to Wharton, and I had no idea what it was! So I started out rather ill equipped but made a vow during my freshman year I would graduate at the top of my class. Upon graduation four years later, I was not only senior-class president, which was the highest elected position in our class, but I was awarded what they call the "Spoon Award," an honor given to the top graduate each year. This tradition started when the university was founded in 1740.

Following Wharton, I was offered tremendous jobs on Wall Street. But I started off selling eggs in Los Angeles, which was about as unglamourous a job as a Wharton graduate has ever taken. The company I joined had major ranches and egg-producing plants throughout the western states. I was part of a team commissioned to develop a plastic egg carton to replace the pulp carton we had known for so many years. We felt that plastic cartons would prevent the escape of moisture and keep eggs fresh much longer because they were not porous like paper. We also thought a plastic carton would prevent broken eggs from making the carton mushy and leaking from one carton to another. While we were going through this process, we merged our fledgling packaging business with Dow Chemical—it was a fifty-fifty joint venture. At the time, I was the executive vice president of the egg company, managing some thirty different egg-processing plants around the country. Then in 1967, when I was just turning thirty, they asked me to be the president of the packaging business. The company had lost a lot of money, and they wanted me to salvage the four manufacturing plants trying to make the new egg carton. The only reason I got the job was because Dow had virtually written this investment off their books. "Let Jon try it; he's done well running egg plants at an early age. He's probably too young to know it can't be done. Since it's already at a low point, what do we have to lose?"

I went in without knowing a thing about plastics, without having a chemical-engineering background, without having had a chemistry course in my life. I didn't understand extrusion equipment, vacuum formers, and all the technical elements of chemical engineering required to manufacture plastics. It was like watching a Chinese language class after speaking English all my life. It became clear to me I had to find people who could do those functions. I also had to take the plants out of the R & D mode they were in during the mid '60s when plastics were just coming into vogue and get something tangible out into the marketplace—and in the process make a profit! Basically, I had to do what I had tried so desperately to do when I was selling eggs: to see that we were making a quality product and that our plants were running at 100-percent capacity. It didn't matter to me at that point whether I was selling eggs, producing toothpicks, making shoelaces or textiles. All I knew was that in order to make a profit, we had to make a quality product, run at full capacity, and do it efficiently enough to be competitive. Those are the basic ingredients of a successful business. So I brought in a new team, and within eighteen months we'd turned a very heavy loss into a rather substantial profit. During the next three years, as plastics were just beginning in America, I decided if we could make egg cartons out of plastics, we could make a multitude of other products. I also realized that if I could turn around a company that was 50 percent owned by one of the largest plastics companies in the world, I could probably do it on my own!

For Christmas that year, I received a gift from Mr. Ted Doan, the president of Dow Chemical in Midland, Michigan. It was a book entitled "The Dow Story." It told how Mr. Herbert Dow started a small company to manufacture bromine and chlorine in a little shack adjacent to his home. He said he would rather work for himself than his existing employer, which was very impressive to me at that point in my life. So I went back to Midland, Michigan, and visited with the person I reported to, Dr. Julius Johnson, who was then senior vice president of research and development. I showed him the book and said, "If Mr. Dow can go out and start his own company, I would like to do likewise." Without realizing the enormous risks and hazards I was about to undertake, I went back and explained to Mr. Olson, who owned the egg business, that I would be leaving the packaging company to launch my own venture—Huntsman Container Corporation. I thought they would cheer me on and say this is the dream that every young man and woman has.

During the two-year period we were building our first plant, I went back to Washington and served as associate administrator of the Department of Health, Education, and Welfare. I was literally the chief operating officer of the welfare and social services programs in America under Elliot Richardson. After seven months in that job, I became a special assistant to Richard Nixon. This was during his first term, so it was before Watergate. My office was in the west wing of the White House, and I was responsible for the ingress and egress of information to and from the president's office: budgets, finances, personnel, perks. During this time, I helped orchestrate the building of our first plant in Fullerton, California. From 7:30 A.M. until 9:00 P.M. every day I was at the White House working with the president. Then until two or three in the morning I was on the phone with my brother and our engineers seeing that our plant got built.

Just before we were ready to open the plant, our financial partner, who was W. R. Grace, pulled the plug on us. They decided they wanted to go into the plastics business alone, which left us high and dry. At the time, I had a successful business going on the side in phonograph records. I would buy these records from Capitol or RCA or Columbia, package them, then sell them through television advertising. We did the "Greatest Hits of Rock & Roll," Christmas albums, and other records. Twenty-one of our first twenty-three records were gold albums, which means they sold over 500,000 copies. So I was making four to five times as much on records as I was selling eggs or in packaging, but I knew the record business was like a bubble—because it could pop at any time, I never paid a great deal of attention to it. Nonetheless, it did provide the cash flow to finance our equipment and pick up some of the slack where W. R. Grace had left off. My brother Blaine and I also raised $300,000 by borrowing on our homes. The rest of the capital came from Hambrecht and Quist, a small investment company that had just started in San Francisco. To make a long story short, I left Washington in 1972 to run the business.

We started producing a plastic egg carton somewhat dissimilar from the one we had produced at Dow Chemical. But our main goal was to be the first to make a host of plastic items for the food-service industry. We developed the first plastic plates, bowls, and dishes for American Hospital Supply. It eliminated the need for washing dishes and therefore the potential of germs being carried from patient to patient. After American Hospital we began to supply restaurants, fast-food chains, and the public at large. In 1974 we developed the first clamshell container for hamburgers. I went to McDonald's to sell the concept, but they turned me down. I couldn't go home without an account, so I caught a plane to Miami and went to see Burger King. I tried to get them to use the container for one of their big-selling items like the cheeseburger or hamburger, but they put their ham and cheese sandwich in it. When McDonald's saw Burger King selling this ham and cheese sandwich in a plastic container, they asked who made it and found out it was Huntsman Container. They came to see me and said, "Why didn't you bring this to McDonald's?" I said, "I waited outside your offices for two days and couldn't get an appointment!" So over the next eight months we worked very closely with McDonald's and by late '74 came out with the first Big Mac container. They immediately converted all their paper items into plastic.

Although we created seventy to eighty new products during that era, about two-thirds of them turned out to be disasters. Our great taco containers that we made millions of were total failures. Our take-out pizza containers never caught on. But the ones that did catch on did very well. So it gave us the enormous advantage of being one of the first companies in America to build the plastics industry in a way that had never been done before. By 1976 our business was extremely successful. At the time, I owned 25 percent, and the other shareholders owned 75 percent. Being a minority shareholder yet having to carry the responsibility of rapid growth with limited capital was somewhat frustrating. So that year, I sold the business to Keyes Fiber Company, one of our competitors in the pulp and fiber industry. It was a good move for them because they could now offer a panorama of both paper and plastic products.

I signed an agreement with Keyes Fiber to stay on as president for four years. I found that when I worked for somebody else I had to dance to their music. But the basic laws of business still applied: We had to produce high-quality products to keep good customers; we had to run our facilities at 100-percent capacity to realize the lowest possible costs; and we had to develop high morale with our employees to motivate them to perform. In the end, those who invested with us early on received thirty-four dollars back for every dollar they invested. Also, the fellows who started in the business with me, but didn't invest any of their own money, did extremely well. Many millionaires came out of that first little company, Huntsman Container.

After fulfilling my commitment to Keyes, the Church of Jesus Christ of Latter-day Saints asked me to serve as a mission president in Washington, D.C., for three years. That was a wonderful hiatus because it gave me the opportunity to focus on service rather than monetary activities. It also gave me a chance to reflect upon what I wanted to do for the rest of my life. So when I left the mission, I knew I wanted to enter the petrochemical business. At the time, many products made of paper, wood, metal, aluminum, and glass had already been converted to plastics. So the industry was building a strong base and becoming a necessary component of our economy.

Having a background in the business, I knew companies I thought might be interested in selling off one of their assets. I began negotiating with Shell Oil Company to buy their polystyrene plant in Belpre, Ohio. They couldn't conceive of an individual paying $42 million for a single manufacturing plant that made polystyrene. When I told them I would put up $500,000 in equity, they just about tossed me out of their office. But since resilience had been my middle name from birth on, I was able to string together the most unique financing arrangement ever concocted. I persuaded Shell to take back a $12-million note that I would pay off over the next ten years. I then met with ARCO Chemical Company and told them I'd buy 150 million pounds of styrene monomer from them each year for thirteen years—the raw material for polystyrene—if they would loan me $10 million up front. They finally agreed to do it over the objections of many of their senior officers.

So with my $500,000, the $12-million note from Shell, and the $10-million loan from ARCO, I was able to persuade one of my former classmates at Wharton, who was now the executive vice president of Union Bank in Los Angeles, to loan me the remaining $20 million. I gave Union Bank a first mortgage on the facility and Shell a second mortgage. To ARCO, I gave my home, the record business, and some buildings and shopping centers I owned. So at the age of forty-five, I pledged everything

I had to buy this one plant from Shell Oil. At the closing, they gave me a statue called the "River Boat Gambler." It's a statue of a gambling man lifting his six-shooters off his hips. They later acknowledged they never believed I could make this thing fly; it was literally hooked together with chewing gum and bailing wire, to say the least.

The plant was breaking even when I bought it, but fortunately everyone involved had great confidence in me. They had all studied my record at Dow Chemical and Huntsman Container and knew I had taken those businesses from heavy losses to major successes. So I had a track record, and thank goodness for that. My experience told me we had to get back to the basics of producing the highest-quality polystyrene and running the plant at full capacity—it was only running at 80 percent at the time. As we got going, it was clear we needed additional capital, so I went out and sold 40 percent of Huntsman Chemical to some private investors. I used that money to help pay off the bank debt. Eventually I was able to buy back the 40 percent, then sell it again to Great Lakes Chemical for $54 million. This money allowed me to take out all my debt and expand into several other plants. One of the plants I bought was another Shell facility in northern England. I bought it quite cheaply because it was old and antiquated. When I first saw it, Shell said, "We're going to close it and lay off our people because it doesn't run effectively anymore." I said, "There's no need to lay off your people; we can make rust work!" At the end of 1984, there were ten quotes of the year in the London Times. The first one was by Queen Elizabeth. The number-ten quote was by "Polystyrene King" Jon Huntsman who said, "We can make rust work," which was exactly what I had bought for a very inexpensive price. But we made the old plant run smoothly and efficiently. Our people were just remarkable!

Anyway, we've gone through twenty-one acquisitions in the last thirteen years. Those twenty-one acquisitions represent more than eighty sites around the world. They are all manufacturing plants. The acquisition of Texaco Chemical Company in 1993 for approximately a billion dollars lifted us to new heights. Up to that time, most of our acquisitions had been divisions of companies with two or three manufacturing sites. But here, we purchased an entire chemical company with a multitude of sites around the world. We now have manufacturing plants in Asia, Europe, Australia, North America.

Our base materials are still petrochemicals and plastics, but instead of one product, polystyrene, we're now one of the world's largest producers of specialty chemicals that go into over 500 uses. We produce the ingredients for appliances, microwave ovens, television sets, cameras. We're one of the world's largest producers of ingredients for soaps, toothpaste, mouthwash, razors, household detergents. Our products go into automobiles—everything from bumpers to dashboards to upholstery to tires. With the purchase of Goodyear Tire and Rubber Company's entire film division, we became one of the world's largest producers of film overwraps for meat, frozen-food bags, and bread bags. We're also the third-largest producer of rubber in the world today. So our products are endless; they literally go into everything from medicines to soaps to appliances to safety bags for automobiles to the tires to the dashboards. There isn't much in life that you can see, feel, or touch that Huntsman doesn't produce in one way or another. Our total sales are approximately $5 billion. Our operating profits are in excess of $800 million. So from very humble beginnings . . .

> We always try to combine a humanitarian project that will genuinely help the people with our business interest. It might be assisting the flood victims in Thailand or the homeless people in Armenia, or helping to relieve starvation in Russia and India and Ukraine.

As you can imagine, with over eighty sites around the world, I travel a tremendous amount internationally. We usually go around the world three to four times a year. It might be exhausting to some people, but it's absolutely exhilarating to me. One of the things I enjoy most is developing relationships with various world leaders. When we build or buy a facility in a country, we become a very significant factor in its infrastructure;

we employ several hundred people in a basic industry, which in turn leads to employment for hundreds more in service jobs. So government leaders are very willing to chat with someone like me who's going to invest a huge amount of money and create jobs for their people. I've found in life that people typically look for quid pro quos; they look for what they are going to get out of a relationship. In our case, we always try to combine a humanitarian project that will genuinely help the people with our business interest. It might be assisting the flood victims in Thailand or the homeless people in Armenia, or helping to relieve starvation in Russia and India and Ukraine. But all the leaders appreciate that very much, and hence we've developed very fine relationships with thirty or forty major countries around the world.

So I would have to say that relationships have really been the key to our success in business. And in a manufacturing setting, it starts with our own people. If our people are motivated and know they are appreciated, any dream can come true. This has been so critical to me, being in a very technical business and not having had a chemical engineering course. I've had to surround myself with a large number of Ph.D.s and chemical engineers, then ensure they are well satisfied with their salaries and benefits, and most importantly, that they know I care about them. Clearly, our most important assets are the people who work with us in the spirit of teamwork—not these mammoth facilities around the world. Even today with 10,000 employees, I still spend at least 50 percent of my time with our people: calling them by name, thanking them for good work, letting them know they are a vital part of our success, trying to recognize birthdays and anniversaries and illnesses, traveling through the night to a funeral or home of a family where an unfortunate death has occurred. Whether it's a production worker or a truck driver or an R & D person—I tip my hat to all those who are masters of their jobs.

So one of my suggestions to young entrepreneurs is to learn to hire the right people. We have two questions we ask job applicants that I think are very important. Number one, "Tell us about the jobs you've had through high school and college." We want to know whether they've learned to work. Having held part-time or full-time jobs through the education process tells a lot about a person's character. The second question we have our people ask is, "Tell us about your failures and how you've overcome them." It doesn't matter to us that people have fallen in life. What we want to know is if they've learned to overcome adversity. As Shakespeare said, which is etched on my mother's tombstone, "Sweet are the uses of adversity." These questions catch people off guard because they think we're going to ask about their college, grades, and degree. I've found that those questions are meaningless. What matters is the character of the individual.

There's another concept I think entrepreneurs need to understand. It's my belief that men and women who have been rewarded financially not only have an obligation, but a very important duty, to place money back into the society from which they have reaped their reward. We have three basic objectives for our profits. Our first is to repay debt as quickly as possible. Our second is to improve our plants and equipment so our employees enjoy the safest possible facilities. Third is to put money into humanitarian projects in our community and world at large. The family has never taken substantial amounts of money out of the business—we've just lived on our salaries. We see ourselves as temporary trustees to redistribute those monies to programs that can do the most good for society. We give large amounts to education, culture, and religious organizations. We recently bought a new boiler for the Episcopal Church, we helped rebuild the Cathedral of the Madeleine, and we're one of the largest contributors to the Catholic Church's effort to feed the poor—Pope John Paul II thanked me personally at the Vatican. We are also funding a $100-million center to help find a cure for cancer. It seems like the more we put back into humanitarian programs, the more we are entrusted with even greater financial affluence, and thus greater responsibility to contribute. All businesses have a bottom line, and ours is

> Until we truly move beyond the profit level and help find cures for cancer, provide for the homeless, and feed the poor, we haven't achieved our corporate objectives.

not the building of profits. Our bottom line is the utilization of profits to enrich the human soul and alleviate human suffering. So until we truly move beyond the profit level and help find cures for cancer, provide for the homeless, and feed the poor, we haven't achieved our corporate objectives.

I don't know if this is the American dream; it's really more of a fantasy. When I was in the egg business in Los Angeles, it was my goal to make $1,000 a year for every year of my age. So when I was fifty, I hoped to be making $50,000 a year; when I was sixty, I hoped to be making $60,000. Then we got into the chemical business, and our dream was to someday reach $50 million in annual sales with $5 million in profits. In our wildest dreams we never thought we would be more than a one-factory operation. This was just over ten years ago. So where we are today is something we never anticipated. I believe America provided us the opportunity to achieve this level of affluence. Although we pay hundreds of millions of dollars in taxes each year, it's a privilege to live in a country where one can start out in a dust bowl in Idaho and build the type of empire we have today.

One final thought: Life is a series of starting over. We start over when we get out of elementary school, we start over in junior high and high school, we start over again in college, we start over when we get married and have a family, then we start over again at the bottom of the heap in a company. So life is a series of, not how we finish, but how we start. We have to have a road map to point the direction we want to go. If we just push the gas pedal of life and don't know where we want to be, we're never going to get there. In every one of these incidents of my life, I've invariably started out at the bottom of the pile. I can't think of a time, right from birth, that it wasn't a grind. Yet I always set goals and made decisions about where I wanted to go, and it became a way of life. I don't know Michael, that's just a little philosophy.

1. **EVALUATE YOUR MOTIVES FOR STARTING A BUSINESS.**

    List the reasons you want to start your own company. If making money is your main motivation, your efforts may be short-term. If you have a genuine desire to help other people and contribute to your community, your chances of success are higher.

2. **IDENTIFY COMPATIBLE COMMUNITY GROUPS TO SERVE.**

    Make a list of all the organizations that need support from local companies. Select several that are compatible with your products and services and are most likely to bring customers to your business.

3. **CREATE YOUR PLAN FOR GIVING SOMETHING BACK.**

    Write out a simple, one-page plan for working with the community groups you have selected. Include the services you can offer early on without spending a lot of money: free products, manpower, sponsorships, and so on. Commit to dates to make the contacts and get started.

EPILOGUE

During most of the twentieth century, large corporations created the jobs, generated the wealth, and made the American dream possible. The important question was, "Which company do you work for?" not, "What do you do for a living?" Throughout this era, entrepreneurs were suspect: they were scatterbrained folks who tinkered in garages and had a hard time fitting into society. No parents wanted their son or daughter to be an entrepreneur, or to marry one, for that matter. Many business sages predicted that small businesses would forever occupy the sidelines in our economy.

Today, we are experiencing the biggest change in American business since the rise of the industrial era. Mammoth corporations are decaying and entrepreneurship is exploding. Small businesses are creating most of our new jobs and innovative products. The support for new venturing has never been stronger. Entrepreneurs are becoming our national heroes, and everyone wants to be one. As this shift from large to small business continues, researchers and practitioners alike are asking fundamental questions: What do entrepreneurs actually do? Are there common steps to starting a new venture? Is success a function of personality traits? Can entrepreneurship be taught?

My three years of "on-the-street" observation offer real insight into the entrepreneurial drama. Having read the stories, you now know that everyday Americans follow similar paths to create thriving companies. They have unusual knowledge of an industry, stumble onto a true opportunity, drum up support from a cast of characters, and work with wonderful resilience. They are masters of efficiency, experts on change, and philanthropists in their communities. After realizing success with one venture, they repeat the process with a new opportunity. While being in the right place at the right time is part of it, *successful entrepreneurs go to the right place at the right time.* The word that best describes the process is *scrambling.* The heroes I interviewed scramble to the opportunities, scramble to meet the right people, scramble to win important accounts, scramble to find solutions to problems, and scramble to keep the company alive.

This vision of entrepreneurship is very different from the traditional, highly structured approach taught by some experts. These authorities advocate a detailed business plan, raising funds, securing a facility, hiring employees, then hoping the venture achieves its projections before the money runs out. While long-range planning is important, my findings show it is not at the heart of success. Instead, the important keys are a great idea, incredible zeal, stupendous tenacity, team-building talent, and a sincere desire to make a contribution— both within the organization and the community. Thriving entrepreneurs commit to new ventures, then continue scrambling until they succeed.

The advantages of entrepreneurship over employment are tremendous. First, it's an exhilarating ride! Building your own company is much more exciting than doing a routine job for someone else. Second, entrepreneurship increases your skills and confidence immensely. After a few successes, you come to believe anything is possible under the right circumstances. The impact is so positive, I think everyone should try it at least once! Third, building your own company can shore up your financial future. Many of the entrepreneurs I interviewed have already sold their businesses and capitalized on their hard work: Sean Nguyen, Bill Fitzgerald, Sally Gutierrez, Dave Burbidge, Zia Wesley Hosford, and June Morris. Selling a healthy company can give you greater freedom than you can ever achieve from employment. I suspect many future entrepreneurs will start companies with the purpose of building equity, selling the business, and moving on to something else. The opportunities are great for those who master the keys to success.

In sum, entrepreneurial skills will be critical in the future. The most important business enterprise of the next century will be *you!* We are returning full circle to a time prior to the industrial revolution when people grew up knowing they had to take care of themselves. It never occurred to anyone that a large corporation would provide his or her livelihood. Consequently, people became blacksmiths, craftsmen, farmers, and artisans, and they developed real skills in small business. And so it is today. Savvy individuals know they need a plan for securing their future. The good news is that you can create a thriving company by following the ten keys to entrepreneurial success. It's a matter of setting up the factors in advance—preparation precedes power in new venturing! Consider this book an operating manual for getting your new business off the ground. Refer to it often, and reread the stories for information and inspiration.

The assessment tool that follows helps you see where you stand on each of the important keys. It's a sequence of questions to make sure you don't launch prematurely. You will get a score for each key and a score for the entire assessment. The more favorably you can answer the questions, the greater your chance of success. Take your business idea and see how you stand. Each time you have a new idea, measure it against these questions. This tool can help you evaluate opportunities for years to come. My hope is that all the ingredients will come together so you can enjoy entrepreneurial success. Whether you are in business, government, or education, these ten keys consitute the leadership skills of the future.

KNOWING THE TERRAIN

	NO!	No	no	?	yes	Yes	YES!
I have extensive experience in this industry:	1	2	3	4	5	6	7
I am familiar with all the major competitors:	1	2	3	4	5	6	7
I know the strengths and weaknesses of other companies' products:	1	2	3	4	5	6	7
I know which companies have the best products:	1	2	3	4	5	6	7
I have many important contacts in this industry:	1	2	3	4	5	6	7
I am familiar with the channels of distribution for this business:	1	2	3	4	5	6	7
I have several good ideas for getting ongoing feedback from customers:	1	2	3	4	5	6	7
I have strategies for gaining up-to-date industry information:	1	2	3	4	5	6	7

Total score for knowing the terrain: _____

If you scored over 40, you have a pretty good handle on this industry. You've either worked in the field or are a serious user of the products. Don't assume you know everything, however. Continue to acquire as much information as you can, now and after launching your venture. If you scored 30 to 40 there is still hope, but you have work to do. Read up on your future competitors, visit their places of business, buy and test their products, attend an industry trade show, and start networking with everyone you can in the field. Until you gain more information, don't move forward. If you scored less than 30, this is not the right industry for you, at least not at this time. Keep your day job or buy a franchise to obtain the "industry knowledge" part of the equation for success.

SEIZING THE OPPORTUNITY

	NO!	No	no	?	yes	Yes	YES!

My product meets a need that is not being
adequately addressed in the marketplace: 1   2   3   4   5   6   7

My product has definite competitive
advantages: 1   2   3   4   5   6   7

I have the required skills and training
necessary to make this business work: 1   2   3   4   5   6   7

I have adequate credibility within this
industry: 1   2   3   4   5   6   7

I know several important players who
can help me get started: 1   2   3   4   5   6   7

I have the basic resources I need to launch
this venture (money, equipment, tools,
office, etc.):   1   2   3   4   5   6   7

I know exactly who my customers are
and how to reach them: 1   2   3   4   5   6   7

I have potential customers who will buy
my product right now: 1   2   3   4   5   6   7

Total score for seizing the opportunity: _____

If you scored over 40, you have a pretty good business opportunity. If you do well on the other entrepreneurial keys, your venture has a high probability for success. Courageously seize the opportunity and start scrambling. If you scored 30 to 40, you have a potential opportunity, but several pieces are missing. You may lack resources, credibility in the industry, or customers who are ready to buy your products. Keep doing your homework until these components fall into place. When they do, don't hesitate to move forward. If you scored less than 30, you don't have a legitimate business opportunity. There's so much work to be done that it might not be worth doing. If you launch a pipe dream, it will vanish into thin air.

FINDING A MENTOR

	NO!	No	no	?	yes	Yes	YES!
My mentor knows me fairly well:	1	2	3	4	5	6	7
My mentor understands my strengths and weaknesses:	1	2	3	4	5	6	7
My mentor has passion for this opportunity:	1	2	3	4	5	6	7
My mentor has significant business experience:	1	2	3	4	5	6	7
My mentor has many contacts who can help us jump-start this venture:	1	2	3	4	5	6	7

Total score for finding a mentor: _____

If your score is over 25, you are fortunate. Your mentor will be a great asset to your new business, particularly if he or she has real passion for the deal. If your score is 25 or less, your future venture is missing an important piece. Keep searching for the right mentor. If you can't find the support you need in one person, you may need several mentors to cover the bases.

RADIATING ZEAL

	NO!	No	no	?	yes	Yes	YES!
I have a genuine passion for my product or service:	1	2	3	4	5	6	7
I have real enthusiasm to succeed in business:	1	2	3	4	5	6	7
Owning my own company will be much more exciting than working for someone else:	1	2	3	4	5	6	7
I can clearly and passionately tell others why my product is better than anything else out there:	1	2	3	4	5	6	7
I have all the key factors in place to make this business venture work:	1	2	3	4	5	6	7

Total score for radiating zeal: _____

To move ahead with a new venture, your score here needs to be greater than 25. If it is, you have enough passion to persuade others to get involved: investors, partners, and team members. Most important, you'll be able to convince customers to try your product or service. If your score is 25 or less, you're not ready to launch. Starting a business is too tough without the power to ignite passion in others. You'll also lack staying power during the difficult times. Perhaps your product or service is wrong. Maybe you're nervous about going out on your own. Try to visualize your future without launching the new venture; this may enhance your zeal for independence.

WORKING WITH TENACITY

	NO!	*No*	*no*	*?*	*yes*	*Yes*	*YES!*
I am willing to work long, exhausting hours on this new venture:	1	2	3	4	5	6	7
I enjoy rolling up my sleeves and doing the "real work" of this business:	1	2	3	4	5	6	7
I am responsible for my own successes and failures in life:	1	2	3	4	5	6	7
When people tell me no I remain calm and try to figure out why:	1	2	3	4	5	6	7
There are always ways to get around obstacles and accomplish business objectives:	1	2	3	4	5	6	7
This venture will succeed if I think clearly and continue to scramble:	1	2	3	4	5	6	7

Total score for working with tenacity:　　　　　_____

If you scored above 30 on this key, you have the mental toughness to succeed in new venturing. You're not afraid to work hard, and you take responsibility for your own actions. This posture is critical to making things happen in business. If you scored 30 or less, you lack the mindset required for entrepreneurship, at least for this particular venture. If you're not prepared to make things work at all costs, they won't. It's better not to start until you're ready to work with tenacity.

GIVING MIND-BOGGLING SERVICE

	NO!	No	no	?	yes	Yes	YES!
I have a good feel for what customers expect in this industry:	1	2	3	4	5	6	7
I know what level of service the major competitors offer:	1	2	3	4	5	6	7
I can overshoot my customers' expectations:	1	2	3	4	5	6	7
I can implement several events when launching this venture that will boggle my customers' minds:	1	2	3	4	5	6	7
I can give my customers better service than they can get anywhere else:	1	2	3	4	5	6	7
I can create systems to maintain superb service with every customer as this business grows:	1	2	3	4	5	6	7

Total score for giving mind-boggling service: _____

If you scored greater than 30, your customer service will provide a competitive advantage. You'll attract people to your business and produce early sales. Make sure mind-boggling service continues to be a priority during all phases of business growth. If you scored 30 or less, you'll definitely struggle, particularly during the launch phase. If you enjoy people and want to serve them well, you need more information or an expert in service systems. If you really don't like serving customers, you had better rethink your interest in starting a business.

BUILDING THE TEAM

	NO!	No	no	?	yes	Yes	YES!
I clearly understand my strengths and weaknesses in business:	1	2	3	4	5	6	7
I know people who are "team players" I can recruit to compliment my skills and experience:	1	2	3	4	5	6	7
I am willing to offer strong incentives to attract and keep top talent in the organization:	1	2	3	4	5	6	7
I have a group of advisors I can work with cooperatively (investors, board members, etc.):	1	2	3	4	5	6	7
I know partners outside the organization I can team up with (suppliers, distributors, manufacturers, etc.):	1	2	3	4	5	6	7
I know how to build strong teamwork throughout the organization:	1	2	3	4	5	6	7
I am able to put my ego aside and work toward a team success:	1	2	3	4	5	6	7
I am willing to make changes quickly if a team member isn't working out:	1	2	3	4	5	6	7

Total score for building the team: _____

If your score here is over 40, you understand the importance of team-work and have critical players in mind to help with your venture. Remember, emphasizing teamwork at all levels in the organization will dramatically increase your odds for success. If you scored 30 to 40, you're off to a good start but need to rethink your attitude toward teams, and perhaps find a few more players. If your score is less than 30, you don't have a team attitude, you don't know the right people, and you're not ready to start a business in today's turbulent environment.

GETTING MORE FROM LESS

	NO!	No	no	?	yes	Yes	YES!
I know how to get this company up and running with limited capital:	1	2	3	4	5	6	7
I know how to find customers and produce cash-flow immediately:	1	2	3	4	5	6	7
I know how to solve problems and get things done with limited resources:	1	2	3	4	5	6	7
I know how to keep my cost structure lower than my competitors in this industry:	1	2	3	4	5	6	7
I am willing to forgo the "images of success" to keep this company healthy financially:	1	2	3	4	5	6	7

Total score for getting more for less: _____

If you scored over 25 on this key, you're in a strong position. Being frugal has real advantages. You can start your company, keep prices down, and pick up market share early. You can also raise your prices and enhance your profit margin over time. If your score is 25 or less, brace yourself for serious financial troubles if you launch your venture. My advice is to hold off until you develop a more creative strategy for getting more from less. This is not an area to take lightly in new venturing.

NOTCHING IT UPWARD AND ONWARD

	NO!	No	no	?	yes	Yes	YES!
I operate according to specific and attainable goals and objectives:	1	2	3	4	5	6	7
I am comfortable with growth and change:	1	2	3	4	5	6	7
I have a clear strategy for expanding the core business:	1	2	3	4	5	6	7
I have ideas for expanding beyond the core business into other products and services:	1	2	3	4	5	6	7
I am willing to change directions when it becomes clear that something is not working:	1	2	3	4	5	6	7

Total score for notching it upward and onward: _____

If your score here is greater than 25, you're prepared to handle the twists and turns of entrepreneuring. You are goal directed, forward thinking, and comfortable with growth and change. If your score is 25 or less, you either lack flexibility or need to spend more time planning for growth and future opportunities. Think about all the possible plan Bs you might implement if plan A doesn't work. Quickly moving to more fruitful areas is critical to entrepreneurial success.

GIVING SOMETHING BACK

	NO!	No	no	?	yes	Yes	YES!
I have a genuine desire to contribute to the community in which I operate:	1	2	3	4	5	6	7
I know several community organizations I can work with that are compatible with my business:	1	2	3	4	5	6	7
I have a specific strategy for working with one or more local community organizations:	1	2	3	4	5	6	7
I plan on making community service an ongoing part of my business:	1	2	3	4	5	6	7

Total score for giving something back: _____

If your score is greater than 20, your generosity will work to your advantage. If you support the community, the community will support your company. You will also bring a great spirit into your organization and have a much richer experience in business and in life. If you scored 20 or less, you need to formulate a strategy for giving something back to your community. While charitable service may not seem that important to starting a new venture, it will help you attract customers and serve the company well in the long term. Don't forget this important key to entrepreneurial success.

OVERALL SCORE ON TEN KEYS TO SUCCESS

List your score on each of the ten keys to entrepreneurial success. Then add them up to get a total score for the assessment.

Knowing the terrain: _____

Seizing the opportunity: _____

Finding a mentor: _____

Radiating zeal: _____

Working with tenacity: _____

Giving mind-boggling service: _____

Building the team: _____

Getting more from less: _____

Notching it upward and onward: _____

Giving something back: _____

Total score for assessment: _____

If your overall score is greater than 300, you have a legitimate opportunity and a great chance for success. Don't hesitate to start your new venture! Just don't fool yourself into thinking you have "arrived." Entrepreneurship requires ongoing education and skill development. Continue to study your industry, search for new opportunities, practice frugality, and develop your team-building skills. Most important, keep the zeal and tenacity high—as they go, so goes the business!

If you scored between 220 and 300, you may have an opportunity, but a few pieces are missing. Review the keys where your scores were weak, reread these chapters, and study the stories of our role models. You probably need to acquire more information, cultivate new attitudes, meet a few more people, and develop additional skills—all of which can be done. In several months to a year, you can become much better prepared. Believe me, it's better to wait and be ready than it is to launch too soon and fail fast. Business is hard enough when you are prepared. Don't make it more difficult by starting something prematurely.

If your overall score is less than 220, a career in entrepreneurship is not in your immediate future. Most likely, all you have is an idea. Obviously, you lack information and skills critical to success. There is no point in launching a venture with a high probability of failure. But there are things you can do. Take a job in your industry of choice, meet as many people as you can, become a star performer, and keep your eyes and ears open. You can also further your education by going back to school. If you really want to start your own company now, bring on partners who have the talents you lack, or pay for a proven system by buying a franchise. This is not a bad way to acquire the information and skills necessary to do something on your own later. If the desire is there, you *can* create a glorious accident. Best wishes!

REFERENCES

Page

3   U. S. Bureau of the Census. *Statistical Abstract of the United States,* 116th ed. Washington, D.C., 1996.

3   "The New Economy Almanac." *Inc.,* Special Issue: The State of Small Business, 1997, 108-21.

4   Case, John. "The Wonderland Economy." *Inc.,* Special Issue: The State of Small Business, 1995, 14–29.

4   McConnell, Sheila. "The Role of Computers in Reshaping the Work Force." *Monthly Labor Review,* August 1996, 3–5.

4   Series of Articles on the Downsizing of America. *New York Times,* March 1996.

5   "The New Economy Almanac." *Inc.,* Special Issue: The State of Small Business, 1997, 108-21.

6   *A Compendium of Statistics on Women-Owned Business in the U.S.* National Women's Business Council, Washington, D.C., 1994.

6   "The New Economy Almanac." *Inc.,* Special Issue: The State of Small Business, 1997, 108-21.

6   Florence, Mari. *The Enterprising Woman.* New York: Warner Books, 1997

6   Carney, Karen C. "Who's Who in Small-Business Research." *Inc.* Special Issue: The State of Small Business, 1997, 56–63.

6   Weihe, Hermann J., and Frank-Rainer Reich. "Entrepreneurial Interest among Business Students: Results of an International Study." In Heinz Klandt, ed., *Entrepreneurship and Business Development.* Auebury, 1993, 179-81.

Page

6   Card, Emily, and Adam Miller. *Business Capital for Women: An Essential Handbook for Entrepreneurs.* New York: MacMillan, 1996.

6   "The State of Small Business 1997." *Inc.*, Special Issue: The State of Small Business, 1997, 11–14.

7   U. S. Bureau of the Census. *Statistical Abstract of the United States,* 116th ed. Washington, D.C.: 1996.

7   Useem, Jerry. "Churn, Baby, Churn." *Inc.* Special Issue: The State of Small Business, May, 1997, 25–32.

33   Jones, Constance, and the Philip Lief Group. *The 220 Best Franchises to Buy: The Sourcebook for Evaluating the Best Franchise Opportunities.* New York: Bantam Books, 1993.

33   Ludden, LaVerne L. *Franchise Opportunities Handbook: A Complete Guide for People Who Want to Start Their Own Franchise.* Indianapolis: Park Avenue, 1996.

33   Hiam, Alexander Watson, and Karen Wise Olander. *The Entrepreneur's Complete Sourcebook.* Englewood Cliffs: Prentice Hall, 1996, 69–79.

55   "The Evolution of the Professional Entrepreneur." *Inc.*, Special Issue: The State of Small Business, 1997, 50–56.

139 Johnson, Michael. *Slaying the Dragon.* New York: ReganBooks, 1996.

140 Sykes, Charles J. *A Nation of Victims.* New York: St. Martin's Press, 1992.

201 Labich, Kenneth. "Elite Teams Get the Job Done." *Fortune,* Feb. 19, 1996, 90–99.

223 Stanley, Thomas J., and William D. Danko. *The Millionaire Next Door: The Surprising Secrets of America's Wealthy.* Atlanta: Longstreet Press, 1996.

253 Kriegel, Robert, and David Brandt. *Sacred Cows Make the Best Burgers.* New York: Warner Books, 1996.

254 Op/ed. *Newsletter for Organizational Psychologists,* 1995.

255 Tichy, Noel M., and Stratford Sherman. *Control Your Destiny or Someone Else Will: How Jack Welch is Making General Electric the World's Most Competitive Company.* New York: Currency Doubleday, 1993.

INDEX

102; on Mello Smello, 102–3; on intellectual property, 104; on distribution, 104–5

Knowing the terrain, assessment tool on, 314

Line, Lorie: on learning to play piano, 156; on contests, 157; on business, 158; on marriage, 158; on night work, 159; on recording album, 159–61; on financing, 160; on Time Line Productions, 160; on marketing, 160–61, 163; on Dayton/Hudson Corporation, 161; on expanding, 162

Marketing: Lorie Line on, 160–61, 163; Pam Walsh on, 203; Hyrum Smith on, 218; Zia Wesley-Hosford on, 269–72

McBride, Teresa, on getting started, 56–57

McCloskey, Rick, 223–24

McDonald's: Marty Shih on, 287–88; as entrepreneur's dream, 288; Jon Huntsman develops packaging for, 303

McMahon, Marti, started Pacific Marine Yachts, 107

Meadows, Annie, on starting ECM Records, 281

Media: Frieda Caplan on, 37; Diane Dimeo on, 60; Chuck Harris on, 130; David Tibbitts on, 177; Robin Petgrave on, 234; Debrah Charatan on, 239

Megahertz as example of exceptional service, 168

Mentors: support of, essential, 18; lifetime and business, 78–82; Tony Conza on, 80; choosing, 82–84; tips for finding, 106; assessment tool on, 316

Miller, Lorraine, on starting Cactus & Tropicals, 138

Millionaire Next Door, 223

Missett, Judi Sheppard: on mentors,

112–13; on teaching, 113; on starting Jazzercise, 113; on advertising, 114; on expanding, 115; on franchising, 116; on financing, 117; on Jazzertogs, 117; on JMTV, 117–18; on the American dream, 118; on work, 118; on change, 118; on time, 118–19

Montgomery, Joe: on business, 45; on the cycling industry, 46; on aluminum, 46, 48, 52; on generating a product, 47; on bicycle products, 47–48; on creating bicycles, 48–52; on funding, 50–51

More from less: as one of ten keys, 22; tips for getting, 247–48; assessment tool on, 321

Morris, June: on getting into business, 259; on meeting needs, 259; on leisure business, 260; on chartering flights, 260–61; on leasing flights, 261; on financing, 262; on the airline business, 262–63; on selling Morris Travel, 263; on change, 264; on going public, 264; on selling to Southwest, 264–65

Mouth guards. *See* Kittelsen, Jon

Moving companies. *See* Sheets, Mary Ellen

Naylor, Mary: on getting the idea, 209; on getting started, 209–10; on financing, 209–11; on expanding, 211; on partners, 211–12; on teams, 212; on business plans, 212

Neese, Terry, on starting Terry Neese Temporaries, 249

Notching it upward and onward: as key to success, 255–58; tips for, 279–80; assessment tool on, 322

Nguyen, Sean: on getting to America, 41; on Multi-Tech, 41–44; on testing modems, 42; on business transformation, 43

Olim, Jason: on music, 181–82; on the idea, 182; on getting started, 182; on